One Korea

One Korea
A Proposal for Peace

SHEPHERD IVERSON

Foreword by Andrei Lankov

McFarland & Company, Inc., Publishers
Jefferson, North Carolina, and London

All photographs © AP/Iviary, 2013

LIBRARY OF CONGRESS CATALOGUING-IN-PUBLICATION DATA

Iverson, Shepherd, 1956–
    One Korea : a proposal for peace / Shepherd Iverson ; foreword by Andrei Lankov.
       p.   cm.
    Includes bibliographical references and index.

    ISBN 978-0-7864-7683-1
    softcover : acid free paper ∞

    1. Korean reunification question (1945–)   2. Korea (South)—Relations—Korea (North)   3. Korea (North)—Relations—Korea (South)   I. Title.
DS917.444.I84 2013
951.904—dc23   2013027508

BRITISH LIBRARY CATALOGUING DATA ARE AVAILABLE

© 2013 Shepherd Iverson. All rights reserved

No part of this book may be reproduced or transmitted in any form or by any means, electronic or mechanical, including photocopying or recording, or by any information storage and retrieval system, without permission in writing from the publisher.

 Front cover: *from left* South Korean and North Korean flags (iStockphoto/Thinkstock)

Manufactured in the United States of America

McFarland & Company, Inc., Publishers
  Box 611, Jefferson, North Carolina 28640
    www.mcfarlandpub.com

Until her dying day my mother, a proud Norwegian American, was a constant emotional support. It is amazing how much mothers give to their sons; I see many of her influences in the deep sentiments of this manuscript. My high school coach and lifelong best friend Dr. Jack Blatherwick must know how much he has meant to my intellectual development.

None of this would have been possible without the loving care of my wonderful Polish wife Beata (Ph.D. physics) and my ultimate inspiration, our trilingual (Korean, English and Polish) 9.7-year-old son, Tomek. I dedicate this book to these four remarkable people, and to millions of Koreans who suffer the deprivations of a premodern existence.

Acknowledgments

It is with considerable joy and gratitude that I thank Dr. H. Russell Bernard. He inspired more than a generation of students with his enthusiasm for empirical research, and when scientific methods were unavailable, he encouraged us to tell a good story. I would also like to acknowledge my indebtedness to the late Dr. Marvin Harris; his popular books were the reason I entered graduate school. His profound theoretical insights have yet to be fully appreciated.

Dr. Andrei Lankov, a Russian from Leningrad who briefly attended Kim Il-sung University, is a pure multilingual social, historical and political scholar, and a passionate intellectual who has spent his life learning and teaching; through his books, articles and conversation, he, more than anyone else, is my number one "informant" and has inspired me to try to understand the Korean situation in more detail. This is why I asked him to write the foreword for this book.

Though excusing them from any implied agreement with my thesis, I also wish to extend my thanks to David Kang, Marcus Noland, William Stueck (my fellow Brown alumnus), and Dick Chadwick for their kind and insightful comments on my original journal article, and to my Korean and Chinese students and several anonymous reviewers.

Ms. Lee Sunyoung, an expert librarian at Jungseok Memorial Library at Inha, has spent many hours tracking down my requests, and I thank her for her professional diligence. My major secretary in the Department of Cultural Contents, Ahn Hyo-Jeong, has been a big help with administrative matters. I would also like to thank professors Kim Mansu, Yook Sanghyo, Cho Byung-Joon and Kang Ji-Soo for their kindness and trust. Finally, on behalf of my family, and myself, I wish to especially thank Professor Lee Jae Il for his friendship and loyal support. This work was supported by Inha University research funds.

Table of Contents

Acknowledgments	vii
Foreword by Andrei Lankov	1
Preface	5
Introduction	11
One. A Model for Peace	25
Two. Theories and Incentives	30
Three. Critical Changes in North Korea	38
Four. Tipping Points	53
Five. The Price of Peace Equation	62
Six. Funding and Acquiescence	72
Seven. Review and Conclusion	89
Eight. Reunification Signing Ceremony	105
Nine. After Reunification	110
Epilogue	144
Chapter Notes	149
Bibliography	171
Index	185

Foreword
by Andrei Lankov

This is an unusual book. It proposes a solution to one of the world's most difficult political problems and does so in great detail. Such books are rare these days, when concrete plans are expected to be produced by policy planners, while books tend to be verbose and imprecise when it comes to policy suggestions and executable plans. One can understand why academics try to be nebulous when predicting the future or even when suggesting ways to a better future. The track record of such efforts over the last hundred years or so has been quite bad, so caution seems to be the best policy.

Nonetheless, some brave people still try, and this book is one such rare attempt. Shepherd Iverson suggests a rather imaginative way to solve the recurrent problem of North Korea. He believes that peace on the Korean Peninsula, as well as its future economic growth, is for sale. He also suggests that interested parties, as well as the international community in general, should be prepared not merely to pay the price necessary but also to create an institution whose task will be to collect and manage the necessary amount of money. The institution, which he dubs the "Korean Peace Fund," will use money provided by donors to compensate the North Korean elite for the loss of power, and also to mitigate the many shocks that will occur during transition.

While Shepherd Iverson is quite specific about the mechanics of his proposal, the present author does not expect the precise blueprint to ever be implemented. But who knows? The book's core idea remains worthy of consideration, even though its eventual implementation might take a form dramatically different from the vision set forth in this book.

Indeed, one of the major stumbling blocks that prevents a peaceful solution to the Korean problem is the vested interests of the North Korean elite. Taking into consideration the yawning economic gap between the two Koreas, as well as the abysmal human rights track record of the current hereditary dictatorship, one should not be surprised by the fact that North Korea's political elite is deadly afraid of both the collapse of their regime and unification. They assume that if such a collapse were to happen, they would lose their power and privileges. Some may even face prosecution.

This is a major difference from the countries of the Middle East, which recently experienced the "Arab Spring" revolutions. A mid-level bureaucrat or military officer in Tunisia could rationally expect that, regardless of the political struggles in the capital, he would keep his position and still be promoted in due course. North Korean bureaucrats, policemen and military commanders do not see things in such a way, and this makes them extremely hostile to the very idea of change.

Therefore, the basic idea of Iverson's book — paying compensation to North Korea's elite in exchange for their willingness to accept change and surrender power — is a sound, if rather paradoxical, notion. If ever implemented, it is likely to be seen as morally dubious by many, but, as Iverson notes, the alternatives are clearly worse. If North Korea's leaders believe that they have a golden parachute in case of a revolution, they are less likely to resort to brutality to maintain the existing system. The existence of a Korean Peace Fund exit option also means that these people will be far less motivated to fight in the case of a violent crisis, if such a crisis is ever to break out in the North.

Another part of Iverson's plan is a massive infusion of aid into what is now North Korea. Without such aid, the North Korean economy is unlikely to break out of its current sorry state. Even if the economic management system and social structures are reformed, the lack of infrastructure and social skills is likely to impede economic recovery in the North. Therefore, massive aid is necessary.

The third major underlying idea in Iverson's proposal is the assumption that in the long run, a stable and unified Korea will serve the interests of all major international players. Therefore, he reasons that it makes sense for the interested parties to invest in the unification and economic restructuring of the Korean Peninsula. Such money is better to be seen as an investment, a way to speed up the arrival of a peaceful and stable Korean Peninsula, whose existence will serve the interests of neighboring powers as well as other international actors.

Foreword by Andrei Lankov

The essence of Iverson's plan can be summed up as follows: First, the North Korean elite should be bribed generously to ensure that they will accept change. Second, there will be a need for massive infusions of capital into post-unification Korea. Third, South Korean taxpayers alone cannot possibly finance such an infusion of money, and since the fast and smooth solution to the Korean problem is in the interests of many parties, one should expect outside donors to be generous.

The major value of this book is in how it outlines both the essential issues that must be dealt with in order to resolve the Korean problem and how such issues can be resolved. There is little doubt that if these ideas are ever realized, the implementation will be different from what is outlined in this book. Nonetheless, this book is important because it shows us what can be done, and it also makes us think in constructive and creative directions. For over half a century we have been searching for a way to achieve Korean peace and reunification, and however remote, this might be one.

Educated in Russia and Pyongyang, Andrei Lankov has been an important multilingual expert on North Korea for almost three decades.

Preface

"Perpetual peace is no empty idea, but a practical thing which, through its gradual solution, is coming always nearer its final realization."—Immanuel Kant

The danger imposed by the inter–Korean partition and the constant threat of war exists in historical context and within a wider contemporary framework where changing balances of power and new geopolitical impulses prevail. The United States has confirmed that over the next few years it will "pivot" its gigantic military toward the Pacific.[1] And as the economic center of the world shifts to the East, export-driven capital accumulation is currently funding an arms race in Northeast Asia. China, Japan, Russia and South Korea spent a combined $250 billion on defense last year. Moscow plans to spend $720 billion on 1,600 new warplanes and attack helicopters by 2020. Although a much smaller amount, North Korea spends more on its military relative to its GNP than any nation in the world.[2] Chinese military spending has increased by more than 10 percent per year over the past twenty years. At current growth rates China will spend $2.5 trillion by 2020; Japan will spend close to half a trillion dollars and South Korea more than half that.[3]

The security dilemma in East Asia is perplexing. Do new military capabilities create more regional stability by increasing deterrent and defensive proficiencies, or do they exacerbate regional tensions and foster mutually reinforcing insecurities and suspicions? There is no definitive answer to this question. However, the military arms build-up and nationalistic rhetoric expressed between East Asian nations is markedly familiar to the military trajectories and ethnocentric nationalistic attitudes of Western Europe prior to the great world wars of the twentieth century. Asian military strengthening may not be a prelude to war, since it is also a deterrent, but there are historical and cultural reasons that suggest otherwise.[4]

The race-based nationalism of geographically and historically isolated Northeast Asian nations is extreme.[5] Affinities of pure blood and notions of ethnic, cultural and national superiority run deep in the newly democratized nations of Japan and South Korea. And in addition to at least two millennia of Middle Kingdom Sinocentrism, China's educational system has implied a natural superiority of the Han Chinese by erroneously teaching students that they evolved biologically apart from the rest of humanity — on a different branch of the family tree.[6] Chinese political science professor Suisheng Zhao has described a primordial form of patriotism in China based on a sense of racial and cultural superiority.[7] Both communist and democratic political leaders manipulate ethnic-nationalist sentiments to win confidences and gain power over the impressionable masses.

The history of Japanese colonialism still arouses bitter nationalist hostilities in the region. After centuries of meddling, Japan formally annexed Korea in 1910 and retained political control for almost two generations, until 1945. The Japanese assassinated the Korean royal family; banned teaching the Korean language; burned historical documents; forced Koreans to take Japanese names and use their language; expropriated agricultural land, businesses and civic properties; enslaved men for labor and women for sex; and imprisoned, tortured and murdered those who opposed their rule. Similar outrages occurred on Chinese soil, where the Japanese expansionist empire was responsible for the deaths of millions of civilians in the 1930s and 1940s.[8]

These early twentieth century imperialist misadventures and World War II transgressions have not been forgotten. Senior Japanese government officials have issued numerous apologies over the past half-century and Japan has made efforts of contrition in South Korea, such as providing development capital (reparation money) for the Korean steel industry in the 1960s after the World Bank declined support.[9] Unfortunately, these formal apologies have not been sufficiently convincing and there is little forgiveness in the region.

Recent Japanese, Korean and Chinese provocations over disputed island territorial claims have elicited resentment, public protest and increasing ethnic-nationalist sentiment in these countries. Toyota of Japan claims it lost over one billion dollars in Chinese sales in 2012 because of nationalist agitation over a maritime territorial dispute that resulted in boycotts. With the shifting intentions and maneuvers of global powers, the escalation of military capabilities and a resurgence of historical race-based nationalism, East Asia is becoming a more dangerous region in which to live. The mid–December (2012) elections of hardliner conservative party candidates Geun-hye Park in South Korea and Shinzo Abe in Japan reduce the likelihood of improving relations with North Korea or assuaging Japan's relationship with China. Indeed, the new South Korean president-elect, Geun-hye Park, says she won't reinstate major projects with the North unless it dismantles its nuclear weapons. The North says it never will.

There is a new "Gangnam Style" generation in East Asian nations, with more transnational attitudes and global perspectives who carry less of the legacy of militant ethnic-nationalist resentment.[10] Unfortunately, the voices of this more cosmopolitan group will be drowned out rather quickly if there is an act of military aggression.

Perhaps the most likely military confrontation is between Japan and China over the Senkaku-Diaoyu islands in the East China Sea. There have been recent naval and fishing boat skirmishes and military posturing, and diplomatic tensions are high in Tokyo and Beijing. Due to these provocations, as in 2005, there have been anti–Japanese protests in several Chinese cities, with angry citizens taking to the streets to smash Japanese cars and attack sushi restaurants; some Japanese companies (Panasonic and Canon) have decided to close manufacturing plants in China as a result of this anti–Japanese sentiment.

Although outgunned 73 to 48 in attack ships, and 3 to 1 in submarines, the more technologically advanced Japanese navy is considered as capable as the Chinese navy.[11] Along with serious trade consequences, probably the worst that can happen if hostilities erupt is a few sunken ships and downed fighter aircraft before both nations come to their senses; it is difficult to see where a land battle could commence and it is hard to imagine missiles or bombers over densely populated areas where the loss of civilian lives would elevate this confrontation at sea into an all-out war. It is unlikely (although within the realm of possibility) the United States would intervene in an isolated sea battle between China and Japan despite its protective alliance agreement with Japan.[12] However, if China threatened Japan's mainland, it is presumed the United States would respond.

Although less threatening, there is also the territorial dispute between South Korea and Japan over the Dokdo-Takeshima islands. These island territorial disputes are ready flashpoints for confrontation and could erupt into small-scale military action, but they are unlikely to lead to full-scale war. Indeed, if bigger fences make better neighbors, the nations of East Asia are fortunate to be separated by the blue water that lies between them.

However, due to the steady growth of Chinese control over seaport terminals along critical shipping lanes and its development of specific weapon systems aimed to destroy aircraft carriers with hyper-sonic shore-based missiles, the United States believes China's military capabilities are becoming more offensive than defensive. Thus, it is strategically conceivable that the United States might use a Japanese-Chinese confrontation at sea as the pretext to challenge the Chinese military before it develops this technology and while the United States still has superior capabilities and an overwhelming advantage. The United States is not likely to cede military control to the Chinese over essential ocean trade routes. From the U.S. military perspective, it is easier to fight now rather than later. In the future, the U.S. Navy may not be as invincible as it is today. Of course, this is purely speculative, but entirely consistent with the highly regarded offensive realist purview of international relations.[13]

If this scenario were to occur, it would strike a severe blow to world trade and the global economy, but this would not be the first time war superseded more pragmatic economic objectives (see epilogue). Further maritime speculation is beyond the scope of this manuscript, since Korean unification would only delay, not prevent, this geopolitical showdown, if indeed it is inevitable.

Some South Koreans believe the presence of outside actors creates the most potential danger for serious conflict in the region. Indeed, the United States may not allow North Korea to complete the production of an intercontinental nuclear ballistic missile that would endanger its shores. If the United States felt threatened, it might act, especially if it was suspected that North Korea was also supplying arms or nuclear material and technology to Iran. The successful three-stage missile launch that put a satellite into orbit in December 2012 has already been termed a Sputnik moment and, along with the February 2013 nuclear test, has intensified U.S. concern.[14]

Preface

Another danger was created when South Korea changed its rules of military engagement in 2011 from a passive to a more aggressive proactive deterrence that includes preemption (a tactic of offensive realism). This policy creates worries about controlling the ladder of escalation once small-scale military actions commence. There are fears that poor communication of intent and a spiral of miscalculation could result in a small skirmish leading to full-scale war.

There has been talk within the South Korean National Assembly of the redeployment of U.S. nonstrategic nuclear weapons. Representative Shim Jae-cheol recently remarked, "The only way to defend our survival would be to maintain a balance of terror that confronts nuclear with nuclear." Other government officials have gone even further by recommending an independent South Korean nuclear deterrent.

There are other dangerous possibilities beyond those generally acknowledged. For example, with an eternal "war of terror" fought between the "haves and the have-nots" of the world, the actions of non-state actors constitute a permanent threat; it can be expected the United States would respond harshly if a terrorist attack on its soil were traced to weapons that originated in North Korea, regardless of who is responsible. And if at any time in the future political leaders in the East or West needed to contain internal revolt or deflect attention away from themselves or the failure of their party's domestic policies, incensing race-based nationalistic hostilities against another nation is one proven way to do this. North Korea is also one of the most likely points of military conflict between China and the United States; Pyongyang's intercontinental nuclear missile development program and belligerence toward the United States represent a clear and present longer-term danger to peace with civilizational implications.

From this list of presumptive dangers, it is clear that there is an unacceptable level of unpredictable variables that could cause catastrophic consequences. Some analysts have referred to Korea as a ticking time bomb. The tense and increasingly confrontational situation in Korea is one of the central geopolitical concerns of our age; it creates regional instability, great powers are converging and solutions remain elusive. Some manner of peaceful unification or confederation is a preferred solution to rising hostilities, but this path seems blocked at every turn. However, dynastic transition and the rise of a new generation of leaders in North Korea may have opened a window of opportunity for a final resolution.

In the pages that follow I will argue that there are an increasing number of tangible and measurable factors pushing and pulling the North Korean regime toward a day of reckoning. North Korea may be less stable than its smooth political transition would indicate, and it may be closer to a tipping point than at any time in recent history. Some experts are taking collapse scenarios seriously.[15] Chinese support that keeps North Korea solvent may be at a tipping point of its own; new Chinese leaders may be ready to consider a policy alternative that offers a permanent solution to the Korean problem if it is in their national interest.

I do not wish to add to the long list of failed past predictions of North Korea's imminent demise. This book does not predict a collapse. It is quite possible North Korea may survive for another half-century under Kim Jong-un's leadership. Indeed, without an external stimulus, the most likely scenario is for the North to limp along, as it has for the past two decades, until a crisis suddenly emerges. But the world community need not wait for the unpredictable repercussions of crisis in Korea.

What if there existed a peace plan that could capture the attention of the world? What if international business elites who recognize that the smooth operation of the global economy may be in peril decided to play a role in solving the Korean problem? What if enough money could be raised from public and private sources to compel the peaceful reunification of a political regime that has few, if any, other good alternatives? And what if the results of this plan benefited everyone in the region and provided a positive outcome for both U.S. and Chinese economic and geopolitical objectives?

The Korean Peace Fund model is such a plan. It calls for the creation of a peace fund that would provide an institutional framework for governments, global elites, and corporations to cooperatively raise a large amount of money and offer it to the North Korean masses, military officers, and political and military elite if they acquiesce and reunify under South Korean political leadership. A potential conflict that might involve the United States and China would be averted, Kim Jong-un would receive the Nobel Peace Prize and become an international hero, and Korea would finally be reunited. If you think this scenario is preposterous or implausible, it is because you have not yet read this book.

Introduction

This treatise is written primarily for elites: government leaders in China, Russia, Japan, the United States and South Korea, and business billionaires who might underwrite a Korean Peace Fund; Kim Jong-un and the North Korean power elite who might agree to this reunification model; and institutions, scholars and activists who might promote it. It is anticipated this book may be translated into Chinese, Japanese, Russian and Korean, and so I try to avoid linguistically and culturally confusing idiosyncratic expressions.

I encourage readers to think about North Koreans not through a media-distorted lens, as goose-stepping saber-rattling soldiers and belligerent missile-launching miscreants, but instead as a culture of mostly innocent flesh-and-blood people, who get married, love their children, cry at funerals and try to get by as best they can in a difficult society. North Korean leaders are trapped in the institutional inertia of the times, as we all are.

This book is an expansion of an article previously published in an academic journal.[1] I am grateful to the Korean experts and area specialists who have been open-minded enough to offer a favorable response to this unconventional strategy for peace and reunification. Perhaps some have been more open-minded and gracious than would otherwise have been the case because the interminable consensus is that there are few, if any, good options in Korea. I believe I have come up with one.

We are already in the second decade of the twenty-first century and it has been 60 years since the end of the Korean War. Much has changed during two generations but the political and cultural divide between North and South remains, and dangerous military tensions still exist. The world seeks a solution to inter–Korean conflict and nuclear proliferation before danger escalates. This book offers one possible positive-sum solution. It is a call to action for the global community to raise money to pay North Koreans to submit to reunification under South Korean political leadership.

I will outline an empathic smart-power strategy to incentivize Korean reunification through the institution of a Korean Peace Fund that would pay North Korean leaders to put down their guns and join the rest of the world as wealthy new members of the international community. According to Marcus Noland, former senior economist with the Council of Economic Advisers in the Executive Office of the President of the United States, paying for peace in North Korea was a topic of discussion during the Clinton administration but was never fully developed. The idea was discarded because it was felt at the time that the "psychic" rewards derived from absolute power were probably too compelling to give up.[2]

However, emerging global political and economic forces and fundamental changes inside North Korea over the past two decades have made this proposal ever more relevant today. The per-capita purchasing power parity in South Korea is a formidable seventeen times that of North Korea ($30,800 versus $1,800). This is the largest economic disparity along a sovereign border in the world today. Indeed, growing North Korean awareness of South Korean prosperity, ubiquitous proto-capitalist behavior, and leadership uncertainties have created a new context for political change. These developments are elaborated on in chapters three and four.

Although there is little expectation North Korea will collapse anytime soon, few experts believe that it can continue on indefinitely without economic reform. It has been argued that North Korea could succeed if it becomes an attractive destination for foreign investment. But corruption and weak legal institutions discourage trade finance and many large-scale foreign investments have gone sour. Except for limited Chinese and inter–Korean trade, illegal activities and arms dealing, North Korea has no significant foreign economic relationships from which to draw capital.[3]

Sanctioned and cut off from foreign capital, most state enterprises perform dismally and a moribund economy has been stagnant or worse for over two decades, with per-capita incomes less than what they were in 1990, agricultural production half its potential, and an obsolete industry operating at a quarter of its capacity. Its national currency is worthless abroad, inflation is a recurring problem, hyperinflation an existential threat, and there is no obvious solution for the regime other than giving up its nuclear proclivities or embarking on the politically dangerous path of economic reform.[4]

Thus, on June 28, 2012, policies were announced (not yet implemented) that would give factory managers more control over production and freedom to set prices; collectivized farms would be broken up and independent households would be given incentives to produce a surplus for sale; farmers would keep 30–50 percent of what they produce, and state-run companies and shops will be allowed to keep 70 percent of their profits. But whether this is the beginning of a new openness and a movement toward a Deng-like pragmatic emphasis on economic development is uncertain. Modest reforms tried in the past have been reversed or modified in implementation. And even if some proposed economic initiatives do go into effect, improved conditions resulting from them will most likely be modest and gradual, and for the vast majority of people they may not appear at all. Policy alone will not manufacture exportable commodities, replenish infertile soil or put food on the table and money in the bank.

Household savings, capital investments and essential improvements in crucial infrastructure underwrote successful reforms in China thirty years ago. But North Korea does not have the capital, and has no place to get it. Without capital investment in factories, rural industry, tractors, fertilizers, transportation, gas and electricity, 30–70 percent of very little amounts to nearly as much. Therefore, a large number of increasingly impatient North Koreans will be forced to survive indefinitely on the edge of starvation.

Presently, the Kim regime has few, if any, good options. The annual $1 billion of food, energy, and consumer and luxury goods from China makes North Korea dependent and vulnerable; its nuclear program angers its last benefactor and increasingly produces negative unintended geopolitical consequences; its control over its military is tenuous; market reforms could lead to a bloody revolution; and economic recovery is nearly impossible without capital investment (which is unobtainable). The Korean Peace Fund offers the Kim regime an honorable escape from this increasingly desperate situation.

Introduction

The central assumption of this book is that peace and reunification can be achieved by changing the underlying incentive structure for all North Koreans and by offering its leaders a safe, honorable and profitable way out of a deteriorating situation. Society-wide knowledge of the existence of a $300 billion Korean Peace Fund (to be disbursed over five years), sitting in escrow and ready to pay out between $100 million and $500,000 to the top 10,000 families of the North Korean political and military elite, large sums to 31,200 military officers, and money equal to several years' income to military conscripts and average citizens, will put enormous pressure on the Kim dynasty to acquiesce with honor and dignity, as Mikhail Gorbachev did just over 20 years ago during the political and economic transformation of Russia.

In addition to inciting political pressure from below, the threat of a reunification-motivated coup d'état would increase, as the Korean Peace Fund is certain to be the elephant in the room among North Korean elites and military commanders, who will be attracted by the wealth, security and freedom they would obtain from this peace offering. But a coup may not be necessary.

If Kim Jong-un were to accept this plan for reunification, he would be awarded the Nobel Peace Prize (as was Gorbachev in 1990 and Kim Dae-jung in 2000) and hailed as the heroic young leader who brought, peace, prosperity and Korean unification to his people. His personal wealth and popularity would keep himself and his family and friends safe. Indeed, he would become an international celebrity in high regard. His father would be the scapegoat.

The Korean Peace Fund model is predicated on the notion that there is nothing more powerfully motivating in human affairs than the alleviation of fear and the promise of personal prosperity. Instead of using negative coercion or impersonal conventional bargaining chips, it is posited that providing personal incentives to the families of a relatively small but powerful North Korean elite might be a more successful strategy for compelling state behavior.

Kim Jong-un is newly married and recently became a father. By accepting the terms of the Korean Peace Fund and passing political power to South Korea, he would not only save his people from their impoverishment but also secure his legacy, the personal wealth and safety of his family, and his heroic standing in the eyes of the world.

Introduction

Twenty-nine-year-old Kim Jong-un and his new wife.

Any discussion of the Korean Peace Fund begs the question of where this money will come from. It may seem preposterous to think governments and private interests would simply hand over hundreds of billions of dollars to the "enemy" through a peace fund. But upon closer examination this makes the most sense. In spite of the appearance of erratic behavior, experts agree the North Korean state is a skilled strategic player and behaves quite rationally. Thus, there is reason to presume the regime would acquiesce if this were its best option. It is incumbent upon the international community to make acquiescence the best option.

Kim Jong-un is currently pressured from every direction by growing modern forces beyond his control, and North Korea faces several inescapable, possibly fatal destabilizing contradictions. Among other things, the nuclear weapons program is resulting in as many losses as gains for the North Korean government, and China is beginning to re-evaluate its relationship with North Korea (see chapter six for more details). In fact, a consensus is emerging among Chinese private citizens

Introduction

and think-tank experts that North Korea's belligerence and adventurism is causing strategic losses for China. And there is a growing consensus throughout China that a stable, unified Korea would be of economic value. Besides creating a barrier to Sino-Korean relations, the presence of a bankrupt, unpredictable and vitriolic North Korea with questionable stability discourages economic development in the Pacific Northeast, an important Chinese (and Russian) objective. And if access to the Pacific is important to China, it is conceivable that South Korea could promise to deed or lease a kilometer-wide corridor of land connecting Jilin Provence with the sea in return for Chinese contributions to the peace fund, long-term development assistance, and withdrawal of aid to North Korea and political insistence on reunification.[5] The positive permanent results of this proposition should be far more appealing to Chinese interests than the current tenuous situation.

A plan for avoiding the possible chaos of an unexpected collapse and stabilizing the Pacific Northeast region for investment and development may give economy-first Chinese political pragmatists more authority to push to strategically disengage with North Korea and compel it to accept this peace offer. Indeed, the Korean Peace Fund model described in this book may provide the platform and impetus for this new consensus, not only within the seven-member Central Politburo Standing Committee but also within the Northeast Asian community.

Considering the vital overlapping interests involved, the expanded supply of global capital, and the vast sums of money spent to solve other international problems and fund militaries to keep the peace, $300 billion is not an excessive price for the creation of enduring peace at a flashpoint of potential conflict that may have civilizational repercussions.[6] China, Japan, Russia and South Korea spent a combined $250 billion on defense last year. China has over $5 trillion saved in foreign exchange reserves and sovereign funds; Japan has over $1.3 trillion, Russia three-quarters of a trillion, and South Korea has over $400 billion saved. It is not difficult to envision how $300 billion could be raised outright or by some combination of foreign reserve or sovereign fund withdrawal and redirected military spending, and then promised to the Peace Fund as grants and loans or as payment for future mineral extraction by China, rail and gas pipeline concessions from Russia, and secure access to the ice-free Pacific port at Rason and other seaports from both China and

Introduction

Russia. A cooperative partnership to share the costs of the Korean Peace Fund would not cause financial hardship on any of these wealthy nations and is not only an investment in the sustained growth of foreign reserves and sovereign funds but would also amount to the greatest humanitarian gesture and security reversal in the history of the world.

China, Japan, Russia and the United States all want a denuclearized North Korea, but each also has reasons to prefer a stable political regime.[7] The growing military strength and geopolitical role of China is changing regional power relationships.[8] Political unification would further alter these relationships and create the possibility of reassessing the U.S. security shield.[9] If there is the chance of a demilitarized Korean Peninsula without a U.S. military presence, China may promise significant sums to the Korean Peace Fund to seek social and political advantage. A unified Korea can reassess its security alliances long after reunification.

The elimination of nuclear weapons controlled by the totalitarian dictator of a failing state in the epicenter of East Asian prosperity is worth a great deal to Japan and other countries.[10] Once the fund gains legitimacy and momentum, Japan would be all in since it is afraid of being completely isolated in East Asia and, with uncertain U.S. support, would want to win favor with an increasingly powerful unified Korea.

Russia does not want to alienate North Korean leadership but would unofficially promise to contribute and, like China and Japan, would be all in once the reunification ball started rolling. Russia needs peace and cooperation above all else because it wants Korean links to its Trans-Siberian Railway system for Asian exports to Europe and a pipeline for energy deliveries to the South.

The United States (and Israel) would prefer it if Asian countries bought more oil from Russia and reduced their dependency on supplies from Iran and the Middle East. At nearly 5 billion barrels per day, this amounts to a $150 billion per year opportunity for Russia if it could provide the fuel.[11] Although it has played only a small part in East Asian affairs since the late 1980s, considering Russia's increasing strength and potential economic gains from a stable cooperative reunified Korea, it should be willing to play a larger role in the future and aid reunification.

The United States is concerned about the growing nuclear threat and the transfer of nuclear technology and materials. For over two decades the United States, Japan and South Korea have seen billions of

Introduction

dollars evaporate in broken quid pro quo promises and have been unsuccessful in eliminating the North Korean nuclear weapons program or preventing vertical and horizontal proliferation.

It is certain North Korea will continue development under the assumption that the world will resign itself to its nuclear capability, as it did with India and Pakistan. The Kim family has seen what happened in Libya to Colonel Gaddafi after he relinquished his nuclear weapons, and therefore probably considers its nuclear program vital to personal and national security. Many experts now concede the Six-Party Talks were predicated on a faulty premise and realize that it is likely denuclearization can only occur with reunification.

Regarding the military situation, China's armed forces are growing in strength, with a robust sea-based nuclear deterrent force and a strong fleet of about 60 attack submarines and, in September 2012, China launched its first aircraft carrier. The United States has a comparable number of attack submarines and eleven operational aircraft carriers. However, China has been developing land-based missile attack systems specifically aimed at destroying aircraft carriers. According to a 2009 report from the U.S. Naval Institute, China is developing a maneuverable low-radar signature weapon that can travel at mach 10 speeds, supported by a network of satellites and unmanned aerial vehicles, which can locate and destroy a U.S. aircraft carrier with a single hit.[12]

Although the past need not portend the future, in a review of 600 years of naval military history, Peter Swartz has shown that "all rising powers with rising navies have eventually collided with other great naval powers in combat."[13] And new fears arose after the U.S. secretary of state announced at the ASEAN[14] Regional Forum in 2010 that Washington would intervene in disputes in the South China Sea, and following the 2012 release of documents revealing plans for a new U.S. national security strategy to pivot its military toward the Pacific, while plans are under way for South Korean and Japanese intelligence cooperation and military enhancement, perhaps including nuclear capabilities. Korean peace and reunification would reverse this contentiousness between great powers, weaken the influence of military hardliners in Beijing, Tokyo and Washington and deflate incentives for an Asian arms race, and could set the stage for unprecedented regional cooperation on maritime territorial boundry disputes.

Introduction

Rapid change over the past several decades has made it difficult to grasp the magnitude of economic globalization. By most accounts, the hegemonic power of the Westphalian system of sovereign nation-states has declined relative to the influence of multinational corporations. Behind the scenes, private interests are ascendant and undoubtedly influential in matters of war and peace. Indeed, the furtherance of globalization depends on continued peace in important trading zones. This could be used to great effect in establishing the Korean Peace Fund. If spearheaded by a single multi-billionaire or CEO, or if a consensus emerged within a corporate consortium or among some power elites who attend the Bilderberg, Trilateral, Davos or Boao annual meetings, this speculative peace proposal could become a funded reality.

There is a vast untapped reservoir of private money and noble intentions worldwide. A Korean Peace Fund could galvanize this international goodwill and become a compelling new initiative for those who understand the persuasiveness of economic incentives and are guided by a sincere sense of enlightened globalism. Indeed, it is possible this peace fund will not get off the ground without a nongovernmental stimulus; governments communicate poorly with each other and their leaders and bureaucracies will be reluctant to support anything out of the ordinary.

Outlier deep-pocket elites could institutionalize this fund, provide seed money, and give it legitimacy by promising large initial donations. And their intimate connections with government leaders could spur multilateral support. International elites could set in motion a partnership between private wealth, international media, business, and global institutions such as the G20 that would fundamentally change the political and economic incentive structure in the region. Although there are less controversial areas in which philanthropic billionaires might put their money or apply their influence, it is possible some may regard Korean peace and reunification as a top priority since regional instability, nuclear proliferation, or an unpredictable war near one of the important commercial centers in the world lie in the balance.

As the global supply of money and the cost and destructive power of weapons increase, at some point it may become obvious that paying for peace will cost less than paying the price of preparing for war, or war itself. Surveying the powerful interests that would benefit from peace and reunification on the Korean Peninsula, the vast amount of money

Introduction

there is in the world, the historic policy failures of engagement, containment and coercion, and the dismal results of the Six-Party Talks, the Korean Peace Fund may actually be the only plan on the horizon that is practical and reasonable.

In the following pages I will outline a plan for creating an incentive for reunification through the institution of a Korean Peace Fund. Although there are historical precursors, this model is theoretically grounded in the modern microeconomics of Nobel Laureate Gary Becker, the classical realism of Hans Morgenthau, and the hybrid liberal realist (smart-power) thesis of Joseph Nye.

A fundamental assumption is that the alleviation of fear and the provision of personal security and prosperity are ultimate bedrock incentives that compel individual and collective behavior. From this perspective, the strategic acquiescence of the Soviet elite is examined and it is suggested that the North Korean elite may be in a similar existential situation, but with insufficient material incentives, and how the payment and personal security promised in the Korean Peace Fund might be the precise motivating force to tip the balance toward North Korean acquiescence and reunification.

The elimination of nuclear weapons from the peninsula, free-market access to Russian energy and North Korean minerals, and a secure political platform for the economic development of the Pacific Northeast are shared objectives that public and private interests should be willing to pay for. The Korean Peace Fund offers a cost-effective, positive-sum, smart-power solution to the Korean problem that would benefit everyone with something at stake in the region.

And the good news from an investment risk-management point of view is that this money is unspent until its objectives are met. There is no possibility of loss. Paper promises can be torn up and electronic donations can be held in escrow and returned if there is no deal. From this perspective, even though this payment idea may seem exorbitant and unrealistic to skeptics, there is no good reason such a fund should not exist and be promoted on the chance that it might work. Indeed, I am aware of no other promising alternative for creating permanent peace and reunification on the Korean Peninsula.

In chapter one I introduce the Korean Peace Fund idea. In chapter two I provide a cursory review of international relations theories and

Introduction

how they have been applied in the Korean situation, and I contrast these approaches with the liberal realist smart-power theoretical preference that, I propose, could lead to a resolution of the Korean problem. In chapter three I discuss the breakdown of social and economic institutions that began during the famine in the mid-1990s; the consequent destabilizing power struggles among the bureaucratic, political and military elite; and the influence of soft-power information flows that have each contributed to a more fragile equilibrium in North Korea today.

In chapter four I provide evidence that suggests the Soviet revolution in 1991 was orchestrated by a pro-capitalist coalition of Russian party-state leaders, and argue that this political-economic maneuver by Russian elites provides a model for North Korean elites to honorably step down. In chapter five I present the Price of Peace Equation, explain how it is tailored to the specific characteristics of the North Korean cultural system and power structure, and provide a detailed accounting of Korean Peace Fund payments by category. In chapter six I argue that deteriorating geopolitical relationships and economic conditions exert pressure on the North Korean elite to acquiesce and that private and multilateral interests may be compelled to underwrite the Korean Peace Fund.

In chapter seven I review important changes that have transpired in North Korea over the past 20 years, discuss the current situation and provide hopeful concluding remarks. In chapter eight I provide an imaginative description of the reunification signing ceremony to help us visualize how the exchange of political and military power for money and personal security will occur. Finally, in chapter nine, I explore an array of concerns in the immediate aftermath of reunification. Projecting into the future may also help us reflect on path dependencies and perhaps imagine alternatives.

It would be a mistake to dismiss this plan simply because it is unconventional or seems at first glance unlikely to be adopted. Dynamic geopolitical changes are currently under way that are altering global and regional incentives. What seemed impossible yesterday may be possible today. It may also seem unlikely that China would discontinue preserving the existence of North Korea as a fraternally allied autocratic state buffer. However, according to a senior Chinese government official and a growing body of research (cited in chapter six), Chinese support for

Introduction

North Korea has been eroding and is no longer a certainty, especially with new leadership.[15] Indeed, the Korean Peace Fund might provide the compelling institutional pivot necessary to produce a new consensus within the seven-member Central Politburo Standing Committee. And in an increasingly interdependent world system based on global trade, it makes sense that corporate and private elites in Hong Kong, China, Russia, Japan, South Korea, the United States, and the rest of the world might cooperate and directly involve themselves (that is, invest) in preserving peace and prosperity. Any one of over a thousand billionaires could put this peace process in motion, and though it likely will not be an easy road to travel, the potential benefits for the international community are too compelling to ignore.

There is a traditional Korean folk tale about how a small beginning can have a great ending. For a recent example of this phenomenon, in early February 2012 a small group of protesters stood across the street from the Chinese Embassy in Seoul, demanding a stop to the repatriation of North Korean defectors. In spite of neighborhood complaints about their presence on the sidewalk, they persisted, showing up every day to express their displeasure with Chinese policy. A few weeks later a South Korean celebrity arrived with 50 teenage North Korean defectors and brought local media attention to the issue. Then a prominent defector, the first North Korean to earn a doctorate degree in South Korea, announced his personal hunger strike.

By early March nearly 500 civic groups had formed a network and began holding protest rallies. Word spread across the ocean. On March 20 a human rights subcommittee in the U.S. House of Representatives passed a resolution opposing China's forced repatriation of North Korean defectors. International celebrities, world leaders and the global media began voicing opposition to this policy and spread attention on this issue worldwide. On April 10, rallies were held in 53 cities around the world. Within 77 days of when that small group of protesters first stood outside the Chinese Embassy in Seoul, the whole world was protesting and there were clear signs that China was considering a change in its repatriation policy.[16]

When quiet diplomacy seemed to be failing, the humanitarian gestures of a few committed people created international awareness of an invisible injustice and moved a great solitary power to reconsider its

Introduction

Kim Jong-un was born on January 8, 1983. Before the age of ten he was sent to boarding school in Switzerland and, in addition to his native Korean, he probably speaks English and German. His former classmates report that he had a particular interest in United States pro basketball. As in many excessively wealthy families in the U.S. and Europe, it is unlikely that he had a very close relationship with his father, who allegedly drank prodigious amounts of cognac and was a philanderer. His mother, Ko Young-hee (1953–2004), was born in Japan and his maternal grandfather was from Jeju Island off the southern coast of Korea. Like many on this island, it is likely his deep ancestry is associated with the Austronesian migration that occurred several millennia ago.[18]

policy.[17] From a small beginning there could be a great ending. One can imagine a similar escalation of support for a Korean Peace Fund once details of this plan become known and knowledge begins to spread. Once this fund gains momentum and crosses the threshold of international interest, no single country will be able stop it, nor could they afford to be left out of the process, since if reunification does occur, everyone will wish to be included in the enormous political and economic benefits that will result from a unified Korea.

CHAPTER ONE

A Model for Peace

This chapter outlines a strategy to incentivize the peace process by creating a Korean Peace Fund. An empathic incentive model is introduced to promote Korean reunification by linking social and economic incentives with personal and political motives. To convince the North Korean leadership to disband their military and proceed with reunification, this model prioritizes three fundamental motivating incentives: (1) private wealth; (2) personal safety and freedom; and (3) honor and prestige.[1]

In addition to this top-down approach, bottom-up incentives are provided to the military and to the general population that recognize the motivating role of women and children and the organic desire for family security. And perhaps most importantly, this model allows the North Korean leadership to save face and honorably opt out of their current predicament with dignity. Saving "face" is a universal value with deeper cultural significance in more rigid hierarchical societies like North Korea, where it is embedded in a longstanding legacy of collective social consciousness.[2] Fully funded, the Korean Peace Fund would change the political and economic incentive structure in North Korea and create underlying material conditions favorable to peace and reunification.

The Korean Peace Fund is explicitly designed to create the personal, economic and political motivation for peaceful reunification. It is based on compelling personal and economic incentives, as well as an empathetic appreciation of the North Korean political leadership and the average North Korean family.

I propose nothing less than paying for the allegiance of 24 million people by offering sums equal to years of work to average North Korean citizens, and publicly honoring the North Korean leadership (for their "heroic" wisdom in stepping down) and buying them off with tangible in-the-pocket private wealth and international assurances of their personal safety and freedom to live and travel wherever they wish. The total price of peace is affordable, and a bargain of inestimable value when one considers the possible alternative of war and the disruption of the global economy.

This model provides enormous incentives to all North Koreans to join in the relative prosperity of the rest of the world. Popular support improves the likelihood of reaching a tipping point for Korean unification. Tipping points are moments of sensitivity when thresholds are reached and small things can have enormous consequences. Stoessinger calls them "moments of truth" when leaders cross thresholds into war (or peace).[3] They can arise unexpectedly and alter the course of history.[4]

It has been said that everything is for sale. What about peace? Can peace and reunification between North and South Korea be purchased? Can war be avoided by simply paying for peace? If war is fought over money (and power and control over the people, land and resources that produce it), why can we not pay in advance to prevent it? I think we can and I will present a model to accomplish this task, recommend who should be paid how much, and suggest where this money might come from. And when all the costs and benefits are weighed, everyone from simple North Korean peasant farmers to powerful geopolitical and global economic interests will end up appreciably ahead.

The potential efficacy of this model is enhanced by cultural diffusion and the word-of-mouth rumor currently spreading across North Korean social networks that the outside world is a better place to live. Cultural diffusion is usually underestimated, and cultural anthropologists have frequently found that people are far more networked and better informed than originally imagined.[5] A porous border with China and increased market activity have created trade networks that have spread South Korean cultural products and outside information much more than outsiders would predict.[6]

Analyzing data from two large defector populations, Haggard and Noland have found "evidence of increasing willingness to defy the government through everyday forms of resistance, such as listening to foreign media."[7] It is clear that information flows are subtly changing perspectives and aspirations throughout North Korea. As personal desperation and the aspirations of a new generation synergize with knowledge of the outside world, more people will realize they are trapped inside a self-limiting political-economic and cultural system and may seek alternatives. With greater access to outside information, the power elites (and their children) are probably acutely aware of this relative deficiency. This model provides especially strong incentives for the power elites to reassess their options.

In every polity there are internal divisions at the highest levels of power and authority. Disagreements undoubtedly exist among elite power brokers in North Korea as crosscurrent objectives of cabinet, party, and military peer institutions clash.[8] The passing of Kim Jong-il has opened a window of opportunity for change before the personality cult of Kim Jong-un is firmly established and while questions remain about the legitimacy of young Kim's leadership. As desperation or opportunity reduces the fear of change, it is possible some members of the leadership might welcome a chance to escape from their current situation and unite to make the now-weakened Kim dynasty an offer they cannot refuse.

An ethnographically informed interpretation of the rapid demise of the Soviet system in 1990–1991 provides a recent top-down historical example of the relatively peaceful historic transition of a totalitarian nuclear-armed government. Interviews with former members of the Soviet power elite suggest that the political-economic overthrow of the Soviet Union was orchestrated by a less ideological faction within the Central Committee that realized the state was declining and saw an opportunity for personal profit.[9]

In spite of recent purges and the reshuffling of leadership, this pragmatic faction must also secretly exist within the North Korean power hierarchy. Therefore, with the right combination of incentives and assurances, these powerful individuals could become the harbingers who guide North Korea into the modern world. But they need an alternative that saves face and provides private wealth, freedom and safety for themselves and their families. By providing a secure framework for this alternative, the Korean Peace Fund model creates a new personal, political and economic incentive structure for the most powerful members of North Korean society. This option is described in greater detail in chapter four.

Social control has diminished since the early 1990s, as growing impoverishment has lead to survival-motivated domestic innovation and widespread corruption and bribery of government officials. Byung-Yeon Kim argues that a "fragile equilibrium" currently exists between state control of police behavior and the potentially destabilizing influence of increased bribe-taking.[10] As the Korean Peace Fund becomes common knowledge, forces for reform and reunification may emerge. An unprecedented general revolt would put pressure on the power elite, who could turn on the Kim family. Or members of the military command could stage an unprovoked coup d'état. But as with Gorbachev, acquiescing to the will of the people may be an honorable way out through the front door.

More than twenty years after the end of the Cold War, Mikhail Gorbachev and his family are alive and well, and many of the old Soviet political elite are members of the new Russian economic elite. The public execution of Romanian dictator Nicolae Ceausescu in 1989, the recent Arab Spring of mass political revolts in Tunisia, Egypt, and Libya, and the fate of Colonel Gaddafi are additional incentives for the Kim regime and power elite to accept the peaceful political reunification this model proposes.

The Korean Peace Fund model is grounded on absolute assurances of personal safety for anyone (including the Kim Jong-un's family, regents and top leadership) in any danger of retribution after reunification, including amnesty from prosecution by local authorities and international institutions. This peace model is also controversial because it calls for a one-time transfer of an enormous amount of money, some of which will be given to high-ranking North Korean officials who have been perceived as the enemy. The 12 percent of the fund offered to elites may seem excessive or even unconscionable to democratic peoples and governments, and therefore it must be obtained from non-public sources. After separating this elite payment from the fund, the political and media focus on the estimated 200,000 political prisoners and the millions of innocent impoverished North Koreans (including over seven million children) who will directly benefit from the fund will create international empathy and help justify the transfer of public money that will permanently unite the Koreas and eliminate the threat of war.

In time every North Korean will come to understand the important details and personal incentives of this offer. With an information highway wrought by twenty years of grassroots social and economic networking, we can assume almost everyone inside North Korea will know specific details about the Korean Peace Fund incentives within days or weeks.[11] And if there is one thing certain about cultural evolution, it is that enticing incentives, whether natural or man-made, usually do not remain unexploited for long.

CHAPTER TWO

Theories and Incentives

Theories of international relations are derived from simplifying assumptions about elite and common motivation, as well as human and institutional behavior. Faulty assumptions, like inaccurate information or deficient knowledge, can lead to incorrect (although logical) and ineffective theories and policies. Theory purportedly informs debate between competing policies about how to most effectively apply power to influence the behavior of others to obtain preferred outcomes; assumptions are often invisible. Figure 1 illuminates this epistemological situation and represents these causal relationships.

Assumptions, Theory and Policy in International Relations

Assumptions → **Theories** → **Policy**
about Motivation   to Apply Power   to Obtain
and Behavior   Preferred Outcomes

Figure 1

Transparent assumptions are introduced below in order to illuminate the substantive differences in past and prospective approaches to peace and reunification in Korea, and to set the basis for the liberal realist smart-power theoretical preference I propose could lead to a resolution of the Korean problem. A cursory review of international relations theories and their policy applications in North Korea will expose motivation and incentive flaws and orient Joseph Nye's liberal realist (smart-power) approach and the underlying rationale for the Korean Peace Fund within a general theoretical and policy framework.[1]

Two. Theories and Incentives

Theories of international relations contain explicit biases based on either materialist (positivist-rationalist-objectivist) or idealist (reflexive-subjectivist-constructivist) assumptions, or some hybrid syntheses.[2] On the materialist side, for over half a century the power politics and classical realist propositions of Hans Morgenthau, the neorealist hardpower focus of Kenneth Waltz and the offensive realist position of John Mearsheimer have dominated international relations theory and profoundly influenced international diplomacy.[3] Abstract impersonal factors such as military strength, state sovereignty, the balance of power and national security are the primary area of concern. Neorealist policies often employ unimaginative zero-sum bargaining and hard-power coercive quid pro quo tactics to advance national interests.[4]

The hardliner "Mutual Benefit and Common Prosperity" (2008–2012) policy of the Myung-bak Lee administration was representative of this neorealist approach. Most observers agree this approach has led to increased tensions over the past five years. Not to be outdone, inconsistent U.S. policies of accommodation, engagement, coercion, containment and isolation, framed at the same impersonal objectivist level of interpretation and analysis, has lead to twenty years of policy failure and resulted in strategic deception, dangerous retaliatory brinkmanship and the perpetual impasse of nuclear negotiations and Six-Party Talks.[5]

On the positivist-rationalist theoretical branch, after the geopolitical and military debacle in Vietnam and the failure of anti-communist U.S. policy in Southeast Asia, a neoliberal approach emerged in the West that advocated objectivist institutional solutions for creating political and economic cooperation and complex interdependencies. These strategies seek to develop norms and common ground on issues of security and conflict resolution.[6] Proponents of neoliberalism shudder when a world leader uses a phrase such as "axis of evil" or "pariah state."[7] Such rhetoric is obviously counterproductive to the strategic goal of friendly engagement.

Kim Dae Jung's "Reconciliation and Cooperation" (1998–2002) and Roh Moo Hyun's "Peace and Prosperity" (2003–2007) policies represent neoliberal initiatives.[8] They were based on the belief that engagement and inter–Korean economic exchange will lead to reform and eventually to reunification.[9] But because neoliberals focus on rational self-interest and minimize the role of fear as the ultimate arbiter of personal and political decisions, they lack the ability to provide realistic incentives to the fearful. I address the political impracticality of this policy option in greater detail in chapter seven.

On the idealist side, since the unexpected fall of the Soviet Union and the inability of objectivists to predict or explain what happened, constructivism gained currency and has made considerable contributions to understanding the intersubjective basis of knowledge and agreement in international relations.[10] The seminal insight is that humans construct their cultural and political reality.[11]

Thus, believing that perceptions shape outcomes, to help solve the Korean conflict some recent reflexive models propose the need for new forms of trust,[12] a commitment to nonkilling,[13] rebuilding of the social Tao,[14] and incremental steps toward advancement and enlightenment.[15] Several theories stress the importance of establishing a consensus or a peace regime.[16] But idealist notions that better knowledge and less misunderstanding will lead to more cooperation are probably overly optimistic if primitive fear and insecurity mask a deeper suspicion.

There is also a general evolutionary hope that contemporary cultural diffusion will blend with Manchurian partisan traditions, postcolonial repulsion, and personal realities, and that modernization, democratization, globalization, and the concomitant rise of civil society will awaken social and political reform.[17] But critics contend that these theories may not apply with sufficient efficacy in a mistrustful, socially atomized, hierarchical, and politically isolated hermit country like North Korea.

Charles Armstrong argues that socialist policy in the 1940s absorbed or "co-opted a potentially critical civil society."[18] Indeed, in spite of growing discontent among the North Korean masses, Marcus Noland asserts, "The country is bereft of civil society institutions capable of channeling that discontent into constructive political action."[19]

In chapter seven I will argue that common knowledge of the institution of the Korean Peace Fund may create a shared cultural construct and provide the impetus for organizing and motivating thoughts and emotions into collective action. The fund provides for a significant payout to 1,200 high- and 30,000 middle-level military officers (who interact with and control the troops on a daily basis), who may function as an armed supra-civil society; they represent an organized middle-level social force that will want to obtain the substantial money offered them in the Korean Peace Fund. It is not inconceivable that if instability ignites, they could unite with more liberal or opportunistic generals to assert their preference.

Other intellectuals complain these universal theories are based on a Eurocentric framing of world history and are biased toward sustaining Western hegemony. Amitav Acharya and Barry Buzan assert, "East Asia may be dressed up in the Westphalian costume, but is not performing a Westphalian play."[20] These critics often cite unique East Asian cultural and historical legacies and argue for theoretic exceptionalism and the inclusion of regional Sinocentric and Confucian hierarchical considerations.[21] However, empirically based materialist explanations of cultural evolution, recent economic history, modern geopolitical alliances, and the World Value Survey call into question the saliency of this Asian values hypothesis.[22]

Despite the Sino-Korean suzerain system during the Ming (1368– 1643) and Qing (1644–1911) dynasties, I doubt modern Koreans or nationalist Korean leaders and elites consider themselves China's (or Japan's) little Confucian brother in some imagined historical East Asian community. This is not to suggest that a powerful China will not exert significant political influence in East Asia in the future. However, if they are useful, neo–Confucian values and sentiments may have a mediating effect on stability or change inside North Korea, but as an ultimate causal factor, pragmatic adaptation to immediate contingencies of survival and well-being are more deeply embedded in the biogram of our species and are more often directly employed during existential crises like those now occurring in North Korea.

Finally, some next-generation Western foreign policy experts critique the underlying assumptions of conventional wisdom and diplomacy.[23] They challenge the old guard to recognize that emerging forces of digital technology and satellite communication, in conjunction with the manifold effects of economic globalization, have revolutionized our age as much as the development of the atomic bomb and mutually assured destruction revolutionized theirs.[24] While deterrence remains essential, conventional hard-power diplomacy has had little influence on North Korea's slow-motion nuclear proliferation over the past two decades and has often resulted in the opposite of its intended effect.

Path dependence theory explains how options in a given situation are often limited by decisions made in the past (history), even though past circumstances (or institutional prerogatives) may no longer be relevant.[25] Warning against path dependency, Victor Cha asserts that it may be dangerous to adhere to familiar policy templates: "The successful strategy that brought peace in one era could bring the opposite result in another."[26] It is presumed there are new and perhaps unconventional paths to peace; checkbook diplomacy is increasingly viewed as more humane, pragmatic and effective than gunboat diplomacy.

Checkbook diplomacy is slowly displacing gunboat diplomacy in the interdependent multinational globalism that flourishes today because costs and benefits have changed. With greater amounts of free-floating capital and larger discrepancies in wealth, a carrot is increasingly more cost-effective than a stick. Money manipulates behavior as never before. Conventional coercive hard-power diplomacy has become less effective, and when it fails, the alternatives are increasingly unpopular and cost-prohibitive.

Critiquing the misconceptions and misjudgments of conventional wisdom, Kissinger associate Joshua Ramo asserts that our leaders "lack the language, creativity and revolutionary spirit our moment demands ... policies designed to make us safer instead make the world more perilous."[27] Indeed, after more than sixty years of enforced division and diplomatic standoff, there is little evidence to suggest that conventional policies and theories from either East or West will bring Korea closer together or lay the groundwork for peace and reunification. If they could, they would have already.

It is therefore possible that the implementation of a modern hybrid model or theory may produce better results. The philosophical neorealist Kenneth Waltz asserts, "Even though one may find it hard to believe that there are ways to peace not yet tried by statesmen or advocated by publicists, the very complexity of the problem suggests the possibility of combining activities in a different way in the hope that some combination will lead us closer to the goal."[28] Indeed, as the tenuous situation evolves in Korea, new or untried policy options become more plausible.

The growing disproportionate cultural and economic context between the North and South presents persuasive possibilities that were unavailable in the past. The border between North and South Korea separates the greatest economic disparity in the world today. The per-capita purchasing power parity in South Korea began to skyrocket in the mid-1980s and is now a formidable 17 times that of North Korea ($30,800 versus $1,800). My goal is to propose incentives in the Korean Peace Fund that will maximize the power of payment and persuasion in this asymmetrical context.[29]

Hard-power money dominates today, and the commoditizing democratizing digital communication revolution is popularizing and asserting this change. Economic context and asymmetries are more relevant today than ever before, as we live in a faster-paced world wide web of computers, attractive commodities and mobile communication devices. These global changes create new leverage points.

In 1992, Gary Becker won the Nobel Prize in Economics for his creative extension of microeconomic principles into sociology and human behavior; he was interested in how incentives influence behavior. Becker devised behavioral models for various aspects of human activities, including racial discrimination, human capital, and crime and punishment, and estimated such things as the costs/benefits of children, divorce, and illegal parking.[30]

Since then, iconoclastic and mainstream economists and social scientists have applied Becker's microeconomic models to explain and successfully predict behavior in diverse realms of human existence. Steven Levitt and Stephen Dubner assert, "Incentives are the cornerstone of modern life. And understanding them is the key to solving just about any riddle from violent crime to sports cheating to online dating."[31] The trick is to strip away the layers of surface phenomena to get at the substructure of human motivation.

According to Becker, most people make decisions to maximize their welfare in every aspect of their lives by comparing the anticipated costs and benefits of different courses of action; this often occurs beyond the level of individual and social consciousness. Human behavior is limited by specific opportunities and constraints and motivated by a rich set of values and preferences. And although behavior is not always driven by personal gain or guided by accurate information and knowledge, physical and material incentives tend to have the most influence, particularly personal safety (when fear exists) and money (or its equivalent). These personal decisions combine to create social patterns of behavior. In his

Nobel Lecture, Becker asserts, "While the economic approach to behavior builds on theory of individual choice, it is not mainly concerned with individuals. It uses theory and the micro level as a powerful tool to derive implications at the group or macro level."[32]

Becker's general economic utility orientation explains the changing conditions and resultant behaviors in North Korea that are creating the social and economic context for political change. Augmenting domestic developments with the bedrock incentives proposed in the Korean Peace Fund may create a dynamic social synergy for change and convince the vast majority of elite and non-elite North Koreans to choose to reunify with the South because it is in their personal interests and the best interests of their families.

Regional geopolitical interests and the international community may consider supporting these peace fund incentives for similar positive-sum, cost-benefit reasons (discussed in chapter six). However, at both the personal and the geopolitical level, when costs seem to outweigh benefits, it is often because of the presence of fear or the perception of risk. Perhaps inspired by the political pragmatism of Niccolò Machiavelli (1469–1527), it was Hans Morgenthau who brought this fact to light in the modern age of international relations theory. Shortly after World War II, Morgenthau introduced a classical realist political theory that for the next two generations would become the foundation for the study of international relations, a handbook for statesman, and a user manual for how the world works.

Part social psychologist, political scientist, and cultural materialist, the consilient Morgenthau argued that normative political and human behavior is not guided by divine forces, revered institutions, cultural heritage, manifest destiny, or abstract ideological or moral principles, but instead is guided by an ever-changing complex matrix of real-world material contingencies.[33] He theorized that ideologies and institutions are meaningful only if they serve the purpose of self-preservation. Logic, rationality, compromise and cooperation are similarly epiphenomenal; ideology is subterfuge. Morgenthau asserts, "Reason is like a light which by its own inner force can move nowhere. It must be carried in order to move. It is carried by irrational forces of interest and emotion to where those forces want to move."[34] Thus, Morgenthau considers fear a prime mover in human relations. From this Hobbesian purview,[35] Morgenthau argues that amid the perceived threat of anarchy and upheaval in social and political relations, there is a compelling underlying fear of survival and an instinctive need for security.[36]

Combining Morgenthau's classical political realism with Becker's cost-benefit microeconomics, I conclude that there is nothing more powerfully motivating in human affairs and international relations than the alleviation of fear and the promise of personal prosperity and security. These are pervasive interdependent, multidimensional bedrock incentives. Thus, incentives that eliminate fear and improve prosperity and security provide ultimate motivation for individual and collective behavior.

Widespread marketization from below, corruption from above, and attraction to South Korean cultural products and standards of living reflect this contingency-based non-ideological adaptive strategy. Defector reports of the diminishing effect of legacy politics, modern propaganda and the decline of ideology, as represented by the commonly acknowledged weakening of the Juche, Suryong, and Songbun systems, reflect new pragmatic cost-benefit microeconomic preferencing.[37] And with an empathic appreciation of the growing uncertainty and frightening realities now confronting the North Korean leadership and elite, we might better understand what could influence them to change course.

The efficacy of the Korean Peace Fund model is founded on empathy and the insights of Morgenthau and Becker, and also on the smart-power thesis formulated by Joseph Nye. Nye defines smart power as a "combination of the hard power of coercion and payment with the soft power of persuasion and attraction."[38] Hard power includes tangible economic sanctions and the threat of military force, but it can also include giving or withholding foreign aid. Till Geiger asserts, "The exercise of hard power such as foreign aid cannot always be separated from the exercise and generation of soft power."[39]

Indeed, payment is a gentle form of hard power, and in the Korean context it may prove to be more cost-effective and determinative. The soft-power attractiveness of South Korean prosperity combined with hard-power payment may create a smart-power solution to the Korean problem. Indeed, there is substantial evidence that critical domestic changes already under way in North Korean society are creating a favorable context for accepting the final solution for peace and reunification proposed in the Korean Peace Fund model.

CHAPTER THREE

Critical Changes in North Korea

Politicians and policymakers armed with private knowledge from sensitive intelligence briefings once viewed academic assessments with skepticism. But scholars are now at the cutting edge of pertinent information about North Korea as they interview smugglers, aid workers and thousands of defectors, refugees and travelers; analyze government documents; filter cross-border news reports; share information; engage in scholarly debate; and assess opportunities and constraints in a more transparent and multidisciplinary manner. Emma Chanlett-Avery claims grassroots information gathering has "democratized the business of intelligence on North Korea."[1] What has been described by the U.S. Central Intelligence Agency as an "intelligence black hole" is much less so today, as insider information has narrowed the difference between knowledge and speculation. Indeed, these informant glimpses of life inside North Korea have laid the ethnographic foundation for this treatise.

For over twenty years experts have predicted the political collapse of North Korea.[2] But the Kim dynasty has held on to power in spite of internal problems that ordinarily topple totalitarian regimes. Daniel Byman and Jennifer Lind have identified an extensive list of tools of authoritarian control the Kims have employed, including the manipulation of ideas and information and the use of force to prevent popular unrest, as well as the co-optation of elites and institutional cross-surveillance to prevent a coup d'état.[3] Through effective use of authoritarian controls and other factors, the Kim dynasty has retained power through at least three waves of virtual economic collapse, successive years of countrywide famine, chronic food shortages, and transitions in hereditary leadership.

In addition to authoritarian controls, the regime has used strategic insecurity and nuclear extortion to convince foreign governments to feed its military and political base in Pyongyang for almost two decades.[4] Since the early 1990s North Korea has suffered structural food deficits, with annual grain harvests more than one million tons short of domestic demand.

Between 1994 and 1998 floods, drought and famine led to the starvation of an estimated 600,000 to 1,000,000 people.[5] Since then, chronic food crises have been moderated by grain donations averaging 800,000 tons per year, valued at $300 million annually. More than 80 percent of this total has been donated by China (27 percent), South Korea (27 percent), the United States (17 percent) and Japan (11 percent).[6] China dramatically increased aid after Japan stopped donating almost a decade ago.[7] Additionally, each year China subsidizes North Korea with close to one billion dollars' worth of energy, consumer and luxury goods.[8] At current levels of material support, the prospect for political instability in North Korea is reduced considerably.

However, famine and the 200,000 tons per-year difference between imports and demand has led to important consequences in the hinterland. Food shortage has caused fundamental changes in several defining socialist-totalitarian institutions. The state-run public distribution system stopped providing food to the public (except in Pyongyang and the military),[9] the people's group neighborhood surveillance apparatus broke down in the countryside,[10] and the travel permit requirement was no longer strictly enforced (except for entering Pyongyang).[11]

Public food distribution was tried again in some places after the famine but once it was realized that government profits could be obtained by selling this largely donated product to markets, even if the state had enough food to give away in good harvest years, there was little incentive to re-establish the old system. Travel permit requirements were eventually enforced again after the famine was over, but once authorities began to accept bribes to augment their meager state incomes, one could "purchase" a permit or pay to stay out of jail if caught without one, thus effectively nullifying the raison d'être for the system in the first place.

In functioning people's groups, one individual monitors the activities of about thirty households (100–150 persons) and reports anything suspicious to higher authorities. Although people's groups continue to function in urban areas for garbage collection and organizing local activities, they are largely inactive in the countryside, and what were once considered political transgressions are much less often reported to authorities these days. These institutional failures have caused an interlocking sequence of revolutionary social and economic consequences.

After the public food-rationing system collapsed, a closed socialist system became capitalist by necessity, as crisis-motivated "marketization from below" proceeded at a rapid pace.[12] As the only solution to starvation, Andrei Lankov notes, "Private commerce boomed, and millions of people began to make their living independently of the state."[13] Although statistics from defector samples can be misleading,[14] recent estimates are that households earn 78 percent of their income through informal economic activities,[15] and as many as 62 percent of farm and 95 percent of non-farm North Koreans get the bulk of their food and daily necessities from the market.[16]

As illegal markets grew and became profitable, they attracted official notice, and bribes became necessary in order to stay in business. New exchange-trust relationships formed, with local government officials as protectors. Initially markets opened to sell food, but soon Chinese digital products and South Korean cultural contents were also sold. With non-perishable products of ubiquitous demand, the breakdown of institutions of social control and the ability to bribe government officials, market networks expanded across the country.

The flow of foreign news, culture and information through these invisible information highways has exposed the truth about a more prosperous South Korea. The effect of this information is cumulative, since once someone knows something, they cannot un-know it. Growing mass awareness of their relative impoverishment, and subsequent cynicism and distrust of government propaganda, is creating a new social context for political change in North Korea.

Developments among the elite have also been substantial. Analyzing the political patterns of government decisions from almost 10,000 speeches and articles written over a twelve-year period (1998–2009), Patrick McEachern has shown how North Korea evolved from a rigid totalitarianism under Kim Il-sung into a more rational, moderate, and pluralist bureaucratic post-totalitarian institutionalism under Kim Jong-il. With less political legitimacy than his father, and therefore less control over state institutions, Kim Jong-il was forced to use a "divide and conquer" strategy to keep powerful factions off-balance and to maximize his influence.[17]

This erosion of control resulted in competitive internecine struggles over bureaucratic power and, along with food shortages and the general breakdown of the socialist economy, created possibilities for opportunistic or pro-business military, cabinet and party elites to seek profits from informal enterprises. Official trading companies were also established in response to Kim Jong-il's appeal for foreign currency. Bradley Martin writes, "Not only high-level government and party organizations but military, agricultural, and industrial units at lower levels, as well, had their own trading subsidiaries."[18] With the Songun "military first" policies in effect since 1995, the armed forces gained control of over 80 percent of the businesses that obtain foreign currency.[19] This has resulted in growing friction between the military and party and cabinet elites, and between socialist ideologues and an emerging generation of more pragmatic leaders.[20]

With weaker authoritarian control and the near collapse of the industrial and agricultural economies, more independent, autonomous and entrepreneurial North Koreans of all social ranks are exhibiting increased personal involvement in profit-making activities. Indeed, Barbara Demick reports that even "defections were arranged like package tours," and for more money you could be treated like a VIP.[21] Usually a guide/fixer, known as a broker, makes the arrangements and is often paid by relatives in South Korea.

In the spring of 2011, a visiting journalist slipped away from his North Korean minder and interviewed several people on the streets of Pyongyang. One person commented, "If you have money, anything is possible in this country." The Chinese journalist compared the current state of mind in North Korea to that in China in the early 1980s. After his visit, he remarked, "If the outside world can give North Korea the right inducement, I think it would open up further, like China."[22]

From the halcyon days of the 1960s and into the 1980s, North Korea appeared to be a shining beacon of socialist central planning and communist management. But it was a façade, an illusion underwritten by Russian external inputs. Without these inputs, in the early 1990s North Korea spiraled downward and social control decreased as rapid economic decline and impoverishment lead to crisis-driven marketization among the masses and widespread corruption among public officials. Wholesale corruption and bribery, unheard of before the 1990s food shortages, are manifestations of a revolutionary change in social and political relations.

The North Korean state has been forced to reconcile contradictory pressures. Since it cannot provide food for its people, it must allow private initiatives to secure at least a survival diet, but these independent initiatives contravene state control over the daily activities of its people. With the government reneging on its socialist mandate and no longer providing sufficient food or survival salaries, allegiances and loyalties switch.

Ralph Hassig and Kongdan Oh assert, "Police officers and party officials are spending more time looking out for their own welfare and less time doing the bidding of the government and the party."[23] Byung-Yeon Kim describes the "fragile equilibrium" that currently exists between the dictator, government officials, and market participants, and the destabilizing influence of bribery, now twice as costly than in the Soviet Union just prior to its demise.[24]

Bribery is a complex and variable cultural phenomenon, especially in politically deprived, legally maligned and economically underprivileged contexts. In their legalist-economic analysis of current cross-border exchanges, Haggard, Lee and Noland observe that bribery and corruption is a "rational response to the lack of property rights protection" and functions as a "mechanism for assuring trade and investment."[25] From a cultural-economic perspective, Mimura Mitsuhiro asserts, "The key to affluence now is bribery; the establishment of social relations based on individual profit and greed has altered the nature of North Korean society, where collectivism and 'honorable poverty' once were official virtues."[26] Scott Snyder and Kyung-Ae Park assert, "The form of capitalism practiced in North Korea at the grassroots level is a ruthless form of jungle capitalism in which individual traders who are trying to survive might face any number of predators and parasites, including demands for bribes and possible expropriation of goods by local authorities."[27]

But ambiguity often exists between bribery and gift-giving in less developed countries. When a North Korean police officer takes a bribe from a market entrepreneur, it can be considered a local tax or friendship offering—a sharing of the wealth, often between one impoverished individual and another. Over time bribes inevitably create binding social relationships and have likely formed extensive exchange-trust networks throughout North Korea. Indeed, many state authorities rely more on bribes than on insufficient government salaries and food procurements, and now have a significant material interest in the maintenance of these market (and information) exchange networks.

These unofficial unwritten social contracts extend beyond peasant entrepreneurs and low-level government officials. Since the systemic failures of socialist economic policy were exposed in the mid–1990s, North Korean elites have aggressively used their position and authority to obtain hard currency by whatever means available. There is evidence of high-level bribery and corruption and the involvement of "socialist" state authorities in private enterprise.

Although high-level bribery is more clandestine, over 10 percent of defectors in one sample reported knowledge of bribes to high-ranking government officials.[28] Chang, Haggard and Noland assert, "Military and police organizations are also prominent participants in informal money lending businesses, presumably owing to their unique ability to collect debts."[29] Stephen Haggard and Marcus Noland note, "Precisely because of its existing organization and resources such as trucks and fuel, the military was ideally situated to perform the role of middlemen distributors."[30] It is common knowledge that large amounts of World Food Program and nation-to-nation food aid have been diverted to private markets across the country.[31]

Since the late 1990s the scale of the private informal economy has grown beyond household production to include small fleets of private passenger buses, flotillas of fishing boats, the extraction of natural resources, furniture manufacturing, restaurants and beauty parlors.[32] Hassig and Oh assert, "Times are changing and a new economic class is emerging, comprising people who are little for party membership but know how to make money."[33] Jae-Cheon Lim and InJoo Yoon have shown how small and medium-sized "shadowy private enterprises" undermine the official sector of the economy, create an insipient economic class, and change the power relationship between party and business management.[34] Private enterprises now represent the primary source of goods and services in most economic sectors in North Korea.

When corruption is so fluid that almost everyone is "on the take" (profiting), it is difficult to ascertain what is public and what is private.

The structural aspects of North Korea's income stream have been compared to the Italian Cosa Nostra, in which a wink and a nod, or the bend of the bow, can signify either a lucrative deal or a shallow grave. To obtain foreign currency from external profits, North Korea operates a criminal syndicate of illicit activities, from processing fake pharmaceuticals and counterfeiting U.S. currency and foreign cigarettes to overseeing the production, manufacture, transport, and export of these products. They have used military vessels, intelligence officials, diplomats and foreign embassies, and a complex web of state-controlled front companies around the world.[35]

Formal state-owned enterprises have also been adapting to currency-stressed conditions. Comparing six central characteristics of standard market socialism with current practices in North Korea, Gary Stradiotto and Sujian Guo have concluded, "North Korea has departed from the traditional command economy toward market socialism."[36] For the past half-decade nearly $2 billion in annual inter–Korean trade and over $2 billion in annual trade with China have earned substantial foreign currency and, because of reported under-the-table dealings, have benefited some North Korean elites more than others.[37] Trade with China has more than doubled over the past several years and currently exceeds $4 billion. And it is growing.

More than half of the inter–Korean trade is associated with the Kaesong Industrial Complex,[38] which was immune to negative sanctions even after the Cheonan and Yeonpyong incidents, while other trade categories suffered losses in the hundreds of millions.[39] Indeed, Kaesong inter–Korean trade increased 36 percent in 2011.[40] The Kaesong Industrial Complex has considerable political support in Pyongyang because it is a foreign exchange earner (perhaps over $30 million annually) and in Seoul because the South has close to a billion dollars at stake through state-owned companies, direct investments, and insuring existing private firms.[41]

In a twist of public sector irony, a malnourished North Korea exported $75 million in marine food products to South Korea in 2009.[42] This underscores the reality that reunification is a contentious issue for those profiting under current conditions; powerful interests on both sides of the 38th parallel may seek personal gain above serving justice, saving lives and reunifying the peninsula.

Fundamental disagreements exist at the highest levels of the North Korean government. Not everyone is satisfied with the current economic situation or with their personal profits. Hyeong Juang Park has described the existence of "moderate and maximalist" opposition to the government within the privileged political elite that favor expanding markets. According to Park, the Manju group (descendants of anti–Japanese guerrillas) and the "new generation" (descendants of soldiers killed during the Korean War) are the driving forces behind market expansion.[43]

Refugee interviews also suggest a growing politicization and discontent within relatively privileged groups,[44] including the next generation of elites preparing to enter the state bureaucracy. The reason college instruction for Pyongyang elites was suspended for ten months beginning in June 2011 may have been partly to honor and prepare for the centennial celebrations, but the decision was made shortly after the Arab Spring revolutions and when anti-government graffiti was discovered at several elite universities.[45] North Korean leaders promptly issued restrictions on public gatherings and a countrywide inventory of computers, cell phones, flash drives and MP3 players among the elite population.[46] From these policies and others, it appears Pyongyang's top elites fear the youth perspective and the elites just under them in the social and political hierarchy.

Profiteering has created more competition and distrust among elite power brokers as cross-current objectives of cabinet, party, and military peer bureaucratic institutions clash over money, power, and prestige. New leadership creates a reshuffling of power holders, but competition and essential cross-purposes remain the same as conflicts increase. The vertical structure of profit taking in formal state and informal private business dealings leading up the chain of power and influence in government is likely to create intense personal jealousies and exacerbate rivalries between elite military factions and bureaucratic institutions.

Some opportunistic elites are skimming more money than others and there have been bold institutional power maneuvers. In the fall of 2009 the military stepped over the party and cabinet and took control of state-owned trading companies that oversee lucrative (foreign-exchange-earning) natural resource exports to China.[47] This sequestration occurred at about the same time that Goldman Sachs reported North Korean mineral deposits worth an estimated $4 billion.

Competition and political friction are likely to increase within and between state bureaucracies as centralized control continues to decline and the socialist economic system is corrupted, co-opted and subsumed by proto-capitalist economic models and relationships. In spite of the cabinet's official responsibility for economic matters, the military is most likely to dominate as control weakens under new dynastic leadership.

During twenty years of Kim Jong-il's "military first" doctrine, the military has been allowed to metastasize into a state within a state. During this time the North Korean military has established itself in investment banking, as a vehicle for staple food and commodity transport, and as the manager of $4 billion of mineral wealth. As previously noted, Jin-Ha Kim estimates, "The military controls more than 80 percent of the businesses charged with obtaining foreign currency."[48] It is speculated that the July 2012 removal of army chief Ri Yong-ho and a rebalancing toward the party and the cabinet is the result of his excessive interpretation of military-first prerogatives. Indeed, it is believed Ri's ouster may have occurred because he spoke out against efforts to remove lucrative mining contracts from army control. Andrei Lankov has noted that in an effort to downsize military-run enterprises, the navy commander and seven or eight district chiefs have also been replaced and the cabinet has retained its supervisory status.[49] And Stephen Haggard has observed, "All four of the top [military] brass who walked with Kim Jong Il's bier are now gone, while all four civilians are still with us."[50] However, in spite of the removal of Ri and others, it will be almost impossible to dislodge the military from essential control over key resources, though it may have to share more of its profits.

Paradoxically, the increase of military control over North Korean material assets may be a positive development for the pragmatic consideration of the economic incentives provided in the Korean Peace Fund. As evidenced by their involvement in a variety of money-making schemes, some generals and commanding officers may be less ideologically inclined and more opportunistically prone and receptive to the generous distribution of money promised them in the peace fund. The significant benefits and lifetime security that military elites and high-ranking officers would receive from the fund probably far exceed their current profits through unstable corrupt activities. And no group is more cognizant of North Korea's existential vulnerabilities than this internationally aware faction of pragmatic elites. If Kim Jong-un is unwilling accept the provisions of the Korean Peace Fund offer on his own, he may if the military makes him an offer he cannot refuse.

Quiet dissent and internecine power struggles may exist in a heightened state for years to come as market forces increase and the young new leader matures, measures his options, and establishes or discovers the limits of his authority. It is impossible to grasp the complexity of conflict and interaction at the highest levels of power. However, it is clear that pressure for change is building at all levels in North Korean society, from the chronically hungry in the countryside to the privileged in Pyongyang, and from an emerging business class to the more pragmatic proto-capitalist factions within the state bureaucracy and power elite, as individuals and small unified groups seek their self-interests in a house no longer made of brick.

In addition to the hard-power lure of money, there is the soft-power attraction of culture. Without examining the probable influence that images and information have on personal motivations, we may overlook increasing everyday forms of resistance that undermine authority, and therefore underestimate the potential impulse for political action that underlies the surface patina of coerced compliant behavior. And without assessing how cultural change and pressure from below impact on the contingent judgment of elites, we may underestimate the possibility of political change from above.

In 2002, Selig Harrison wrote, "Only the top echelon of the Workers Party has more than an inkling of what the rest of the world is like."[51] But even then this was changing fast. At the time of his writing thousands of free-tuning radios and digital communication devices were being smuggled across the Chinese border by traders and desperate people trying to make money to feed their families. Mostly due to stress migration, Lankov notes, "Some half a million North Korean refugees have crossed into China between 1995 and 2005, and most of them eventually returned to North Korea bringing home stories of China's success and the almost unbelievable prosperity of South Korea."[52]

The perceived wealth of South Korea and the conspicuous display of prosperous lifestyles in media productions are attractive aspects of what Nye refers to as soft power.[53] Soft-power is usually comprised of intangible cultural factors and is based on persuasion and attraction.

Media censorship is a response to the fear of appealing and disruptive soft power influences. The flow of media from South to North Korea is particularly sensitive because the poems and pixels of southern prosperity highlight the backwardness of the North. These cultural flows challenge the official anti–South meta-narrative and weaken the legitimacy of state authority.

As previously mentioned, "there is evidence of increasing willingness to defy the government through everyday forms of resistance, such as listening to foreign media."[54] In spite of some targeted frequency jamming by North Korea, numerous radio broadcasts from the outside are reaching an interested and expanding audience. Voice of America, Radio Free Asia, Korean Broadcasting System, Open Radio for North Korea, Radio Chosun, and Free North Korea Radio are among the most popular stations that broadcast a radio signal into North Korea.[55] In one large sample of recent defectors, more than 50 percent reported that they "watched or listened to foreign news or entertainment programs."[56] Among the favorite U.S. films of the Pyongyang elite are *Titanic* and *Gone with the Wind*.[57] But South Korean cultural products dominate. Young Sun Jeon asserts that the government believes "hallyu (South Korean popular culture) is a risky agent that could accelerate the dissolution of the North Korean system."[58]

However, the government has been unable to prevent the flow of culture and information. Since the late 1990s the Korean wave (*hallyu*) of television soap operas, popular music (K-pop), and action film thrillers have swept across the cultural geography of East Asia and filtered into North Korea. These high-tech mega-produced cultural products depict modern luxurious images of general opulence and urban elegance that are far removed from anything seen or imagined in North Korea, while indigenous cultural contents are mere reproductions of a bygone era, uncharged by the vigorous international hybrid influences that inspire South Korean popular culture.[59]

In spite of government prohibitions and censorship, technological and cultural diffusion is pervasive and inspires modernity and symbolic displays of freedom and resistance; in the capital seat of power in Pyongyang, tweens to twenty-somethings dance disco while middle-aged adults copy the hairstyles and fashions of characters in South Korean television dramas.[60] Hassig and Oh assert, "Today, not only has the ideological dye faded throughout North Korean society, but people are becoming more individualistic in their appearances and lifestyles."[51] In 2007 Lankov noted, "The time lag between the North and the South has never been so narrow, and now last year's Seoul fashion is a hit in Pyongyang."[62]

Some elite youth secretly receive private instruction from choreographers to sing and dance like South Korean music idols, while other students play K-pop tunes on MP4 players (with the lyrics erased to avoid controversy) and dance together outside the central train station. Nat Kretchun and Jane Kim assert, "Armed by their parents with new technologies and a sense of relative immunity, it appears as though elite youth are beginning to push the boundaries of approved behavior more than other groups in North Korea."[63]

Orascom 3G mobile phones are now common for party officials conducting business, and among Pyongyang youth they serve as conspicuous symbols of privilege. The Egyptian conglomerate Orascom has promised a $500 million investment — the largest non–Chinese investment in North Korea since the end of the Cold War.[64] Over 1,500,000 people now have mobile devices, but without international calling access. Notebook computers are available to the children of the elite and the first Apple iPad tablet device was seen in public in the fall of 2011.[65] But there is still no connection with the outside world. The modern communication network infrastructure built in the mid–2000s has yet to be turned on and there is no public access to the World Wide Web.[66]

Communication with the outside is prohibited. Viewing and listening to foreign cultural content is illegal, but defectors report that, if caught, paying a bribe usually settles the matter. The wealthy Pyongyang elite can afford bribes and are an irrepressible captive audience whose central focus is often on international news and the pristine backdrops of video footage, as they wonder what it would be like to live in a world of such wealth, freedom and splendor.

The vast majority (89 percent) of defectors report word-of-mouth as their primary source of information.[67] At great personal risk, those who smuggle in foreign cultural products, and those who talk about them, have instigated a word-of-mouth epidemic that has critically changed the cognitive landscape of North Korea. As North Koreans view and disseminate information about the outside world, they become more cynical about the state of affairs in their own country and pass on this disaffection to others, often within the small groups that gather to play card, board or stick games, or in one of the ubiquitous markets that feed a majority of the population outside Pyongyang.[68]

After more than a decade of outside influences, now almost everyone has an idea or image of the relative prosperity in South Korea. Victor Cha predicts, "The increased flow of information will ultimately spell the end of the regime."[69] Oh and Hassig assert, "The Kim regime is built on lies.... If the truth is ever revealed, the Kim regime will collapse."[70] Analyzing defector surveys just prior to Kim Jong-il's death, Jun Hyeong Park and So Yeol Kim reported, "It seems likely that Kim Jong Il can currently command the support of around or slightly less than 50 percent of the North Korean population."[71] In spite of his Paektu bloodline and the efforts of state propaganda, this proportion will probably weigh more heavily against Kim Jong-un as time passes.

Perhaps thinking of Vaclav Havel and the Czech Velvet Revolution,[72] the late South Korean president Roh Moo-hyun is said to have remarked that *hallyu* would someday unify the peninsula. Considering the overwhelming level of paramilitary authoritarian control, it is more likely that soft-power cultural change is a necessary but insufficient causal force for political change. However, glimpses of modernity through South Korean news reports and cultural content are quietly changing the perspectives and aspirations of an increasing number of North Koreans as word-of-mouth rumors of the inordinately better life just beyond the border saturates cultural impressions and creates a new social context for political change.

While there are liberalizing developments inside North Korea, foreign policy and economic and military strategies have often had the opposite effect. For example, many believe the Lee administration's "over-emphasis on security has boomeranged, leaving South Korea more vulnerable."[73] Patrick Cronin asserts that the Lee administration's decision not to give North Korea something for nothing resulted in a more assertive pushback from Pyongyang, and that the decision to constrict investment in North Korea has accelerated China's rise as North Korea's dominant economic partner.[74]

Symbolic threats of violence from U.S. and South Korean border-area military exercises create fear and empower military-first hardliners in the North, entrench belligerent behavior, and nourish a seemingly intractable diplomatic standoff. And while it is politically difficult to argue against tit-for-tat coercive economic sanctions, they have not succeeded in substantively changing North Korean behavior. It would seem there is need for a more effective strategic model for influencing North Korea.

Former South Korean cabinet member and distinguished professor Chung-in Moon of Yonsei University asserts, "Empathy is a chief functioning principle in obtaining harmony and co-operation in international relations."[75] I agree — thus the Korean Peace Fund model is based on an empathic understanding of the overall context in which this next generation of North Korean leaders will assume power. And combined with critical changes occurring inside North Korean society, the Korean Peace Fund creates a smart-power approach to incentivize peace and reunification. A graphic representation of the critical change variables that may lead to reunification is pictured below.

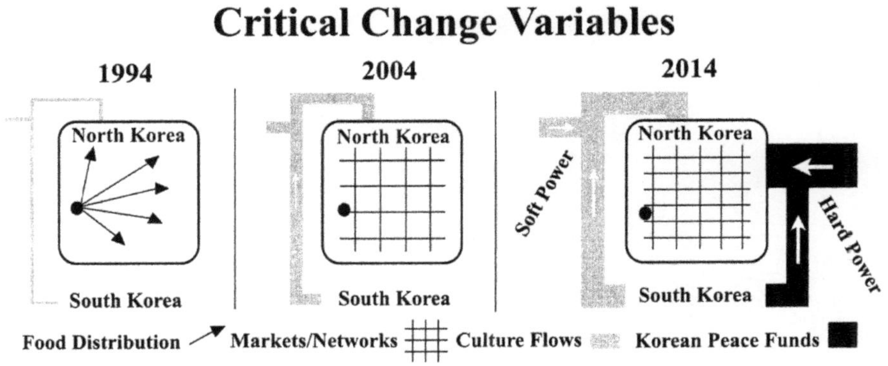

Critical Change Variables

Figure 2.

Figure 2 depicts the collapse of the public food distribution system, resulting in universal marketization, the creation of extensive exchange-trust networks and the formation of an underground information highway. A porous border with China has led to soft-power culture and information flows that inevitably challenge the government monopoly on information and its meta-narrative about South Korea. Since knowledge is cumulative, disaffection increases over time and puts more pressure on elites to reform or reunify. The institution of a Korean Peace Fund would give a compelling reason to the masses and the North Korean power elite to re-evaluate their current situation in light of the personal wealth, freedom and security they are offered. Information about the fund will spread quickly through these established underground networks. The critical change variables outlined above, acting in combination with hard-power payments and soft-power attractions may provide the information and incentives needed to tip the balance toward peace and reunification in Korea.

CHAPTER FOUR

Tipping Points

Tipping points are moments when thresholds are reached and seemingly small events can have large consequences. Who would have predicted a Tunisian street vendor would set off the Arab Spring revolts or that the assassination of the archduke of Austria would set off World War I? Without reform or reunification, it is probable internal stress will eventually reach a tipping point in North Korea. Although some experts speculate this may take more than a decade, totalitarian regimes tend to be brittle. Social and political change is often gradual, but slow and hidden until a sudden, unpredictable "Black Swan" set of cascading events leads to the rapid creation of a permanent alternative political reality. In historical retrospect, it is often easy to identify how the concatenation of antecedent events builds toward a tipping point.

Reverse engineering implicates a succession of causal events leading to the collapse of the Soviet Union. By encouraging *perestroika* (political and economic restructuring) and *glasnost* (a free press and public debate), Mikhail Gorbachev and the Russian power elite unleashed a process that could only end in social, political and economic revolution. Interviews with former members of the Soviet elite suggest the political-economic transition was orchestrated by a pro-capitalist coalition of Russian party-state leaders who realized the socialist system was fracturing and could not compete with international capitalism, and who saw an opportunity for personal gain. Elites quickly abandoned ideology for the pragmatic pursuit of material privilege and continued power in a free-market system.

David Kotz and Fred Weir have provided a detailed account of how this revolution was instigated and managed by those at the top. As early as 1987, several years before privatization became official policy, party-state elites began positioning themselves to take over state industries and take advantage of the changes they were about to make.[1] In the final months of 1991, they did little to stop the growing populist revolt and, after shoring up their material interests and securing their personal safety, they told their troops to stand down, and then sat back and watched the relatively bloodless revolution unfold on CNN along with the rest of the world.

Indeed, Mikhail Gorbachev and his family have lived comfortably in Moscow for the past two decades and many of the old Soviet political elites are members of the new Russian economic elite.[2] This political maneuver by Russian elites provides a model for North Korean elites to honorably step aside, but they must have sufficient material incentives, honorific expectations, and international assurances of personal safety to motivate them. In order to encourage North Korean elites to step aside and reunify with the South, tangible economic incentives must be offered from an external source. Elites must have a high level of confidence that after money is disbursed from the Korean Peace Fund, they will be more secure than they are now, or that they may legally purchase the business enterprises they already surreptitiously control.

In spite of public ideological zeal, North Koreans privately want, first and foremost, to secure the best for themselves and their families. Instead of using impersonal bargaining chips, perhaps providing personal incentives (through a Korean Peace Fund) to a relatively small and powerful North Korean elite would be a more successful strategy for compelling state behavior. As the older generation dies out, North Koreans should be viewed less as perpetrators and more as victims of history. As with second-generation Soviet elite reformers (after the Khrushchev de-Stalinization era), the post–Kim Jong-il North Korean power elite need a secure and profitable exit plan from the failing Stalinist system they inherited.

Growing fear and pressure from social forces may also affect elite expectations about the future and influence their decisions. The dramatic social and economic changes described above and increasing levels of defection and desperation suggest there may be a whispering countercurrent of conversation among people who have absorbed enough truth to feel angry and betrayed. Through ethnographic narratives and personal observation, Nancy Ries has produced an intimate account of living in a collapsing state system and the suffering and aspirations of Muscovites during the last years of *perestroika*. She notes that "talk was ener-

Four. Tipping Points

getic, fervent, and full of vivid images and emotions ... a cluster of tragic, paradigmatic questions, variously phrased, were circulating widely in private conversations."[3] Sounding similar to the saga unfolding in North Korea, David Hoffman writes, "A chasm separated them [Russian citizens] from the state.... They knew that even as the system declared its greatness, it was stagnating, rotting from within....They survived thanks to a vast, unofficial second economy — a shadow economy — that somehow provided a cushion against the harsh realities of life."[4]

This was a time of growing scarcity of basic foodstuffs, household supplies, and a decline in public services in Russia and its satellite states. And as in North Korea, people were becoming aware of the abundance of high-quality commodities and prosperous lifestyles just beyond their borders. When Lech Walesa first ventured outside Poland to participate in an international conference, he was struck by the sheer volume and variety of commodities available. Through word-of-mouth it eventually became clear to most people in the Soviet satellite states that their lives would improve by separating from the Soviet Union and joining the free world. Speaking from personal experience in Leningrad, Andrei Lankov observes, "Admiration for Western consumption goods was an important ingredient of the Soviet youngsters' disappointment with their system. Now it seems that the same story is being repeated in North Korea."[5]

Faced with overwhelming evidence of economic decline and stirrings of protest, Gorbachev first admitted to the deterioration of Russian living standards in 1985, a few years before the dissolution of the socialist state. Similarly, faced with growing public awareness of the South's relative prosperity, in 2000 the North Korean propaganda apparatus openly admitted South Korea's higher standard of living.[6] Almost a decade later, the unprecedented apology for the disastrous 2009 currency reform was the first time public discord had been acknowledged by the North Korean government. After confiscation of personal savings and monetary revaluation caused market closures, the price of a kilogram of rice rose from 22 to 220 won in just two months and resulted in public protests and near riots in some places.

It was reported the policy architect was publicly shot by a firing squad. Haggard and Noland speculate, "The stumble may have exceeded even the regime's coercive capacity and that at least some accountability is required to sustain elite if not mass support."[7] The state even officially allowed markets to reopen in the spring of 2010, since they were already ubiquitous anyway. The masses are growing angry and elites who are in touch with the pulse of the people must be increasingly fearful for their positions in a crumbling society, as propaganda is paying diminishing returns. North Korea may be reaching a status Miroslav Nincic refers to as an "unstable equilibrium," a point of volatility at which positive inducements may have the most effect.[8]

States lose legitimacy when they don't fulfill their promises. Nancy Ries notes, "By 1989 the promises of perestroika had worn out for most people; the utopian visions of a free and prosperous society that characterized the early perestroika years (roughly, 1985–88) seemed to have evaporated."[9] In a short time dissatisfaction reached a tipping point and the Soviet system collapsed. Though less organized and apparent, a similar sequence of events is occurring in North Korea. People no longer believe their troubles are related to the death of their Great Leader Kim Il-sung or are the result of a natural disaster. The substance and sheer weight of thousands of defector interviews provides strong evidence of growing discontent, as "common people are beginning to doubt they live in a workers paradise."[10]

This has been an eventful gestation in power for the young Kim, which included the unsuccessful spring 2012 launch of a $850 million long-range missile, the billion dollar centenary celebrations, the successful launch of a three-stage missile and orbiting satellite in December and a successful underground nuclear test in February 2013.[11] Alexandre Mansourov asserts that successful military exercises "will further boost Kim Jong Un's domestic legitimacy, increase his political capital, undermine potential critics, help him silence military discontent, and increase his international stature and bargaining power."[12]

However, the influence of such spectacles is short-lived and cynicism and dissent will increase again as promises to become a "strong and prosperous nation" fail to materialize. Fewer North Koreans are fooled by parades and propaganda, as increasingly desperate people want tangible improvements in their lives. One successful missile launch or nuclear explosion is unlikely to change the growing ground-level perception of relative deprivation, a sense of general decline among the masses living outside Pyongyang, the yearning of a new elite generation to become part of the wider world, and the anger among excluded groups inside Pyongyang who have witnessed an increase of economic status among elites but have enjoyed few benefits themselves. There were signs and indicators on the horizon many years before the belated reforms and ultimate demise of the Soviet Union. It would seem that North Korea is following a path that has a predictable destination.

But political revolutions are not Newtonian billiard ball events. North Korea is not the Soviet Union. Patterns and similarities can be deceiving. There may be invisible variables. The surveillance state is stronger in North Korea and the controlling elites may be too distrustful of each other for cooperative stealth. Communication is better controlled; state narratives may be more convincing, social atomization more complete. Lack of transportation and communication may be key stabilizing factors, or hunger-induced apathy and a well-armed security force, or foreign currency profits to a smaller and more insulated selectorate and controlling elite, or energy and food aid shipments at crucial times, or the partial impact of multiple factors that tip back the fragile balance.

After severe economic retrenchment due to the cessation of Russian friendship energy prices and the decline in Soviet trade from $3.25 billion in 1990 to just $100 million in 1994,[13] experts discussed what might bring North Korea to a tipping point and force it to cross a threshold into the free-market modern world. The most popular scenario was industrial collapse and economic depression combined with widespread food shortages. A natural experiment testing this model occurred in the mid–1990s, when, after years of economic mismanagement and steep industrial decline, floods, drought and famine lead to the starvation of an estimated 600,000 to 1,000,000 people.[14] But this massive desperation and dislocation did not portend political revolt in Pyongyang, because it was mostly outlying provincial and rural people who starved and they either were too hungry for politics or had no way to get to Pyongyang to protest. Except for a few government vehicles and slow-moving wood-fueled trucks, roads are mostly empty in North Korea. South Korea has 730 times the number of private cars (18,260,000 versus 25,000), and over 100 times the total length of paved roads (only 3 percent of roads are paved in the North). Don Oberdorfer once commented in his journal that it is "a strange land left deserted by some invisible plague."[15] The restricted ability of the population to travel keeps them in a virtual geographic prison. Even bicycles were banned until the early 1990s.

Internal revolt is also suppressed by an inhuman "tainted blood" three-generation family punishment system whereby a protestor's punishment extends to parents, grandparents, brothers, sisters, nieces, nephews, cousins and children. Few who speculate on future political crises in North Korea predict the participation of the rural population (41 percent of the total) will play much of a role in any possible scenario.

With resources disproportionately diverted to Pyongyang, the provinces of North Korea have some political and economic similarities to the satellite states in the former Soviet Union; dissent increases with distance away from Pyongyang (or Moscow). As with presaging protests in the Soviet client states, one can envision revolt spreading in the provincial cities across North Korea. Peter Hayes and David von Hippel imagine a "fiefdom situation, where rival warlords begin to struggle for territory or power."[16] And now with mobile phone coverage expanding to 100 cities across North Korea, there is more of a possibility of coordinating communication links between cities and provinces. In addition to $145 million in revenue, Orascom founder Nuguib Sawiris mentioned this expanded phone coverage to a *Forbes* magazine reporter in November 2012. Wider use of communication technology increases the plausibility of the Hayes-von Hippel scenario. However, without significant military support, isolated provincial revolts could easily be contained, as the one in North Hamgyong province was in 1995.[17]

The most viable location for effective populist revolt is the elite capital Pyongyang, a fortress city of about three million people. According to one high-profile defector, there are about 500,000 privileged core members of the workers party in North Korea (15 percent to 20 percent of Pyongyang's population) who are especially key to the regime's survival.[18] Another estimate is that 200,000 people compose the core political and military elite.[19] Applying either estimate, a minimum of 80 percent of the politically excluded Pyongyang population might be especially receptive to incentives provided by external factors—like those proposed in the Korean Peace Fund.

Pyongyang is often thought of as "a Potemkin village, an elaborate artifice for the benefit of outsiders."[20] Behind the façade of this Hollywood set is another, more desperate Pyongyang. In spite of some recent investment in home construction, over two million less privileged residents of Pyongyang live along dirt roads behind the opulent high-rise apartment-lined main streets in small brick-and-clay huts, without refrigerators, running water, and (for many) televisions; they use public (cold water) showers and toilets and rely on coal-based stove-pipe heating.[21] Recently, even people living in some of the high rises have had to move out during the winter months because they cannot get enough heat.[22] And with new aspirations of a more informed generation, inflationary dangers, and over a million people with cell phones, there is a significant proportion of this population that could spread trouble.[23] Cha asserts, "It is hard to imagine enlightenment out of utter poverty, but this is what is happening slowly in North Korea. And when this anger erupts, it will be violent and bloody."[24]

A less chaotic solution to the Korean dilemma is a scenario of elite acquiescence similar to the 1991 Russian revolution. But in the Russian situation there were significant state-controlled resources to distribute among the elites. This is not the case in North Korea. The current North Korean economy is more than 40 times smaller than Russia's was in 1992; the difference in GDP is $1.15 trillion (1992) versus $26.5 billion (2010).[25] Thus, in order to encourage the North Korean elite to step aside and reunify with the South, significant tangible economic incentives must be offered from external sources.

The Kim family and the North Korean power elite are caught in an insoluble power struggle with reform-minded opponents and trapped in a contradictory social, political and economic conundrum. If they denuclearize or allow economic reforms and social freedoms, they risk losing political control, and if they do not, they also risk losing political control. Kim Jong-nam, the older half-brother of Kim Jong-un, is quoted as saying, "Without reforms, North Korea will collapse, and when such changes take place, the regime will collapse."[26] Seung-Ho Joo contends, "Time is on Seoul's side.... No matter how the power struggle turns out, the Kim dynasty is doomed."[27]

Indeed, there is potential danger for the elite from top to bottom. The memory of Ceausescu's demise, and more recently that of Colonel Gaddafi, creates more fear of their own people than of any imagined external threat. Cha speculates the Kim family might consider alternatives if their personal security were assured, and asserts that the Kim family needs the United States to promise it "will not allow the House of Kim (that is, Kim Jong-un, his aunt and uncles, and other relatives) to collapse as Pyongyang (partially) denuclearizes and goes through a modest reform process and opening to the outside world."[28] As unlikely as this scenario seems, this personal concern may be of paramount importance in promoting for peace and reunification to this top-heavy post-totalitarian government.

North Korean leaders, who command a 1.2 million–man professional army (and 7.5 million reservists), also have personal lives, families, grandchildren, and hopes and dreams for a peaceful and prosperous future. David Kang submits that modern North Koreans inherited "circumstances they did not create ... they live their lives, marry, worry about their children, go to their jobs, and try to get through the day as best they can."[29] They are rational and pragmatic people who are amenable to compelling incentives and might consent to a uniquely enriching opportunity for themselves and their families if their personal safety and well-being are assured.

Therefore, personal security is a fundamental promise in the Korean Peace Fund model. Of course, if Kim Jong-un accepts the terms of the peace fund agreement, the House of Kim must gracefully relinquish political power. But Kim Jong-un will be awarded the Nobel Peace Prize and hailed as the heroic young leader who brought peace, prosperity and Korean unification to his people. And for North Korean elites, the Korean Peace Fund model offers absolute assurances of personal safety for anyone in any danger of retribution after reunification, including amnesty from prosecution by local authorities and international institutions. Leaders will be safe from harm and can begin to live a new life with honor, wealth and security in a forward-looking reunified Korea, or anywhere else in the world they choose.

American economist John Kenneth Galbraith once wrote, "Politics is not the art of the possible. It consists of choosing between the disastrous and the unpalatable." As was the case after the Soviet collapse, there can be no truth-and-reconciliation commissions or international tribunals. Would North Korean leaders give up their guns if they had any reason to fear the worst? Amnesty from punishment is an essential precondition of this peace model even though we know human rights abuses have permeated North Korean society and its gulag prison system for decades.[30] As a practical matter, it may be necessary for North Korea to give up a few notorious human rights violators in order to appease strong prosecutory voices. A few guilty North Koreans may escape to China or elsewhere and live in exile to avoid prosecution.

There will be exposures of labor camp horrors and reports of terrorism, abductions and murder, and there will be political temptations for reprisal. Healing will be painful and take years, but in spite of deep resentment and the desire for retribution, this one-time pragmatic forgiveness will be necessary in order to obtain the release of an estimated 200,000 political prisoners and to permanently solve an increasingly dangerous international situation that ultimately threatens the lives of millions.[31]

CHAPTER FIVE

The Price of Peace Equation

In a previous paper, I wrote, "If war is fought over money, and power and control over the people, land and resources that produce it, why cannot we pay in advance to prevent it?"[1] In response to this question, I drafted a Korean Peace Fund proposal to pay the North Korean military and ruling elite to put down their guns and join the modern world as wealthy new members of the international community. To this model I now turn in detail.

The Korean Peace Fund model is built around the notion that there is nothing more powerfully motivating in human affairs than the alleviation of fear and the promise of personal prosperity. Instead of using negative coercion or impersonal conventional bargaining chips, it is posited that providing personal incentives to the families of a relatively small but powerful North Korean elite might be a more successful strategy for compelling state behavior. As stated before, the fundamental assumption is that peace and reunification can be achieved by changing the underlying incentive structure for all North Koreans, and by offering its leaders a safe, honorable, and profitable way out of a difficult and deteriorating situation.

Joseph Nye defines smart power as a "combination of the hard power of coercion and payment with the soft power of persuasion and attraction."[2] By adding hard-power payment to the significant social changes and soft-power cultural influences described in previous chapters, the Korean Peace Fund completes a full complement of smart-power incentives acting upon North Koreans to compel preferred outcomes. Payment is a gentle form of hard power, and in the Korean context it may prove to be more cost-effective and determinative.[3]

With North Korea as its only military threat, South Korea has spent

Five. The Price of Peace Equation

$500 billion on defense since 1974 (one trillion adjusted to 2012 dollars). The budget for defense between 2006 and 2020 is assessed at over $600 billion.[4] Compare this to the $39 billion estimate for buying off the entire North Korean political and military power elite, including security forces and high- and middle-ranking military officers.

In spite of ideological smokescreens and political posturing, from a materialist perspective it is clear that war and peace are essentially about money (as well as power and control over the people, land and resources that produce it). In August 2010 South Korean President Lee Myung-bak proposed a tax that would fund reunification.[5] Economic projections have been on the table for years. Money is always a central issue. Fortunately, more than enough money is readily available (see chapter six). Indeed, it is possible that most, if not all, of this money can be raised from international sources, allowing South Korea to better afford the long-term costs of economic integration.

To allocate money and quantify the price of peace, we need the following:

(1) A comprehensive cultural map of the power elite in North Korea
(2) An understanding of what would be a sufficiently motivating amount of money for individuals in various sectors of society
(3) An estimate of the number of people to be compensated at each level

Experts working together on both sides of the 38th parallel can determine the specific details of this allocation program. Categories and estimates introduced here merely provide a framework for future discussions.

The aggregate Price of Peace Equation is outlined below:

$$(PE \times \$) + (M \times \$) + (UR \times \$) + (RF \times \$) + (C \times \$) + (S \times \$)$$
PE = power elite; M = military; UR = urban residents; RF = rural farmers; C = children; S = special

It is notable that the Kim family is excluded from this benefits package. In spite of the death of Kim Jong-il, after years of bitter resentment it is politically impractical to ask South Korea (or the rest of the world) to offer money to the Kim family, whether it comes from more abstract sovereign funds or from international sources. This will preserve Kim Jong-un's dignity and honor (face) when he steps down. Money is probably not a principal motivating factor anyway, since the Kim family is known to have large sums in foreign banks.

The power elite (PE), which includes the highest-ranking military commanders, has layers of authority and access to power, and therefore will have several pay rankings. The rest of the military (M), about 1.2 million personnel, or 5 percent of the total North Korean population, has a ranking structure to guide differential payments.

According to the 2008 population census, the total population of North Korea is about 24 million, with 59 percent living in urban areas and 41 percent in rural areas.[6] After arbitrarily subtracting 1.2 million military personnel, there are 8.6 million adult urban residents (UR). This model may unfairly lump urban professional, industrial and service workers into the same payoff category, but what is fair? Pay scales will adjust after reunification. An estimated 6.8 million adult rural farmers (RF) compose a more uniform impoverished class and can also be paid equal amounts. An estimated 7.4 million children (C) under 18 years of age represent approximately 31 percent of the total North Korean population. They will likewise receive equal amounts.

The above payment categories are suggestions. The final aggregate equation can be smoothed and dissected into as many payable categories as are deemed necessary. This simplistic model discriminates at the higher end and equalizes in the middle and lower end. The following numbers are segmented monetary averages to be paid to the six major sectors or categories of people in the Price of Peace Equation:

PE — (10,000 members of the political and military power elite) — The first 100 families at the top of the power hierarchy will be paid on a graduated scale between $100 and $50 million and the next 100 will be paid $50–20 million ($11 billion);[7] the next 800 elites will receive graduated payments between $20 million and $10 million ($12 billion); the next 1,000 families will be paid between $10 million and $2 million ($6 billion); the next 1,000 families will be paid between $2 million and $1 million ($1.5 billion); the next 7,000 families will be paid $1 million to $500,000 ($5.25 billion). The total amount paid to power elite families will thus be, $35.75 billion. This will create 10,000 families worth over half a million dollars and spread incentives well beyond Pyongyang. By comparison, with double the population, 150,000 South Koreans have a

Five. The Price of Peace Equation

net worth of a million dollars or more (mostly due to high incomes, decades of saving and dramatically increased property values).

M — 1.2 million members of the military will receive money based on a multi-tiered graduated payment schedule. Officers below the rank of general and above the rank of captain/major will receive payment between $600,000 and $400,000. Based on common worldwide military command structures, it is estimated this group would comprise about 1,200 officers who command 1,000 soldiers each at the battalion level ($600 million). Payments between $200,000 and $50,000 will be given to 30,000 officers including and between the rank of captain/major, who command 200 soldiers, and platoon leaders, who command 50 soldiers. Assuming four times as many lower-ranking officers in this category, this payment will be $2.4 billion.

This extra $3 billion payout to military officers will put additional pressure up the chain of command on those at the top who may be profiting from corruption and thus reluctant to cede control. These 31,200 high- and middle-ranking military officers (who interact with and control the troops on a daily basis) may function as an armed supra-civil society, since they represent an organized middle-level social force that will want to obtain the substantial money offered them in the Korean Peace Fund. If instability ignites, they could pose a threat to their unwilling generals.

The remaining 1.17 million soldiers will each receive $20,000 ($23.4 billion). The total amount paid to the military (excluding military PE) is $26.4 billion.

UR — 8.6 million adult urban residents will be paid $15,000 each ($129 billion).

RF — 6.8 million adult rural farmers will be paid $10,000 each ($68 billion).

C — 7.4 million children (age: 0–18) will be paid $5,000 each ($37 billion). Parents will be happy to know this money will be held in an interest-bearing escrow account until their children's eighteenth birthday. It is likely most of this money will re-enter the economy through college tuition payments.

S — includes three special social categories that are considered for extra payment: (1) people's group heads; (2) party members; and (3) the Guard Command. This special group has 750,000 members, who will be paid varied amounts ($6 billion).

As part of the state surveillance apparatus, people's group heads monitor the activities of about thirty households (100–150 persons) and report anything suspicious to higher authorities. It has been previously noted that this neighborhood system of social control has been disintegrating in the countryside and has lost its effectiveness in provincial cities because people have stopped telling on their neighbors. It does, however, remain prevalent in Pyongyang.[8] If these individuals were offered an additional $5,000 each, multiplied by (an overestimated) 200,000 heads, this would amount to a bonus payout of $1 billion. Aligning the interests of people's group heads with reunification might influence their surveillance activities and turn some into valuable communication assets.

As estimated by a high-ranking North Korean defector, there are about 500,000 privileged core members of the workers party (15–20 percent of Pyongyang's population) who are especially important to the survival of regime.[9] A $9,000 bonus payment to these individuals would amount to an additional $4.5 billion. Enriching this Pyongyang purse may result in more influence over this important populace.

And for an additional cost of $500 million, it may also be strategic to offer a bonus of $10,000 to each of the estimated 50,000 members of the Guard Command, who directly handle the personal safety of the Kim family and other high-ranking officials. Considerations could likewise be made for the parallel paramilitary protective forces, the Pyongyang Defense Command and the Military Security Command. All of these payouts are additive bonuses to original payment categories. These targeted payouts may ultimately prove decisive.

Thus, to solve the Price of Peace equation:

$$35.75 + 26.4 + 129 + 68 + 37 + 6 = \$302.15 \text{ billion}$$

This is the potential cost of permanent peace and reunification on the Korean peninsula. Of course, there are other possible numbers that could reduce the payout, but it is important to make the initial incentives as attractive as possible. It is better to pay extra up front since this money will be the primary incentive for reunification and will prime the economic pump after reunification, and when the alternative is the even greater price of war. Table 1 summarizes the Price of Peace equation.

Five. The Price of Peace Equation

Table 1. The Price of Peace

Group	Average Amount (thousands)	Recipients	Total Amount (billions)
PE	3,575	10,000	35.75
M	22	1,200,000	26.4
UR	15	8,600,000	129
RF	10	6,800,000	68
C	5	7,400,000	37
S	8	750,000	6

Korean Peace Fund benefits are tailored to the specific characteristics of the North Korean cultural system and power structure. Since the extended family is the central core organic institution and women comprise more than half of the North Korean population, women, children and grandparents are explicitly included in the direct distribution of money. In this way, the primacy of the Confucian age hierarchy and the security of the family are honored, and the intangible influence of these important invisible sub-cultures is incentivized.[10] The essential inclusiveness of this fund should result in broad-based enthusiasm and motivate individuals to take action to make reunification possible. A detailed accounting of payments by category is provided on the next page.

This money should be dispensed over the course of five years to create more stability and commitment to social and economic integration. However, a large initial payment of one-third of the total amount should be offered up front. Twelve billion dollars will be transferred to the North Korean elite on Reunification Signing Day. Military payments will commence soon after disarmament and the masses can have access to money as soon as banks can open around the country.

An urban family of four whose parents are not party members will receive a total of $40,000 over five years; if they were party members and one was a people's group head and the other a member of the Guard Command, the family would receive $73,000. Although more incentive money will be paid to those with more power, permanent peace with inequality is the lesser of other possible evils. The vast majority of North Koreans can expect the monetary equivalent of several years' work deposited into their bank accounts. The economic incentive for peace and reunification will be overwhelming to those at the top, middle and bottom.

Table 2. Korean Peace Fund Payments

	People	Amount (millions)	Total (billions)
Elites	100	100–50	7.5
	100	50–20	3.5
	800	20–10	12.0
	1,000	10–2	6.0
	1,000	2–1	1.5
	7,000	1–0.5	5.25
	10,000		**35.75**
Military		(thousands)	
high officers	1,200	600–400	.6
mid-officers	30,000	200–50	2.4*
others	1,168,880	20	23.4
	1,200,000		**26.4**
Masses			
urban	8,600,000	15	129.0
rural	6,800,000	10	68.0
children	7,400,000	5	37.0
	22,800,000		**234.0**
Special (additional)			
group heads	200,000	5	1.0
party	500,000	9	4.5
Guard-Cmd	50,000	10	.5
			6.0
TOTAL	**24,000,000**		**302.15**

*Assumes 4 times more low-ranking officers in this category

Considering the price of war, the $300 billion price for peace is not unreasonable and would be the greatest gesture of humanitarian goodwill ever undertaken. The cost of German reunification was seven times this amount over twenty years. Credit Suisse estimated Korean unification would cost $1.5 trillion. Other estimates range from two to five trillion dollars to reach certain levels of equality over various lengths of time.

Of course, the incentive money used to fund peace and reunification will be only the beginning of the total price of economic integration. But this initial money will seed an economic foundation and be recirculated within the Korean economy and compounded over time as the notions of banking security, savings, and borrowing settle in among the people. It is possible some money may end up in offshore bank accounts

Five. The Price of Peace Equation

or fund anti-democratic revanchist objectives. However, almost 90 percent of the peace fund money will be given in small sums to poor people who are likely to spend it on themselves and their families.

Capitalist market incentives may not take long to develop, as the reduction or elimination of state provisions has forced the hand of private enterprise and already led to widespread, crisis-induced marketization.[11] Defectors report the existence of a vibrant system of communication, underground economy and widespread engagement in private economic and entrepreneurial activities.[12] Andrei Lankov and Seokhyang Kim note, "North Korea's switch to markets began from below, and this constitutes a major difference from the post-communist transformations of the USSR and China, where the authorities took the lead."[13]

North Koreans are a literate, educated people living in broad social exchange networks. As this peace plan becomes a "word-of-mouth epidemic" and circulates through the population, many details will be discussed.[14] But the bottom-line incentive that will be talked about is the amount of money each person will personally receive. These cash incentives, combined with unpredictable future destabilizing events, may eventually create a tipping point for peace and reunification.

Wide publication, radio transmission and diffusion of the general details and specific incentives of the Korean Peace Fund will provide bottom-up pressure for Korean reunification. It should be communicated across the border that a deposit banking system would be established for money to be distributed locally into private accounts. Inexpensive food will become widespread and improved seeds and fertilizer will be given to farmers, and tractors imported. Job and travel freedom and the legal establishment of private property should be stipulated.

Every household will be promised a tablet computer and sold additional ones at some fraction of the cost for the first year. Given that only 4 percent of the population has ever even held a cell phone, this will be an exciting offer. The network infrastructure for Intranet, Internet and mobile phone communication has been in place since the mid–2000s.[15] In addition to incentivizing reunification, the ownership of personal communication devices will help ease the culture gap after reunification, contribute to productivity, and underwrite the basis for a future market.

The digital revolution will make reunification cheaper, quicker and easier.

Of course, this promise begs the question of a reliable supply of electricity. This must be an immediate priority. Realistic assessments for the energy infrastructure should be shared up front to avoid later dissension. Independent of the serious shortage of chemical fertilizer, North Korean rice seeds produce only 86 percent of the yield of South Korean varieties.[16] Food problems can be eased with seeds, fertilizer, tractors, and cheaper rice imports that would also relieve inflationary pressures.

Democratic voting rights of North Koreans should be restricted for at least five to ten years in order to preserve political consistency during the early vulnerable stage of transition. Indeed, it might be expedient to prohibit Kim Jong-un and other North Korean elites from seeking political office for some period of time. The promise of future suffrage along with immediate promises of job freedom, property ownership, agricultural inputs, an energy infrastructure, tablet computers, international communication, health care, food security, and personal bank accounts will give people hope for a better future and incentives to take action to make it possible.

The fund should be administered by a G20 institutionalized organization to inspire trust, record promises, collect contributions, and accord legitimacy within the international community, the North Korean elite and all Koreans. An optimistic scenario is that once this plan for a Korean Peace Fund is finalized and unfolds, media and political leaders from around the world will promote it and publicize its growth until it is fully funded. Full funding may take several years of vigilant international political and media attention. Or it may happen quickly

The international community will have a sense of working together to raise the money. The new collaborative, self-organizing, transformative power of our digitally connected world to amass global resources and broad-based political support may play a decisive role. Creative Internet fund-raising firms could make this fund go "viral" and collect contributions from diverse elements of the international community.[17] However, after the fund gains international legitimacy the bulk of funding will most likely come from a limited number of governments that want more influence over the final result.

I do not mean to say that we should expect a Panglossian velvet revolution or that international and domestic cooperation will be seamless. There may be serious acrimony along the way — internal factions may fight. But internal political instability should not result in dangerous aggression since the peace fund will be an internationally constituted initiative and globally funded institution.[18] As in other social and political upheavals, some people may pay the ultimate price as the process works itself out. However, it is possible that with sufficient incentive, the leadership and/or the vast majority of literate and reasonable people in North Korea will decide to take advantage of this opportunity and change the course of Korean history.[19]

CHAPTER SIX

Funding and Acquiescence

New ideas often face considerable resistance, especially when politics or the redistribution of money is involved. Beyond ideological divisions, individuals and groups share basic assumptions about how the world works, and what is realistic, unrealistic, practical, impractical, or cannot be discussed because it is the elephant in the room. At first glance the idea that a peace fund could rally a popular revolution or pacify a fearful and belligerent North Korean elite seems implausible, and that it could be funded to the extent of $300 billion seems even more far-fetched. But upon closer examination it is possible to imagine how this could happen.

North Korea's nuclear weapons program has received priority funding since 1993 because, as Don Oberdorfer notes, it is their only internationally respected "bargaining chip for trade recognition, security assurances, and economic benefits."[1] But the United States and neighbor states that North Korea has intermittently depended on for aid are increasingly frustrated, restrictive, and nervous about this progressive threat and are not responding to brinkmanship with benefits as they have in the past. Thus, China is currently the sole provider of aid to North Korea. It is improbable the regime could last more than a year or two without Chinese support, but this relationship may be more fragile than conventional wisdom suggests.

It is conventional wisdom that China prefers to keep the peninsula divided in order to preserve the existence of a fraternally allied communist-authoritarian state as a buffer between itself and U.S.–garrisoned democratic South Korea. However, a continued consensus of support within the new seven-member Central Politburo Standing Committee is not assured.[2] Although for now policy conservatives and cautious traditionalists seem to dominate government policy discussions, their tolerance may not be unlimited. Pragmatism has a way of changing attitudes, along with the most recent analysis of costs and benefits.

Six. Funding and Acquiescence

China's foreign policy establishment increasingly regards North Korea as a "strategic burden" and a provocative threat to regional stability because of its nuclear ambitions.[3] Myeong-hae Choi argues that the general opinion now among Chinese experts "is that North Korea's 'adventuristic' actions are causing 'strategic losses' for China."[4] Shen Dingli contends that as Beijing moves further toward reconciliation with Taipei, the strategic utility of North Korea as a distraction to U.S. military assets is diminished.[5] More importantly, Sangit Dwivedi asserts, "Pyongyang's utility as a buffer state between Chinese and U.S. forces is increasingly invalidated as Pyongyang's provocations invite greater U.S. military presence in the region."[6]

Indeed, Korean unification and a prevailing peace in East Asia would leave the United States with little left in the region to fight over and few reasons to reposition its navy in the Pacific or direct its military toward East Asia, unless China decided to flex its muscles against Taiwan, the Philippines or Vietnam, but this is unlikely.[7] China does not wish to cause problems with the United States and its relations with Taiwan have never been better. China has become Taiwan's largest trading partner and it is most probable that they will reconcile their differences peacefully. As economics increasingly dominate political relations, Taiwan and China are likely to increase cultural exchanges and become better partners.[8]

In spite of perceived past benefits of an alliance with North Korea, China is growing increasingly uneasy about having an unruly rogue state on its border that at some point might provoke a U.S. military response. Chinese diplomacy expert, former national security advisor and U.S. secretary of state Henry Kissinger is also uneasy about this growing threat. Fareed Zakaria quotes Kissinger from a recent personal conversation: "The Chinese will not want to be seen as abandoning an ally or colluding with Washington in planning its demise. They know that there is now a real danger of an accident, incident or miscalculation on the Korean Peninsula. If that happened, there is danger that China and the United States would end up reacting quickly, viscerally and in ways that might make things much worse — even lead to conflict. To prevent this scenario, we should propose serious strategic talks. My instinct is that the Chinese are ready for this conversation."[9]

This threat reached a new level of concern after Pyongyang successfully launched a three-stage missile in December 2012 and then, two months later, conducted its third underground nuclear test in seven years. China's support for United Nations sanctions (March 2013) has been accompanied by an unusual and harsh array of comments against North Korea from high places.[10] Fudan University professor Shen Dingli wrote in *Foreign Policy* that "China has reached a point where it needs to cut its losses and cut North Korea loose," and Deng Yuwen at the elite Central Party School in east Beijing[11] wrote in the *Financial Times* that "China should consider abandoning North Korea [and] take the initiative to facilitate North Korea's unification with South Korea." Xie Tao of Beijing Foreign Studies University also recently wrote, "Having an unpredictable, ungrateful, and totalitarian regime armed with nuclear weapons is the last thing China wants on its border."[12]

There has been speculation that new Central Committee member Zhang Dejiang may blindly support North Korea because of his conservative credentials and because he graduated from Kim Il-sung University as a twenty-four-year-old, and was party secretary of Yanbian Prefecture (1990–1995) and Jilin Province (1995–1998).[13] But this may be a false assumption. He, more than any other Chinese political leader, has witnessed the desperation of people coming from North Korea during the famine in the 1990s, and with his Korean language skills he is likely well aware of the changing social and political dynamics inside North Korea. This background may influence Zhang Dejiang to take the lead and look favorably on the Korean Peace Fund model as a relatively inexpensive permanent solution to a seemingly insoluble security problem. Indeed, he may be the first to hear about this plan and introduce its thesis to the other six members of the standing committee.

Government policy in China is increasingly influenced by public sentiment and the voices of intellectuals. Contrary to old-school Western opinion, Sunny Lee asserts, "Chinese scholars are active participants in policy suggestions and formulations that ultimately shape China's foreign policy."[14] An Internet-facilitated web of discussion has created more transparency and self-reflection, and it is partly responsible for a new China that is undergoing rapid changes—the growing influence of public opinion is one such change.

According to Debin Zhan and Hun Kyung Lee, a reunified Korea is the preference of average Chinese citizens and many scholars and bureaucrats.[15] The Chinese public has a decidedly negative opinion of North Korean leadership and recent provocations have embarrassed party leaders. The Chinese blogosphere erupted in May 2012 when North Korea detained 28 Chinese fishermen in the Yellow Sea and held them for 12 days, as Beijing seemed powerless or uncaring. Stephanie Kleine-Ahlbrandt asserts, "Netizens called on the government to cancel aid to North Korea."[16] That Beijing has allowed scholars and the media to publicly debate its relationship with North Korea is seen as both a warning to Pyongyang and a signal that China may be ready to reverse its North Korea policy.

There seems to be growing sentiment from a variety of sources that it is now in Beijing's best interests to distance itself from Pyongyang for both political and economic reasons. Indeed, the presence of a bankrupt, unpredictable and vitriolic North Korea with questionable stability discourages economic development in the Pacific Northeast, an important Chinese (and Russian) objective. Zhang Liangui, professor of international strategic research at the elite Party School of the Central Committee of the Communist Party of China, has noted that a unified Korea would prompt significant Chinese economic investment.

Chinese scholars arguing for a more hardliner approach, harsher sanctions against North Korea, and more cooperation with the United States are called "strategists," as opposed to "traditionalists," who take the opposite view.[17] A plan for avoiding the chaos of an unexpected collapse and stabilizing the Pacific Northeast region for investment and development may give Chinese policy "strategists" and economy-first political pragmatists more authority to push to disengage with North Korea and compel the North to accept this peace offer.

As China becomes more concerned about geopolitical developments resulting from North Korean provocations, the Korean Peace Fund may appear as the ultimate solution to a situation that is becoming more intolerable. Indeed, the Korean Peace Fund model may provide the platform and impetus for this new consensus, not only within the Central Politburo Standing Committee but also within the East Asian community.

There is some speculation North Korea could grow out of its problems, that an export-led model of development or Chinese- or Vietnamese-style rural reforms could stimulate the economy and appease public opinion.[18] But neither China nor Vietnam had a large population of inordinately more prosperous, politically separated, cultural-ethnic brethren on their borders. The foreign-imposed 38th parallel artificially divides the greatest economic disparity between people in the world today. As mentioned previously, the average South Korean is about 17 times wealthier than his northern counterpart. This disparity vastly increases the possibility that reforms may lead to unification pressures and political instability. Even strictly economic reforms may be potentially destabilizing because, if they are successful, they will empower people and may lead to greater access to information about the South.

Mimura Mitsuhiro asserts, "To succeed, North Korea must become an attractive destination for foreign investment. To win public support, the new government must improve the overall economic situation."[19] In September 2012, 150 Chinese business entrepreneurs privately convened to assess the prospects for investing in North Korea. A similar gathering is being organized by China's Ministry of Commerce that will include Russia and Egypt.[20] Already billions of dollars in foreign investments have been earmarked to develop the resource-rich areas in the northern region. But these will be resource-targeted investments that may benefit the local labor force and a few North Korean elites more than the general economy.

Most business interests are cautious, as many past investments have gone sour. In just the past year, North Korea's decision to expropriate $1.5 billion in Hyundai Asan assets invested in the Mount Kumgang tourist project and allegedly hundreds of millions ($37.8 million officially and the rest in bribes) from a Chinese steel and mining company (Xiyang Group) are two examples from a long list of forfeiture and loss.[21] And without significant nuclear concessions there is little possibility onerous international economic sanctions in place since 2006 (and tightened in 2009 and 2013) will be lifted anytime soon.[22] Except for resource-targeted Chinese investment, the Kaesong Industrial Project, illegal entanglements and arms dealing, North Korea has no significant foreign economic relationships from which to draw capital.

Sanctioned and cut off from foreign capital, most state enterprises perform dismally and a moribund economy has been stagnant or worse for over two decades, with per-capita incomes less than what they were in 1990, agricultural production half its potential, and an obsolete industry operating at a quarter of its capacity. Its national currency is worthless abroad, inflation is a recurring problem, hyperinflation an existential threat, and there is no obvious solution for the regime other than politically dangerous economic reform. Andrei Lankov notes, "North Korean elites know that the greatest threats they face are internal, not external, and that resisting reform is the most effective way to control the population."[23] However, with pressures mounting, everyone knows this can only be a temporary solution.

So far Kim Jong-un and at least some elements of the North Korean leadership have indicated they may agree with this assessment. There are reports of new economic cooperation initiatives and potential economic reforms, including the resurrection of two long dormant special economic zones in Rason (Rajin) and Sinuiju-Dangdong. After a year of construction, in August 2012 the paved road connecting China with the port in Rason was completed and "power substations are being built, railway lines are being linked to Siberia and piers at the port are being expanded."[24] In addition, the June 28, 2012, new economic management system policies may give factory managers more control over production and freedom to set prices; collectivized farms would be broken up and independent households would be given incentives to produce a surplus for sale; farmers would keep 30–50 percent of what they produce and state-run companies and shops may be allowed to keep 70 percent of their profits.[25]

Citing the possibility of a new openness and realism in North Korea, Yonsei University scholar John Delury asserts, "Kim appears to be heading in what he describes as a 'new, creative and enterprising' direction, nudging the national compass away from a fixation on his father's 'military-first politics' toward a Deng-like pragmatic emphasis on economic development."[26] However, Haggard, Noland, and Ryu are more skeptical: "The modest reform efforts that have been tried in the past have almost all been reversed outright or picked apart in implementation."[27] And even if some proposed economic initiatives do go into effect, improved conditions resulting from them will most likely be gradual, or, for the vast majority of people, nonexistent. Successful reforms in China were underwritten by capital investments in crucial infrastructure.[28] North Korea does not have the capital, and has no place to get it. Therefore, a large number of increasingly informed and impatient North Koreans will be forced to continue to live on the edge of starvation.

Though conditions for Pyongyang elites have marginally improved in the past few years, there is no freedom to travel outside the country and personal activities are constrained by surveillance.[29] Greater knowledge of the outside world must be creating secret cynicism; their children are probably asking questions they dare not try to answer. And if some are concerned about the plight of people living outside Pyongyang, they cannot be pleased, and likely sense the growing unrest. Indeed, the future must look bleak for most North Korean elites as they cautiously maneuver around new leadership purges and try to hold on to what they have. Under these circumstances, an offer that substantively changes their incentive structure and offers a lifetime of personal wealth and security may attract their attention.

Patterns of social behavior reflect the choices made by individuals as they try to minimize costs and maximize benefits. On an individual basis it is reasonable that someone might accept a large sum of money and retire in peace and prosperity and honor their family with unimaginable wealth as their friends and associates do the same. Therefore, with enough payment and absolute assurances of personal safety, it is plausible that this individual choice model might scale up to the entire North Korean power elite.

However, support for the Korean Peace Fund model may not be ubiquitous. Some elites are profiting and living well under current conditions. But if profiting elites or nationalist factions oppose reunification with a "U.S. puppet," not only would these individuals and their families be excluded from the payout, but they will be opposing over 10,000 elites at the top of a power hierarchy who will receive benefits between $100 million and $500,000 each ($3.5 million average) and security forces, military officers and conscripts who will also obtain substantial benefits from reunification. Indeed, once it is decided to take the money and reunify, significant bandwagoning could be expected.

Presently, the Kim regime has few, if any, good options. The $1 billion annual contribution of food, energy, consumer and luxury goods from China makes North Korea dependent and vulnerable; its nuclear program angers its last benefactor and increasingly produces negative unintended geopolitical consequences; market reforms could lead to a bloody revolution and economic recovery is nearly impossible without capital investment that is unobtainable. The Korean Peace Fund offers

Six. Funding and Acquiescence

the Kim regime an honorable escape from an increasingly desperate situation.

Society-wide knowledge of the existence of a $300 billion Korean Peace Fund, ready to be disbursed, will put enormous pressure on the Kim dynasty to acquiesce with dignity, as Gorbachev did just over twenty years ago. The Korean Peace Fund is certain to be the elephant in the room, as the masses will clamor for reunification and high-level military officers and the power elite will be attracted by the wealth, security and freedom they would gain (e.g., a second home in the Maldives, Macau, or Hawaii; a family vacation anywhere in the world; a peaceful, carefree life; and an inheritance for their children). Once the money is on the table, it will be difficult not to accept this peace package.

These arguments beg the question of where the money will come from. There is a high level of mistrust and considerable donor fatigue, and it may seem preposterous to think governments and international private interests would simply hand over hundreds of billions of dollars to individual North Koreans, through a peace fund. But upon closer inspection this makes the most sense.

North Korea is backed up against a wall where even a mouse may bite a cat; the Korean Peace Fund proposal solves a series of combustible international problems. The elimination of possible military conflict, an end to nuclear proliferation, the creation of a stable political framework for free-market access to Russian energy and railroads and North Korean minerals and ports, and the economic development of the Pacific Northeast are universally shared interests. And in the context of the vast amount of money printed, earned, taxed, tariffed, stockpiled and flowing around the world today, this is not an unreasonable amount (over five years) for the combined resources of China, Russia, Japan, the United States, South Korea and the rest of the global community.

The Korean Peace Fund model is a multiple-win opportunity for the South Koreans, since (if their contribution is necessary) they will be using money they already know must be spent on reunification to create the incentive for reunification, and they will benefit from international donations. In addition to peace and security, the estimated value of human capital, infrastructure and natural resources that South Korea can expect to obtain from reunification is significant.

The *known* value of mineral wealth in North Korea is $4 trillion.[30]

While South Korea has little mineral wealth and imports virtually everything it uses, the North has abundant quantities of strategic minerals, including coal, uranium, magnetite, iron, copper, and nickel. The valuable rare earth metal molybdenum also exists in large quantities. Alan Ferrie notes, "There are approximately 200 minerals in North Korea which have an estimated value thirty times greater than South Korea's resources."[31] In addition to foreign contributions and mineral wealth, South Korea can enjoy a peace dividend by transferring some of the $30 billion it spends each year for protection to productive reinvestments in a new nation.

From an economic perspective, this peace fund payout is similar to a corporate buyout. For a price, a significant amount of land (production capacity) and people (employees), and a large quantity of unexploited resources (capital stock), will become available to South Korea, and the costs of preparing for war can be avoided. North Korean elites will get a fabulous amount of money and personal security, while the rest of the North Korean population will get large amounts of money and the consequent security of economic integration with a wealthy nation. South Korea will get an enormous package of human and natural resources and a permanent healing peace. An elemental representation of the pragmatic inter–Korean exchange of material benefits is illustrated in figure 3.

Inter-Korean Material Benefits Exchange

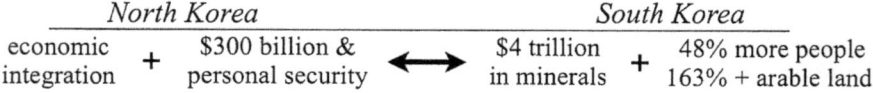

Figure 3

From a geopolitical standpoint, the elimination of nuclear weapons controlled by the totalitarian dictator of a failing state in the epicenter of East Asian prosperity would be worth a great deal to Japan and other countries. Japan has already agreed in principle to pay reparations for its colonial misdeeds in the North and would probably be willing to pay more if this would permanently pacify a hostile nuclear neighbor that has missiles pointed at its shore. Noland estimated in 2000 that compensation commensurate to that paid to South Korea in 1965 would

Six. Funding and Acquiescence

amount to a minimum of $20 billion, plus an extra $5–8 billion to settle the "comfort women" issue.[32]

However, Japan is a conservative democracy and there is no guarantee it will support the peace fund initially. Japan has conflicting geopolitical interests. Although North Korea is considered a threat, a stronger united Korea is not as preferable as a divided Korea embattled with itself. Thus, Japan may not be an early supporter of the Korean Peace Fund. But once the fund gains legitimacy and momentum, Japan would be all in since it is afraid of becoming more isolated in East Asia and would want to win favor with an increasingly powerful Korea to offset its fear of China. Japan's contribution would be contingent upon assurances that a unified Korea would give up its newly acquired nuclear weapons, as the Ukraine and Kazakhstan did after the disintegration of the Soviet Union. Of course, the United States would also insist on this.

Japan has another geopolitical concern. Since its defeat in World War II the growth and capacity of its military has been restricted by the United States. This constraint is perceived as becoming ever more dangerous to its national security with the rise of a potentially hostile China and the successful December 2012 North Korean missile launch and February 2013 nuclear explosion. With the conservative center-right Liberal Democratic Party winning a majority in the Diet's lower house and party leader Shinzo Abe becoming prime minister again with strong support from the right wing, there will be a new push for national security objectives.

Now that the election is over Japanese belligerence may subside, but maybe not. Indeed, Japan has already been implicated in a potential currency war.[33] After almost twenty years of economic stagnation Japanese leaders are searching for a new path toward economic growth, even though Japan has a negative population growth rate and South Korean corporations are successfully competing with its products in the international market.

On paper the United States has agreed to defend Japan, but this promise may not include military confrontations over disputed uninhabited islands in the East China Sea. Nor is Japan's promised alliance with the United States unconditional. However, if the Korean Peace Fund creates reunification, Japan may relinquish or compromise its disputed maritime territorial claims and jump on board with the rest of East Asia.

Indeed, cooperation in a strong and vibrant East Asian economic community is probably Japan's best option for a secure and prosperous future. Korean reunification would likely motivate an unprecedented era of political and economic cooperation in Northeast Asia. The revival of economic growth in Japan and the continuation of growth in South Korea may be contingent upon increased exports to China and their folding into an aligned and cooperative East Asian community. Free-trade talks among economists are already under way.

Fear can drive geopolitical alliances. Sangit Sarita Dwivedi's realist application of Stephen Walt's balance-of-threat theory to East Asian alliances convincingly shows how the perception of intent (aggressive or nonaggressive) by South Korea and the United States influences the relationship between China and North Korea.[34] Thus, hardliner policies by the United States and South Korea have forced North Korea to rely more on China.[35] And with increased fears of political instability following Kim Jong-il's stroke, and after hardliner South Korean policies eliminated aid to North Korea, China stepped up its engagement policies to strengthen ties with Pyongyang and bring it more into its orbit, as China has an economic interest in North Korea's abundant mineral resources.

Gill Bates contends, "Certain elements within the constellation of Chinese foreign and security policy seem to be gaining an upper hand in shaping policy toward North Korea." These elements include "individuals and institutions related to CCP [Chinese Communist Party] international relations and propaganda bodies, the Chinese military and internal security apparatus, provincial governments in China's northeast, and companies with growing economic interests in North Korea."[36] This may seem like a daunting coalition but it is a loose coalition and can be reconfigured by circumstance, co-opted by the promise of stable long-term profits, and influenced by the incentives of the Korean Peace Fund.

Despite public pretense, China and North Korea are not close allies. Living under the shadow of the Chinese imperial state for millennia, North Koreans have multiple reasons to be resentful and suspicious of the patronizing Chinese. There have been major disagreements before and after the Korean War and North Korea's nuclear policy makes it clear that Pyongyang is unwilling to be a pawn in China's geopolitical chess match. Jennifer Lind has pointed out that when China and North Korea formed their alliance, both countries were weak, resentful, iso-

Six. Funding and Acquiescence

lated, and the target of Cold War containment by the United States and its allies. China is no longer in this category. In addition, Korea has a different history; like Poland, for centuries it has been attacked from two sides. There exists a compelling legacy of nationalistic introversion and survival ethnocentricity.

In spite of the symbolic "lips and teeth" rhetoric, ethnic-nationalist prejudice is deep and modern economic relations are strained by what Cha calls a "mutual hostage relationship," whereby China currently wants to prevent the North from failing in order to retain a strategic political buffer zone, while North Korea reluctantly accepts China's rapacious economic policies because it needs hard currency.[37] Drew Thompson argues, "Mutual mistrust characterizes the relationship ... North Korea is ... wary of being 'hollowed out' by Chinese investments in its extractive industries, particularly in the mining sector."[38] Cha asserts, "Beijing has been following a deliberate strategy of economic predation with the North" aimed at satisfying its voracious mineral consumption needs.[39] He continues: "North Koreans increasingly chafe at their growing dependence on the haughty Chinese, who treat them like dirt and dictate the terms of the relationship."[40]

Reunification would dissolve this strained relationship, create a favorable climate for Chinese and international investment, and secure unlimited future access to Korean minerals at fair market prices. Current subsidies to North Korea could turn into Chinese-owned economic investments in a unified Korea. Similar fair market practices would apply to Chinese and Russian leases and access to the most northerly ice-free port on the Pacific in Rason, or the port at Chongjin and others along the coast. China's supposed strategic military passage to the East Sea (or Sea of Japan)[41] and speculative improved doorway to future Arctic shipping would lose a degree of saliency once Rason becomes part of a friendly unified Korea inside a cooperative inter-regional economic development framework.[42]

Although it may not initially want to appear up front in this peace initiative, China would be all in once the fund gained international legitimacy because, in addition to these economic benefits, political unification would lead to a reassessment of the U.S. security shield.[43] If there is the promise of a demilitarized Korean Peninsula without a U.S. presence, China may contribute large sums to the Korean Peace Fund.

Recently exposed diplomatic cables intercepted from a senior Chinese government official suggest China would be willing to accept a united Korea if there is more cooperation between Beijing and Seoul.[44] Since bilateral trade with China already exceeds South Korea's combined trade volume with the United States and Japan, it can be expected that Sino-Korean relations will improve once the North Korean dispute is settled. A unified Korea can reassess its security alliances long after reunification.[45]

Russia, too, like China and Japan, would be all in once reunification got under way. Georgy Toloraya notes, "Russia is aspiring to become a regional energy superpower by tapping East Asian markets."[46] To promote these interests President Putin in May 2012 launched a new Ministry of Development of the Russian Far East.[47] The United States (and Israel) would prefer that Asian countries bring more oil from Russia so as to reduce their dependence on supplies from Iran and the Middle East. Currently South Korea buys 10 percent of its oil from Iran for about $6 billion per year, while Japan buys $6.5 billion of Iranian oil per year. Overall Japan imports close to 90 percent and South Korea 70 percent of its oil from the Middle East,[48] providing an excellent opportunity for Russia to step into the breach.

Any future conflict in the volatile Middle East or along ocean shipping lanes would jeopardize vital East Asian oil supplies. Thus, greater reliance on Russian energy appears to be in everyone's interests and, along with a nuclear-free Korean Peninsula, is a basis for multilateral cooperation.[49] Russia has already forgiven almost $10 billion in North Korean debt because it wants to move forward with cooperative projects. Considering Russia's potential economic gains from a stable, reunified Korea, it should be willing to contribute significant sums to the Korean Peace Fund.

Denuclearization likewise promises significant benefits to the North's neighbors and other countries invested in the region. For example, recognizing North Korea's advanced stage of nuclear technology (compared to Iran and Syria) and its need for foreign currency, Joshua Pollack warns there is "considerable potential for North Korean sales of uranium conversion and enrichment equipment, along with uranium supplies."[50] Selling nuclear technology is grievously destabilizing and it is a top security priority for the United States (and Israel) to prevent

North Korean nuclear technology transfer and arms deliveries to the Middle East, and to stop inter-continental ballistic missile testing and development, because, as Victor Cha notes, Taep'odong missiles (including the Unha) will make North Korea "the first country besides China and Russia to be able to target U.S. cities with nuclear weapons, possibly within four years."[51]

The U.S. Central Intelligence Agency suspects China has sold materials, manufactured equipment, and supplied components suitable for ballistic missile and chemical weapon programs in North Korea, and it is widely believed that China has "served as a transshipment point for ballistic missile related items between North Korea and Iran."[52] In May 2012 South Korean authorities seized 445 graphite cylinders that are usable in ballistic missiles from a Chinese cargo ship docked in the southern Korean port at Busan. A closer economic relationship between China and North Korea will make detection of shipments more difficult.[53] If partially underwriting the Korean Peace Fund would make these dangers go away, the United States, Israel, and other countries should be willing to contribute vast sums (although this may require considerable statesmanship in the recession-ridden United States).

From a geopolitical perspective, compelling conclusions can be reached by the artificial solvency of a disputed nation that is developing nuclear ballistic missiles it threatens to launch at the United States and its Asian neighbors, that is exclusively supported by and owes its very existence to China (especially since Chinese military expenditures have more than quintupled in real terms since 1997 and have recently surpassed $100 billion annually).[54] According to U.S. Secretary of Defense Leon Panetta, the "pivot" in U.S. foreign policy to the Asia-Pacific area is because of "real threats" posed by North Korea.[55]

Korean peace and reunification could set the stage for unprecedented regional trust, cooperation and harmony. It is even possible the Dokdo-Takeshima (Korea/Japan), Senkaku-Diaoyu (Japan/China/Taiwan) and Kuril islands (Russia/Japan) territorial disputes could be settled. Japan's significant reparation contribution to the Korean Peace Fund will symbolize its contrition. This donation may well create a spirit of cooperation and goodwill, increasing the possibility of a resolution to the Takeshima/Dokdo dispute.[56] As conflicts are resolved by accepting new political and economic realities, an agreement with China over the

Senkaku-Diaoyu islands would anchor Japan in the emerging East Asian community. From a foreign armchair perspective, it is difficult to contemplate how a pile of bird-stained rocks amid dubious underwater resources between Japan, China and South Korea could arouse such acrimony. *Korean Times* journalist Jason Lim explains the historically bound emotion-laden sentiments when he writes, "Dokdo is ... something that needs to be healed, not analyzed or negotiated. In other words, it's more a spiritual issue than a diplomatic one because, ultimately, it's about reconciliation."[57]

Whatever the cause of this enmity, without greater cooperation tensions will mount. The rise of ethnic-based nationalism and possible military conflict in the region would be harmful to global corporations that depend on East Asian commodity flows. Toyota estimates it lost over $1 billion in sales in 2012 because maritime disputes led to increased Chinese nationalism and a boycott of its automobiles. And this might only be the beginning if matters get worse. Northeast Asian trade accounts for about 20 percent of global trade volume. The United States and China represent one-third of global GDP and their volume of trade is enormous. Considering the complicated logistics of transnationally fragmented assembly-line production and the import-export dependence of East Asian countries, any conflict between these two economic behemoths would be devastating to regional and international commerce. Fareed Zakaria notes, "A serious U.S.–Chinese rivalry would define the new age and turn it away from integration, trade, and globalization."[58]

Therefore, it may be possible to persuade vulnerable corporations to redirect dividends and a portion of their profit margins for a few years to support an initiative that will provide incentive for regional peace and eliminate an obvious flashpoint for military conflict. An economically cooperative unified Korea will weaken the political influence of military budget hardliners in Beijing and Washington and deflate incentives for an Asian arms race. Private commercial interests will benefit from reduced tensions and the release of $300 billion into the regional economy.

Regional peace and innovations in transportation and communications have led to unprecedented profits from world trade over the past several decades. Over this period the global money supply has grown enormously, spread to more places, and is held in more private purses than ever before. In today's multilayered global balance of power, private interests represent a formidable countervailing, and often unifying, force in the competitive nation-state system of world governance.

In this emerging world where two percent of its people own half of all global wealth, 100 financial institutions own one-third of the world's financial assets, and 250 corporations account for one-third of global GDP, it makes theoretical and practical sense to consider the role of global elites in an economic solution to the Korean problem.[59] Unconstrained by the parochialism of public opinion, international power elites could set in motion a partnership between private wealth, international media, business, and global institutions such as the G20 or the United Nations that would fundamentally change the political and economic incentive structure in the region.

A few thousand people effectively control $100 trillion in global assets; as of March 2013, there were 1,426 billionaires in the world, with over 200 in East Asia and 25 in South Korea (including at least seven high billionaires worth multiple billions).[60] China is now second only to the United States in the number of billionaires (100+ versus 400+), while Russia has almost 100 billionaires. The rich are so rich that the top 50 could give $6 billion each and underwrite the entire Korean Peace Fund with barely a dent in their wallets. In 2012 alone the net worth of the top 40 multi-billionaires increased by almost $100 billion.[61] Bill Gates and Warren Buffet have separately made $30 billion of commitments to philanthropy, so there is no reason to think that they and their peers would be unable or unwilling to contribute to the peace fund.

Considering these vital overlapping interests and the vast sums spent to solve other international problems or fund militaries to keep the peace, this is not an excessive amount to invest for permanent peace on the Korean Peninsula.[62] And although the Korean Peace Fund offers political and economic benefits to every government and corporation that has an interest in the region, universal cooperation is not essential. Due to North Korea's level of dependence, Chinese support for the Korean Peace Fund might be sufficient to compel reunification, but China's support is not necessary; nor is the success of this proposal dependent on the support of any particular nation.

Evolutionary biologists have shown that cooperation is deeply embedded in the DNA of our species.[63] From humankind's primordial epigenesis to the emergence of world trade and global culture, the fittest individuals and groups are more often those who cooperate, intuitively grasp seminal change, and alter their perspectives and behaviors accordingly. A new perspective that injects the persuasive power of money into the peace process may be necessary now in order to overcome path dependencies that could lead to confrontation and war. With the financial instigation of international elites and the cooperation of government leaders and the international community, the underlying conditions and incentives for peace and reunification could be created in Korea by supporting the Korean Peace Fund.

Chapter Seven

Review and Conclusion

Scholars and analysts are currently collecting an expanding universe of information about North Korea from an increasing number of defectors and other sources. This body of carefully weighed empirical evidence suggests that soft-power culture flows have contributed to reconstructing the attitudes and aspirations of a substantial number of North Koreans as word-of-mouth cultural diffusion builds an undercurrent of political dissent.

The defector sample is now large and diverse enough to be reasonably confident that their sentiments represent a substantial proportion of the North Korean population. The overwhelming preference expressed by defectors is for unification under South Korean leadership. In a recent sample, only one person out of 300 supported the political status quo. Haggard and Noland note, "The respondents also indicated that their own views mirrored those of their peers remaining in North Korea."[1]

Although Korean nationalist sentiments remain strong, support for the privileged regime in Pyongyang has never been weaker among the majority population. Economic and ideological changes in North Korea over the past two decades have created a more favorable cultural context for reunification. Support for the regime has declined since the 1990s (especially among people living outside Pyongyang), after a confluence of crises led to the collapse of the government food distribution system. When the state stopped providing food, institutions of social control began to disintegrate, and markets and trade networks emerged. People either migrated toward food or went hungry. One million people starved; half a million people traveled back and forth across the Chinese border to feed their families. Exchange-trust, market and business relationships developed. Hungry and underpaid local authorities began taking bribes of food or money and protected the growth of trade and information networks across North Korea. For almost a generation these networks have spread horizontally and vertically and deepened as state socialism morphed into small-scale entrepreneurial capitalism.

An unintended consequence of these markets and networks, originally established for food and essential commodity distribution, is that they also facilitated the flow of news, culture and information. Digital miniaturization, from videotapes to DVDs, and now to flash memory sticks, has made it increasingly easy for traders to conceal these illegal cultural products. Digital technology has allowed traders to carry compact radios, DVD players, and high-impact visual information across the border and throughout North Korea without detection, and if detected, it is likely a bribe will keep the trader in business and out of prison.[2] According to recent (2012) reports, DVD players can be purchased in Pyongyang for US$13, radios for $3 and DVDs for 50 cents.

Through illicit media many people saw the wealth and abundance of South Korea for the first time with their own eyes, and word-of-mouth carried this secret knowledge along an information highway of established underground networks to the North Korean masses. State propaganda is experiencing diminishing returns. Culture flows are convincing the population that government sources of information have deceived them about the South. And the government is increasingly worried about such awareness.

Public executions tripled last year. The army has shoot-to-kill orders along the Yalu and Tumen River crossings into China. Death threats have been posted for the use of Chinese-made cell phones or the possession of foreign currency, and the gulag prison population has increased.[3] But awareness is cumulative. In spite of renewed government repression, cynicism and disaffection are growing as hunger and economic stagnation continue.

Change has been no less dramatic among the elite, many of whom are now involved in proto-capitalist activities and in constant search of opportunities to obtain foreign currency. Ideological convictions are fading and market mentalities are in ascendance. Weakened central authority and control has led to more competition among elite factions. The evolution of more rational, moderate and pluralist post-totalitarian bureaucratic institutions, combined with new dynastic leadership, has created growing fear and uncertainty, as well as pragmatic reformist impulses at higher levels of power.

Seven. Review and Conclusion

But as interest in Korean reunification increases in the North, it is declining in the South. The more isolated younger generations naturally tend to care less about their northern sisters and brothers than their parents and grandparents who suffered or fought for the freedoms they enjoy. It is politically expedient to worry about immediate short-term issues, while discounting the more remote possibility of a distant destruction. Denial may also repress a sense of urgency. Studies have shown that the people living immediately under a dam are paradoxically less likely to be afraid and more likely to deny the possibility that the dam could burst than people living more safely downriver. This may be the current psychic situation among many South Koreans.

In addition, biased economic assumptions conspire against reunification sentiments. Economic reports on Korean unification often focus on the costs to South Koreans and ignore or minimize investment and business opportunities that will occur. Thus, many South Koreans are under the impression that unification would have a serious deleterious impact on their standard of living. One poll shows this general impression is shared by about half of the South Korean population.[4] These people are afraid of what might happen.

Some models based on German-style integration, the relevance of which is increasingly called into question, suggest a modest decline in economic growth in the South.[5] Most economic analyses rely on extreme guesswork and multiple questionable assumptions, and, of course, none have accounted for the $300 billion input of capital over five years from a peace fund. This factor alone changes the value of every important variable and economic and demographic assumption these models rely on.

Reunification may not be as costly as some have speculated and the benefits may be significantly larger than originally anticipated. Indeed, a 2009 study by the conservative global investment giant Goldman Sachs suggests that the huge growth potential of North Korea could help offset the slowing growth of South Korea, which is burdened by limited natural resources and a fast-aging population.

Reunification comparisons with Germany are a worst-case scenario, since there are more positive results if you look more broadly at China and Hong Kong, Eastern Europe, Mongolia or Vietnam. The author of the Goldman study, Goohoon Kwon, asserts, "North Korea has strong untapped potential, which could be unleashed once meaningful economic reforms start and investment flows in. We would highlight three main factors: (1) an abundant and competitive labour force; (2) ample room for synergies between South Korean capital and technology, and North Korean natural resources and labour; and (3) the potentially large gains from productivity and currency appreciation typical in transition economies."[6] Kwon continues, "The least expensive option would be a China/Hong Kong–style integration, which allows two economic and political systems to coexist in a country with limited inter–Korean migration. The post-integration growth performance of China–Hong Kong was better than Germany's, further bolstering the case for gradual integration."[7] The report highlights the $4 trillion in mineral wealth the South would gain and other strong synergies that would likely make a united Korea wealthier than France and Germany in as little as 30 years.[8]

South Korean skilled and educated workers may enjoy a generation of full employment, since their knowledge and skills will be in high demand in the North. And the business class will gain valuable human and natural resources, an investment territory that promises close to 10 percent growth per annum, and new and expanding markets.[9] Ironically, one new potential market opportunity for Korea is in nuclear energy. In March 2014, the civil nuclear energy agreement between South Korea and the United States will expire. Given the significant interests that are at stake for each state, negotiating its renewal has been difficult. South Korea wants to become a competitive global nuclear energy supplier and is pushing for greater nuclear sovereignty, including the right to enrich and reprocess U.S.–supplied nuclear materials. Oppositional forces contend that approval of these sensitive nuclear activities might negatively affect global non-proliferation efforts, diplomacy with North Korea and regional stability. Reunification may change the situation dynamics enough to allow South Korea into this new market.

Before political and cultural speciation is permanent between the North and South, there is a window of opportunity at this transitory moment in Korean history to effect reunification by using the smart-power solution proposed in this book. It is appropriate to try a new approach to unite Korea, since conventional strategies have failed for over half a century, and considering that more than three million people lost their lives in a war just 60 years ago, a peace agreement has never been signed, military provocations have occurred, and North Korea is enriching uranium, miniaturizing a warhead and testing missile delivery systems, and has declared the 1953 armistice invalid and threatened that nuclear war is only a matter of time.[10]

With the world-awakening October 2006 nuclear test, the increased frequency of ballistic missile and nuclear tests, and the Cheonan sinking and Yeonpyeong shelling, this amplified frequency of brazen military provocations suggests North Korean leaders are increasingly desperate. As prospect theory predicts, North Korea is taking more risks as its situation deteriorates.[11]

Prospect theory introduces instances of irrationality in rational choice models when risk is involved. Cha asserts, "Sometimes even rational actors, when they become especially stressed, can do dangerous things," and at some point, "it becomes perfectly rational to contemplate a desperate action."[12] Even though North Korea may currently lack the ability for a nuclear strike,[13] and is not likely to initiate a full-scale attack on the South,[14] its threatening nuclear weapon and ballistic missile development programs increase its chances of a surgical strike by the United States, with unknown response. In March 2013 the United States flew B-2 stealth bombers nonstop from the mainland United States to the skies above South Korea to emphasize this threat.

And there are other complications and unexpected potential dangers. In March 2011 South Korea changed its rules of military engagement from a passive to a more aggressive proactive deterrence that includes preemption. Preemption was U.S. President Bush's model for waging war in Iraq. In spite of pleas to follow the "principle of proportionality," this policy creates worries about controlling the ladder of escalation once small-scale military actions commence. According to Abraham Denmark, there have been 221 small-scale North Korean attacks since 1953, an average of four per year.[15] Concerned about the results of another Cheonan or Yeonpyeong incident, a former member of the National Security Council, Victor Cha, in testimony before the U.S. Congress, expressed his concern that "the spiral of miscalculation can lead to war."[16]

Indeed, the history of enduring rivalries and conflicts around the world is not a comforting one.[17] Nation-states that experience decades of continued animosity frequently go to war again. And now, with the omnipresent "war of terror" being fought between the "have and the have-nots," the possibility of non-state actors influencing the situation has grown. Cha asserts that if a terrorist attack on the United States were traced to weapons that originated in North Korea, "the regime's days would be numbered."[18] The Korean situation may be a ticking time bomb; political tensions and military preparedness await a perfect storm or the arrival of a Black Swan.

There is no time for status quo diplomacy or complacency. The Six-Party Talks (dormant since 2008) have made little progress, and recurrent hard-power/soft-power diplomacy, depending on the political administration, has only led to further mistrust and confrontation.[19] It is wishful thinking (if not institutional insanity) to keep doing the same thing and expect different results. Conventional thinking has failed to find a resolution to this conflict, leading some emerging next-generation experts and leaders to believe the conventional wisdom of our day and the current consensus of elite last-generation policymakers is based on the wrong image of the world. And this has dire and perhaps tragic consequences.

Trying a new approach to unite Korea is essential, since conventional strategies have failed and the alternative to peace is unimaginable. Bradley Martin refers to the North Korean military as "a gigantic cocked weapon."[20] Only 25 miles from the DMZ, the Seoul corridor of 22 million people is vulnerable to missile attack and from the largest artillery force in the world. It would take 45 seconds for an artillery shell to reach Seoul. With an estimated 13,000 artillery systems, numerous multiple-rocket launchers and more than 650 ballistic missiles aimed at Seoul that may be armed with nerve gas and blistering and choking agents or biological weapons such as anthrax, cholera and smallpox, one-third of Seoul could be in ruins and hundreds of thousands of people could die in the first 24 to 72 hours before these weapons could be neutralized, and many more deaths would ensue in the weeks and months after.[21] And if China and the United States started fighting each other, anything could happen.

The alternative approach proposed in this model for the institution of a Korean Peace Fund represents a proactive challenge to historical tendencies of inter-state warfare. New initiatives that promote smart-power solutions should be considered, if for no other reason than to open our minds to new possibilities. In agreement with Andrei Lankov's foreword to this book, I concede that the specific model presented here may not be the answer, but it may contain a kernel of the answer, or inspire a new way of looking at the problem. In the context of extreme relative poverty, a generation of discontent, and political transition in North Korea, the Korean Peace Fund may represent a historic opportunity for leaders of an emerging global society to use smart-power appeal to reunite a people and prevent a war that might divide the world.

One important and controversial theme in this peace fund model is the empathetic approach taken toward the North Korean ruling elite. Although the 200,000 political prisoners currently in labor camps elicit our sympathy, their release may paradoxically be contingent upon empathy for the children of those who imprisoned them. Inhumane policies and institutions promulgated by leaders long since deceased victimize everyone, including their children. With empathy we can put ourselves in the shoes of current North Korean leaders and begin to realize that they are every bit as obliged to the inertia of institutional policies and path dependencies as we are. They live in constant fear and insecurity, as they inevitably go-along-to-get-along, trapped in an inhumane and unworkable system without a promising alternative.

The Korean Peace Fund offers North Korean leaders a unique opportunity to escape their dire and perplexing predicament, and it also secures the release of 200,000 people from the labor camps. But it is only by not seeking retribution that we can secure their release. Therefore, personal security is a fundamental promise in the Korean Peace Fund model. This one-time pragmatic forgiveness is necessary in order to permanently solve an increasingly dangerous international situation that threatens the lives of millions.

Popular support improves the likelihood of reaching a tipping point for Korean unification. This model provides enormous incentives to all North Koreans to join their brethren in the relative prosperity of the rest of the world. From aggregate information and the reports of thousands of defectors, refugees and travelers, it seems likely that the majority of common citizens are ready for a change and may welcome reunification under South Korean political leadership.

In a world where culture counts, Samuel Huntington has convincingly argued that people separated by ideology but united by blood and culture will eventually come together again.[22] The combined smart-power influence of monetary incentives, attraction of South Korean culture, and ethnic-based nationalism may reunite a people and bring permanent peace to the peninsula.

But the Korean Peace Fund is not the only possible peaceful solution. Many South Koreans and Korea watchers remain convinced by Kim Dae-jung's thesis that small steps of engagement over an indefinite period will lead to reduced tensions and eventually to peace and reunification.[23] I am not in disagreement. This might be an effective plan if externalities could be ignored and North Korea stopped developing nuclear weapon and missile technologies that threaten and incense the United States and its neighbors, and if the United States did not have a political-military interventionist faction that is easily aroused and in any given four-year period might be summoned to power. Similar confounding political dynamics exist in South Korea and Japan. Indeed, the reelection of the conservative party candidate Geun-hye Park in South Korea and Japan's conservative political alliance that returned Shinzu Abe to power are likely to make sustained cooperation with North Korea difficult for at least the next half-decade. Although the hardliner policies of the past Lee administration have currently lost favor with the Korean public and some form of re-engagement has grown in popularity, putting exclusive faith in the revival of the Sunshine Policy may be impractical given the unlikelihood of preventing nuclear escalation and the uncertainty of political cycles. Even a more balanced approach between inducements and sanctions that may be a more popular South Korean strategy would be subject to the inherent dangers of a long drawn-out process.[24]

Considering recent military actions, newly instituted military rules of engagement, unknown factors and increasing military preparedness, it may be wise to employ non-invasive incentives to speed up the process and encourage a peaceful result. In this respect the Korean Peace Fund is the ultimate Sunshine Policy, offering a more rapid path to reunification.

Every so often over the past twenty years, it has appeared from the outside that the fortress state might implode or disintegrate. There were such predictions in the spring of 2010 after serious grain shortages, hunger and disastrous self-inflicted currency reforms. But the Kim regime proved resilient. And while succession is often the Achilles' heel of tyranny, there has not been a discernible ripple of rebellion during dynastic transition.

Seven. Review and Conclusion

Growing dissatisfaction from the masses may exert considerable pressure on those in power, but the essential motivating influence for change must come from an external source like the Korean Peace Fund that targets benefits to powerful decision-makers. Unlike Soviet Russia, Pyongyang elites have few state resources to divvy up and therefore an external payment is necessary in order to enrich their incentive package and change their perspective.

Due to effective tools of authoritarian control; large donations of food, energy and luxury goods from China; foreign currency profits; a lack of transportation and communication; and a variety of other reasons, without an external impetus it is unlikely mass political revolt or a coup d'état will bring down the dynasty anytime soon. The existence of the Korean Peace Fund may provide the essential motivation to tip the balance toward positive change.

As it becomes apparent the government promise to become a "strong and prosperous nation" will not materialize, there is likely to be more skepticism and erosion of support inside North Korea. Common knowledge of the institution of this peace fund may create a shared cultural construct and provide the impetus for organizing and motivating thoughts and emotions into collective action. And at the top, awareness of this fund among North Korean leaders may countermand conventional min-max considerations, or what Richard Chadwick refers to as the Korean "prisoner's dilemma,"[25] because instead of death and defeat it is cash and conciliation at their doorstep." The future promise of suffrage, along with immediate promises of job freedom, property ownership, an energy infrastructure, tablet computers, worldwide travel and communication, food security, and money saved in personal bank accounts, will give North Koreans hope for a better future and incentive to take action to make it possible.

If the Korean Peace Fund obtains the necessary funding, both elite and impoverished North Koreans will be compelled to change the course of Korean history. In addition to the promise of vast sums of money, North Koreans would legally own their property and be able to select employment from a diverse assortment of new jobs according to their personal preferences and abilities. They will receive tablet computers and will soon be able to access the World Wide Web with a reliable supply of electricity. For the first time in over two decades they will have adequate health care and affordable access to an inexpensive and abundant variety of food for their families.

A new generation can begin to discover and assimilate the many alluring enticements of the outside world. Students can learn on computers. Adults can appreciate a new freedom in life choices (i.e., change jobs, start a business, buy a car, express their faith, criticize their leaders and form civic groups). More than 10,000 elites and semi-elites will have enough money to provide an elegant lifestyle for their families without ever having to work again. Senior citizens will have a secure nest egg. And finally, in addition to getting plenty of nutritious food to eat, children will benefit from proper health and dental care, and they will also be given a modern world education and savings for college. There will be an amazing renaissance of cultural and economic activity in the North.

The Korean Peace Fund is a positive-sum investment for geopolitical and regional economic interests. Currently, the presence of a bankrupt, unpredictable, corrupt and possibly unstable North Korea inhibits economic development in the Pacific Northeast, an important Chinese and Russian objective. A plan for stabilizing the region for investment and development may give economy-first Chinese political pragmatists more authority to push to strategically disengage with North Korea and compel them to accept and contribute to this peace offer.

As previously argued, making the peace fund a reality is not beyond the realm of possibility. If Japan, Russia, China, and South Korea promised a one-time withdrawal of only 5 percent of their foreign reserves, this would completely underwrite the Korean Peace Fund. And there is also private money; a few thousand corporate elites effectively control $100 trillion, two-thirds of the world's total assets. $300 billion could easily be raised through private and public donations and by some combination of foreign reserve withdrawal and redirected military spending.

The perception of large payments to the North Korean elite may create a fund-raising and public relations problem. The 12 percent of the fund offered to elites may seem excessive or even unconscionable to some, and therefore this portion must be obtained from non-public sources. After separating this elite payment from the fund, political and media focus on the estimated 200,000 political prisoners and the millions of innocent impoverished North Koreans (including over seven million children) who will directly benefit from the fund will create international empathy and help justify the transfer of public money.

But this is more than an economic initiative or regional humanitarian proposition. In a world endangered by war and nuclear proliferation, it is an international matter of large-scale human survival. The global community should be willing to promise significant sums of money toward a possible permanent solution to the Korean dilemma, especially for a no-risk peace fund.

Korean reunification would create a secure East Asia that benefits everyone. The United States gets non-proliferation and the dissolution of a perceived military threat; Japan gets promises of building contracts, new export markets and safety from missile attacks and weapons of mass destruction; Russia gets rail, gas and oil profits, as well as year-round passage to Pacific shipping; China gets secure and dependable free-market access to Korean minerals and the ice-free port at Rason, Korea's cooperation in developing its northeast provinces, and the probable retreat of U.S. military forces from the Korean Peninsula and perhaps East Asia; and South Korea gets permanent peace, a more reliable supply of energy, $4 trillion (probably much more) in mineral resources, 50 percent more people and more than double its current territory.

There is incentive for China, Korea and Japan to settle old lingering disputes, in spite of nationalistic hubris, and to expand cultural relations and form a strong economic free-trade union. This free-trade association is already "under examination," according to the Korean Ministry of Foreign Affairs and Trade (as of April 2012).[26] This grand new Confucian alliance of cooperation and harmony in a peaceful Northeast Asia would become the most important and powerful trading bloc in the world. And by diffusing a dispute that has civilization-level military implications and eliminating all flashpoints for conflict, multinational corporations will have long-term security for commodity and capital flows and will be unencumbered in the economic development of the resource-rich Pacific Northeast.

Once the Korean Peace Fund gains notoriety and acquires international legitimacy, it may begin to receive massive private and public financing. North Korean elites will be attentive as the fund grows. And once the elephant enters the room, it may be only a matter of time before the forces of reason and hope align and resolve to do what makes the most sense.

The great unknown is Kim Jong-un. He may or may not have a

plan for his people that cannot be revealed at this moment as he navigates a political sea of subterfuge and uncertainty. Victor Cha contends that even if Kim Jong-un were an enlightened leader who has courage, "he would be dealing with a generation of institutions and people that are the most isolated in North Korean history."[27] Cha's nomothetic understanding underscores why significant cash payments might be the precise incentive needed to tip the balance toward reunification at this transitional stage in North Korean history.

Although Kim Jong-un has been granted leadership titles such as the supreme commander of the Korea People's Army, first secretary of the Korean Workers' Party, and the first chairman of the National Defense Commission, it is likely he has had little or nothing to do with the threatening brinkmanship that has played out since his dynastic crowning. He is probably largely controlled by the collective decision-making of his "council of regents" and cannot make important decisions unilaterally. These people are mostly in their late 60s and 70s and have "played decisive roles in North Korean decision-making for the last 10 to 15 years."[28] This period of apprenticeship protects the integrity of young

Kim Jong-un enjoying a laugh with his generals.

Seven. Review and Conclusion

Kim's image and makes the Peace Prize possible. But these elder statesmen cannot prevent powerful new universal incentives and sentiments from catapulting North Korea into a better future, as events may well take a turn unanticipated by the council.

The generous compensation offered to military elites and officers will increase the possibility of a coup d'état if the regime is unwilling to reunify, and decrease the chances of a counter-revolutionary coup d'état by those who reject this plan, after the decision has been made to reunify. The top 1,000 generals and power elites will each become multi-millionaires; 10,000 elites and their families will enjoy a lifetime of financial security; 1,200 high-ranking officers will receive half-a-million dollars each and 30,000 junior officers are well compensated. This payout up-and-down the military chain of command gives incentive for a large armed force of middle-ranking officers to claim the significant rewards offered them in a reunified Korea.

Enjoying thrills at an amusement park.

It is also possible the fund might lead to mass civil unrest, bloody insurrection and its suppression. However, with pressures mounting from all directions and the right package of incentives and assurances, Kim Jong-un might surprise everyone. As a recent college graduate thrust into a very difficult situation, young Kim has virtually no reputational baggage. If he accepts this plan he would not only eliminate impoverishment and misery, he would be hailed as the heroic young leader who brought, peace, prosperity and unification to his people. He would secure the personal wealth and safety of his family, and become an international celebrity with enormous personal credibility. The potential gains for his people and himself (including a possible Nobel Peace Prize) may be too tempting to resist.

The scapegoat for North Korea's malfeasance and human rights violations will be Kim Jong-un's father; his grandfather's legacy would remain enshrined as a liberation fighter and non-threatening (albeit failed) idealist without relevance to a modern, unified free-market Korea, with statues intact for the gaze of curious tourists. It is now incumbent upon the new world order to give this 30-year-old an attractive option that could win his support and that of those around him.

I began this effort with this simple question: If war is fought over money, and power and control over the people, land and resources that produce it, why can we not pay in advance to prevent it?[29] In response to this question, I drafted a Korean Peace Fund proposal to pay the North Korean military and ruling elite to put down their guns and join the modern world as wealthy new members of the international community. I have argued throughout this book that the soft-power attractiveness of South Korean prosperity, combined with hard-power payment, may create a smart-power solution to the Korean problem.

Although there may be a low probability this peace model will obtain the kind of response I intend, nonetheless, now that you have read this book, that possibility has increased. Chadwick asserts, "What seems idealistic and visionary, unrealistic and counter-intuitive today can in the end be the vision that, in its implementation, yields the fruits of stability, prosperity and peace."[30] This model for a Korean Peace Fund proposes the largest peace offering and policy-assisted transfer of wealth the world has ever known. If successful, this initiative would unite a divided people, disarm a growing nuclear threat, and create peace after more than 60 years of hostility.

Seven. Review and Conclusion

Incentives that eliminate fear and maximize welfare provide ultimate motivation for human behavior. The Korean Peace Fund is based on reliable theories of how to most effectively apply the power of incentives to influence the behavior of others to obtain preferred outcomes. It offers the North Korean people a solution to their desperate poverty, as well as an honorable and profitable exit plan for the North Korean ruling elite, with tangible in-the-pocket private wealth and international assurances of their personal safety and welfare, and the freedom to live and travel wherever they wish. This fund is affordable for the combined resources of the international community, and it offers an opportunity for an isolated, impoverished and failing state to enter the global system in the middle and merge with one of the most progressive and successful states of the Twenty-first Century. Political stability, access to material resources and free markets on the Korean peninsula will benefit multinational corporations and all countries with something at stake in the region, as reunification will stimulate the economic development of the greater Pacific Northeast and provide synergies that will likely make a united Korea one of the most geopolitically secure and wealthiest nations in the world.

The impressions most people have of North Korea have been formed by international media reports of human rights abuses, military provocations, and nuclear threats. But the real North Korea consists of over 30 percent children endowed with the innocence of youth and a vast majority of blameless people trapped in a situation not of their making. The next-generation elites who will determine North Korea's future have also inherited circumstances they did not create; they are rational and pragmatic people who are amenable to compelling incentives and might consent to a uniquely enriching opportunity for themselves and their families if their personal safety and well-being is guaranteed.

North Korean leaders are victimized by social conformity and the historical inertia of path dependencies just as they constrain the creativity and conceivable policy options of international diplomats and security experts. It is as if the institutions we created to help better manage our world have come to control us by limiting and constraining alternative paths and perspectives. The personal and geopolitical incentives provided by the Korean Peace Fund transcend conventional path dependencies and may awaken a new hope and sensibility for achieving peace and reunification on the Korean Peninsula.

Transcendent perception and policy require thinking outside the box: everything that has prevented agreement in the past becomes inconsequential at this higher level of abstraction, where only the bare essentials matter (e.g., "let's pay them and end this" or "let's take the money and run"). By presenting an alternative path that may create a safer more productive future, this model for making peace is a challenge to the rational foresight of a new world order to envision how it can avoid being dragged into another war.

Once established, an awareness of this fund will eventually, filter into the hearts and minds of North Koreans and be widely discussed. The mere existence of this fund will change the political and economic incentive structure in North Korea and became an institutional and transformative organizing force for change. If data and theory on cultural evolution and the trajectory of the historical record have predictive value, then opportunistic forces of personal self-interest, security and survival will eventually prevail, and this peace fund will provide the tipping point for reunification and permanent peace on the Korean Peninsula.

The Korean Peace Fund model offers a no-risk, cost-effective, positive-sum, smart-power solution to the Korean problem that would benefit everyone and may prevent a war. I am aware of no competitive or cooperative argument in the marketplace of ideas similar to the one proposed here. There are no theories, suggested policies or promising diplomatic strategies ready and available to solve the Korean crisis (except this one). This book's legacy may be either one of social science fiction or one of helping bring peace to Korea and changing the geopolitical face of the Earth.

CHAPTER EIGHT

Reunification Signing Ceremony

What will it feel like waking up in the Land of the Morning Calm that first morning after reunification? In the South, it will be the first day in three generations without the threat of war. In the North, it will be the first time in 20 years parents will feel sure they can feed their children. For the power elites on both sides of the parallel, it will be a time for retirement and repose, or exciting new economic opportunities, or a chance to learn about each other again and form new relationships with people who share a deep common history. And for all Koreans, it will be a reunion of the human spirit.

This is a WIN-WIN-WIN-WIN result for everyone, from individuals to geopolitical state interests, transforming into harmony, unity and peace what was otherwise projected as over one million people dead, 30 percent of Seoul in flames and rubble, and Pyongyang completely annihilated.

Due to the unique nature of this proposal, it is particularly difficult to imagine how reunification might be finalized and how the exchange of political and military power for money and security will occur. Who will go first? How can everyone trust this agreement will be honored? Left unanswered, these questions may even impair the reaching of the agreement itself. Therefore, I have drafted a brief imaginative description of the signing event that may help us grasp what could happen and reassure anyone who has doubts about the integrity of the final result.

This chapter is about a new world being created by people who realize they must learn to live together in a shared future. As North Korean leaders mull over their current options, their judgment will undoubtedly be influenced by their fears and projections. Gary Becker asserts, "Behavior is forward-looking ... [people] try as best they can to anticipate the uncertain consequences of their actions. Forward-looking behavior, however, may still be rooted in the past, for the past can exert a long shadow on attitudes and values."[1] With such a bitter and turbulent past, it is understandable that the North and South would be skeptical of each other. Therefore, due to decades of distrust, the international community should be involved in legitimizing the final peace and reunification agreement.

Once Kim Jong-un and North Korean elites agree in principle to reunify under South Korean leadership, the complex process of making this happen can begin. It is particularly difficult to imagine how reunification will be finalized and how the exchange of political and military power for money and security will commence, because nothing like this has ever occurred before. Imagining the wonder

Reunion of the human spirit.

and splendor of this moment in time may improve the possibility of this final resolution, and it may also help allay North Korean fears and produce positive expectations among Kim Jong-un, his family and selectorate, and the controlling power elite — and make this public signing ceremony a reality. If this book obtains the influence I intend, the North Korean leadership will read, along with you, this possible scenario of the Peace and Reunification Signing Ceremony.

After everything is agreed upon and signed and sealed behind closed doors, the formal symbolic transfer of political control should be a highly produced international spectacle with epic theatrics and aplomb directed and choreographed by creative experts. This signing celebration will be an international media extravaganza. The high art of ritual and symbolism should be brought to bear on this historic occasion when the people of North and South Korea agree on a world stage to become one nation again.

This should be accomplished in high style in Kim Il-sung Square, with thousands of international news media present and foreign leaders, major donors and dignitaries looking on. Kim Il-sung Square is one of the largest squares in the world and can accommodate over 100,000 people. This momentous event will be presented to a global television audience of billions as the most historic political event of the twenty-first century and should have a production quality and worldwide coverage comparable to the opening and closing ceremonies of the Olympics. This mass coverage will legitimize the peace process before the eyes of the world and create a sense of security among the North Korean elite and help everyone feel more comfortable and reassured about the finality of the process and the reality of reunification.

There will be a grand elevated signing table for the two government leaders, who will stand before their armies. The proceedings will be projected on large screens around the square so military personnel can also view the signing of the document reunifying Korea. Both leaders will turn to face their armies and give a short speech (prepared previously for simultaneous translation to the world) to their people. The leaders will then bow to each other, turn 90 degrees to sign the documents, and then stand before each other for a long moment before shaking hands and embracing. In a signorial stroke of the pen, Kim Jong-un will become the most famous person in the world and announcers and commentators from around the globe will begin speculating about his winning the Nobel Peace Prize.

After the obligatory handshake and hug between leaders, $12 billion will be electronically transferred to the North Korean elite, and simultaneously, as a symbolic gesture of new openness and unity replacing isolation and separation, the Juche Tower across the river will be dramatically blown up and crumble to the ground as billions of people around the world watch and weep with joy. News broadcasters will announce plans for the construction of a new and even more monumental tower that will symbolize a united Korea.

Video cameras on rooftops and in blimps overhead will capture the magnitude of this gigantic spectacle, as forty thousand South Korean and forty thousand North Korean unarmed soldiers march into each other's ranks, merge into an overlapping body, and, on cue, break file and introduce themselves with a bow, handshake or hug as regional versions of the Korean folk song "Arirang" are piped in through an enormous sound system (later used for a K-pop celebration). Both militaries will then discard their shirt uniforms and pull on matching unification military attire. Young Kim and his South Korean counterpart will be center-stage, hands clasped and raised in jubilation, as this great symbolic gesture of unity and reunification will be broadcast on large outdoor screens in every major city center across the Korean Peninsula and on smart phones, personal computers and television sets around the world.

Elevated private booths will show North and South Korean military and civilian elites participating with equal enthusiasm. Soju will be on hand for symbolic friendship toasts. Special pre-produced documentary features about Korean society and culture will be shown to an international audience of billions. Since a large number of North Koreans will only be able to listen to the proceedings, the radio broadcast must have special emotion and verbal attention to detail, described by enthusiastic professional North and South Korean announcers and commentators. This enthusiasm may be unnecessary, since the promised payout from the Korean Peace Fund will be the essential motivator of joyfulness across the land.

Roving reporters will capture everything. There will be a live video feed to and from similar ceremonial festivities occurring at North Korea's nuclear sites and in cities across the Korean Peninsula. People in Pyongyang will see people celebrating in Changjin and Chongjin and cities in between, and people throughout North Korea will see South Koreans celebrating as live feeds from Seoul, Busan, Daegu, Gwangju and other cities show people celebrating in the South. There should also be a video feed from Koreans in America and other parts of the world that producers can cut to, thus showing that these celebrations are international. This will be a moment in Korean history more significant than anything that has ever happened before — a giant Korean family reunion shared with the world.

After the political and cultural symbolism is concluded, live K-pop music performed on an enormous stage off to one side of the square will soon turn the event into a mass celebration, punctuated intermittently by speeches from celebrities and world leaders. International celebrities will be on hand for interviews and songs. Several pre-staged fun activities and venues symbolizing unification will be intermittently shown on the large screens that surround the square.

Somewhere in Pyongyang there will be hundreds of North and South Korean children (distinguished by different color T-shirts) playing together in a fountain. Live video shots of acrobatics and dancing will be projected on the large screens as an Arirang Mass Games Reunification Edition begins at the May Day Stadium, with 30,000 children holding up colored cards to create huge mosaic pictures with unification themes as 50,000 gymnasts perform their synchronized acts on the field. At some point North and South Korean parachuters will drop from the sky into the square holding hands in a show of unity.

The most creative minds in the entertainment and news industry will be charged with making this the greatest broadcast spectacle of all time. It will be remembered as a landmark in world events when, for the first time in history, peace and reunification in a divided country was created by the global community coming together and smartly sharing the wealth of nations.

CHAPTER NINE

After Reunification

The Peace and Reunification Agreement is signed and the North and South are now one united Republic of Korea. Imagining this amazing moment in time, and some of the challenges in the immediate aftermath of reunification, may provide us with a new perspective on its historic possibility. This final chapter has evolved into something more than merely a few additional filler pages to fulfill the publisher's request. Focusing on immediate challenges may make this plan seem more plausible and encourage forward thinking. Indeed, considering the aftermath gives an emotional boost of sorts and makes the possibility of reunification seem all the more real.

This final chapter will transport us forward into the days immediately following reunification. After the radio and television broadcast of the reunification signing celebration, there will be enormous hope and expectation for a better future. The level of excitement should be almost palpable. What next?

Exchanging a scholarly approach for a more speculative one, in this final chapter I will briefly consider an array of immediate reunification challenges. Among some of the issues I will consider: the crucial material exchange of money for weapons, the introduction of banking and legal institutions, private property, a unified military, and the impact of improvements in transportation and communication. I will also highlight some economic issues that uniquely emerge from the $300 billion infusion of money, including the economic and demographic impact of household savings, and identify several issues that arose following Chinese economic transformation and reunification with Hong Kong, the Russian political and economic transformation, and the German political and economic reunification that may apply to the Korean situation. Some of this information may serve to ameliorate South Korean economic and demographic concerns.

Nine. After Reunification

I will argue for a gradualist social and economic transformation that carefully monitors wages, staple food prices, the import of nonessential commodity items, and migration. The role of international non-governmental organizations (NGOs) is discussed in terms of their key role in helping children, the hungry and the imprisoned, and in providing for the health and welfare of hundreds of thousands of North Koreans who are in immediate need. I also offer some cursory considerations on a variety of subjects, including education, media, volunteerism, tourism, and the cultural renaissance that is sure to commence once the North opens up to the world.

Money for Weapons

Long before the official Reunification Signing Day, a list of 24 million people must be compiled from information in the 2008 North Korean Population Census and with the assistance of North Korean experts. Payments will be determined with the cooperation of population professionals from both sides of the 38th parallel.[1] All of this information must be electronically collected, sorted, itemized and eventually made available to the emergent deposit banking system. This will be an extraordinary task.

Determining payment to elites is an immediate concern. The North Korean elite will be transferred one-third of their total payment ($12 billion) on the day of the historic reunification signing ceremony. Elite payments will be quite large, particularly for the top 2,000, who are to be paid on a sliding scale between $100 and $2 million. A slight difference in rank may be worth millions of dollars. Therefore, it may make the most sense for Kim Jong-un to provide this ranked list of 10,000 military, civilian and political elites, perhaps with the provision that all military generals be included and more than 1,500 elites be selected from outside Pyongyang.

All generals will be required to retire after reunification but their inclusion among the elite in the peace fund payout will give them a comfortable status in the future society. The rationale behind this second stipulation is that spreading incentives more widely should encourage a stronger sense of inter-provincial inclusivity and might co-opt possible sources of opposition.

The transfer of nuclear materials and armaments from the North to the South must be planned and organized. International experts will take control of nuclear materials and determine how to neutralize and dispose of them. North Korean military officers will be well compensated by the fund and should be highly cooperative. Most smaller armaments can be decommissioned, collected and stored or destroyed at a few central provincial processing locations in the first week(s) after reunification. Military personnel can begin receiving payments after all weapons have been secured. There will be a great deal of incentive for this process to run smoothly and proceed quickly.

Military

Non-elite high- and middle-level officers will be paid next. As noted earlier, 1,200 officers below the rank of general and above the rank of captain/major will receive payment between $600,000 and $400,000, and 30,000 officers including and between the rank of captain/major will receive payments between $200,000 and $50,000. This will be a significant amount of money for these soldiers. Their original one-third payment can be spread out over 24–36 months, with the remainder also contingent upon their remaining in the military during this critical early reunification period. Their professional leadership and personal authority will be important in the transition to a unified military and in organizing their troops for vital nation-building tasks such as the construction of new public infrastructure. In addition to roads and bridges, they can help build courthouses, parks, playgrounds, hospitals and schools.

Except for the children of Pyongyang party elite, college education has been severely restricted and most young adults are sent into the military until they are in their late 20s and early 30s. Approximately 5 percent of the total population, or 1.2 million men and women, currently serve in the North Korean military. Many of these young conscripts would make contributions to Korean civil society if they were free of restrictive military obligations. Therefore, careful analysis must be given to the disposition of the rank-and-file military after reunification.

It would be counterproductive to prevent those who are the most talented and enterprising from getting an education and participating in this new economy as professionals and entrepreneurs. Therefore, it might better serve the needs of the new nation to allow 10–30 percent of soldiers with the best prospects to test out of the military (while retaining their original peace fund pay grade) to enter higher education and technical schools.[2] The quality of primary and secondary education must be brought up to South Korean standards as soon as possible and the traditional Confucian system of selecting the highest-quality students for college and social advancement must be re-implemented in the North. Opportunities for advancement will inspire an eager new generation of Koreans to find their place in the new economy.[3]

Many elite and non-elite North Koreans will want to attend college in the South. This is a positive development, since the demographic decline of the South Korean population has just commenced and soon there will be more space for new entrants throughout the educational system. College scholarships for North Koreans will be needed, since most will come from impoverished family backgrounds. A testing system and tutoring facilities must be set up throughout the North to prepare students for college and to determine who shall be admitted.

The current 5–10-year mandatory internment of North Korean soldiers is excessive and it should be announced that this will be reduced, perhaps first to five years during the initial ten-year rebuilding period, and then to the approximately two-year commitment currently imposed in the South. This promise will produce goodwill and boost morale. Indeed, after ten years, and without the threat of war, perhaps the period of obligatory military service can be reduced for all Koreans.

However, many would agree that in principle this kind of unselfish public service early in life is not only of value to the country but also contributes to the personal and emotional growth of the next generation and the sense of working together for something greater than oneself. This is a noble calling and helps young people appreciate the sacrifices their elders have made and also provides a perspective on civil society and the social contract in a modern age where tendencies for self-centered materialism and individuation prevail.

In the meantime, salaries may be made more attractive for military personnel who have put in their five years to encourage them to stay, and raised for everyone. This will be a transitory period for both militaries. The function of North Korean military personnel may be unclear after munitions have been locked away in a general disarmament.

The use of guns should be de-emphasized throughout the military, since former North Koreans will not have access to weapons until they are fully integrated with South Korean forces. In the past, the North Korean military has been a valuable source of labor for state projects; the importance of this future role should be re-emphasized. The absorption of the North Korean military into the South Korean command structure can begin, along with refocusing the central role of a united military on transforming a feudal infrastructure into a modern one.

Or it may be advisable to keep military units separate for a few years to avoid rank-and-file jealousies over pay scales or conflicts over cultural differences and so forth. The results of initial experiments in reintegration can inform a more effective and successful process. Some sort of timetable may be set for the complete integration of the two militaries and equalization in pay.

One possible goal might be for salaries in a totally unified military to reach parity within ten years. Whatever plan is determined most reasonable, the rebuilding of the North should be promoted as the patriotic duty and abiding focus of a new Korean military. The peace dividend of cheap labor for patriotic public construction projects will help underwrite economic growth and save the new nation hundreds of millions of dollars in construction costs.

Banking

An immediate priority will be to construct brick-and-mortar banking facilities. Banking is a central institution in every society, but North Korea does not currently have a trusted and functioning deposit banking system. Hassig and Oh report, "Even state organizations have avoided using banks."[4] Therefore, the new banking system will be owned and operated by South Korean banks that previously bid for the rights to set up business in the North. Private South Korean banks will construct this system with the help of the central bank, the military, and government assistance and oversight.

As banks are built or refurbished, and before people have access to money, everyone must have enough to eat. Therefore, international humanitarian food agencies will be granted immediate and complete

Nine. After Reunification

geographical access inside the North so they can begin to provide food to the hungry and assess critical needs.

The central bank of North Korea has over 200 branches. The banking industry will have to determine how many additional deposit banks are needed and where to build them. It should be understood that brick-and-mortar facilities will open for business countrywide to provide access to money within six months (or some reasonable time frame). A determination will have to be made on how the river of money will flow: Is it better to let it out slowly or all at once? By region? In alphabetical order? This has never been done before and the answer to this question will require careful micro- and macroeconomic analysis. This flow of capital must also be coordinated with temporary controls and other aspects of the new economy.

Picture identification cards must be issued to nearly 20 million people over the age of ten. This card may also serve as a bankcard and identification for travel to the South, as well as other legal purposes. Processing facilities can be set up in banks and at post offices and government facilities (perhaps even farmers' markets) throughout the North. Mobile units could be used to produce identity cards in more remote rural areas.

The South Korean banking industry will be challenged to provide service, but the potential remuneration is large, as initial deposits will be in the tens of billions of dollars and the North is expected to develop rapidly. Professional people will have to be brought in from the South to manage loan departments and train new bank managers and employees. The distribution of money to an eager population may not run smoothly at first. There is bound to be some confusion; everything will be a learning process.

To avoid a run on the banks, it may be necessary to put some rules in place, perhaps limiting withdrawals to 20 percent of total assets per week unless special permission is given by the bank manager. Automatic bank machines can be installed countrywide with video directions on how to use them. The first bank openings will inform a more efficient process for future openings. A secure banking system trusted to hold household savings, and with sufficient capital to invest in local and regional development schemes, will be one of the foundations to economic growth.

Enormous amounts of money must be printed and driven around the country to be held in these small banks. The exchange rate for North Korean currency must be set. Cashing out this money will be made easier by the 2009 reforms, which wiped out private savings so that few citizens have much to exchange. An upper limit should be set so that counterfeiting is discouraged. This will simplify banking operations. Of course, it would be even simpler to not honor North Korean currency, and this option should likewise be considered. Since individuals will be given large amounts of new currency, complaints about not honoring the old currency may not be a serious problem.

South Korean banking experts will be challenged to devise a smooth system for expeditiously introducing North Koreans to the modern world of banking and finance. Radio, television and Internet communication should be used to assure people that money in a bank is theirs to keep — that it is stored in a safe place, guaranteed with interest, and available anytime they need it. An early and thorough education about this fundamental social institution will be of utmost importance for confidence building and to provide a sense of personal security among the people. An established banking industry, a stable currency, and low inflation are critical to the success of economic integration.

Economics

In 2000 Noland, Robinson and Wang wrote, "Greater North-South economic integration ... could have profound effects on both economies, yet scant effort has been devoted to constructing economic models to analyze this possibility."[5] Over the past decade economists have responded to this challenge and more work has been completed.[6] Unfortunately, none of this highly speculative scholarship is even vaguely relevant to a unified Korea influenced by $300 billion in peace fund allowances.[7] However, some valuable insights and limited generalizations can be obtained from German and China–Hong Kong political reunification, and also from Russian, Chinese and Vietnamese economic transformation, about which much has been written.

Economic reunification will benefit greatly from South Korean institutional and management expertise. Holger Wolf asserts that Korea has

Nine. After Reunification

the advantage of "immediate access to an efficient, market-proven system of regulations and institutions, including (very importantly!), skilled and experienced administrators."[8] Indeed, South Korean economists and policymakers have a successful track record of balancing macroeconomic factors and producing favorable results. Their skills will be needed to eliminate distortions and manage the critical elements of the reunification economy as the North and South gradually equilibrate.

Even with conscientious efforts, Korean reunification and economic integration are likely to have idiosyncratic problems and elements of partially controlled chaos. Almost every decision in the transition process will be subject to debate, corruption and abuse. Perfectly sensible solutions may have serious unintended consequences. Money will be moving in many directions; profits and livelihoods will be at stake. Opportunities for unfair advantage and excessive recompense will be everywhere. The moral fabric of Korean society will be tested. Therefore, diligent supervision will be important and safeguards must be put in place to discourage taking advantage of economically naïve and financially inexperienced compatriots who suddenly have large bank accounts and money in their pockets.

Let us not forget that this will be the first time in economic history something like this has happened. The Germans and Russians did not have a $300 billion peace fund infusing money into their processes. Special transitional laws for a civil society may be necessary to discourage arbitrage and prospering from unfair advantage. An agency may be given direct authority (with punitive powers) to monitor and govern all domestic transactions in order to avert corruption, thievery and price gouging.

Economic development cannot take place without a working legal system. Legal institutions have a central place in societies that protect private property and enforce principles of fairness and equity. In spite of North Korean efforts to establish a legal infrastructure to facilitate international business activities, new property ownership and economic exchange will be protected by the rule of South Korean law.[9] Educational materials and news reports shared through newspapers, radio, television and the Internet may be helpful in educating people about these new laws and protections.

Courthouses must be built. A new civic bureaucracy and legal system must be installed to adjudicate disputes, license businesses, and record and protect private property rights. South Korea will not need to limit graduating lawyers for the next several years, as their services will be in high demand in the North. Lawyers will be involved in every aspect of establishing a new economic system and organizing the legal basis for a civil society. This will be a messy time-consuming affair fraught with errors and disputes.

Northern nouveau riche elites may try to control state assets and quickly and quietly turn them into private enterprises, like the elites did in Russia a generation ago. Perhaps these usurpations should be allowed to stand after unification for properties valued at less than a few million dollars, since these new owners will likely have an in-depth knowledge of the business and can keep them productive. In due course, state property, factories and production facilities should be valued and sold to private ownership in a transparent manner.

Privatization may create a host of subsidiaries of South Korean companies, as it did in Germany.[10] During the German transition, political expediency often stood in the way of efficient economic reform as corrupt transfers of property and subsidies encouraged rent-seeking activities. Rent seekers are often politicians or bureaucrats (gatekeepers) who try to obtain money by high-level extortion — demanding a share of wealth that has already been created. This can be avoided in Korea with transparency and vigilant independent oversight. Mistakes made in the secretive and hurried German privatization process should forewarn Korean privatization policymakers.[11] Everyone should be given a fair chance in a free market.

Reunification will also impact the South in specific ways. Some Korea watchers have predicted reunification would have a deleterious short-term impact on the standard of living in the South, an impression shared by about half the South Korean population.[12] This scenario might have more credence under normal conditions, but the Korean Peace Fund would profoundly change the basis for these calculations. Even without this $300 billion input, some economists have predicted the macroeconomic impact of economic integration on South Korea would be relatively small.[13] What is most likely is that the massive investment and blossoming of new markets, and the acquisition of natural and human resources by the South, will create growth for the overall Korean economy in the short and long term.

Nine. After Reunification

Original material factors play an underlying and sometimes determinative role in economic stability and prosperity. One reason the Japanese economy is almost four times larger (based on GDP) than the South Korean economy is because of its geographic and demographic advantages. Japan is 350 percent larger and has 250 percent more people and triple the labor force. Adding another 24 million people and 122 percent more territory with a 450-kilometers (300-mile) coastline with warm water ports to Korea will reduce this gap. Korea is currently only about 7 percent behind Japan in purchase power parity (PPP).[14] There is every reason to be optimistic about the future, as human and natural resources will add a new dimension to Korea's productive base and more diversity and stability to the Korean economy.

Over a generation of sustained rising standards of living in South Korea may give a false sense of economic strength and stability. The Korean economy has several underlying vulnerabilities. It is dependent on Middle East oil and natural gas imports, and just two corporations, Samsung and Hyundai, are responsible for almost half of its foreign-exchange earnings. Energy imports from nearby Russia, mineral sales to China, and the economic development of the Pacific Northeast and its ice-free ports will diversify the economy and create more intrinsic economic stability.

In 2000, it was estimated it would take about $2 billion per year to balance the North Korean economy and support minimal living standards; the purchase of grain, energy, fertilizer and pharmaceuticals accounted for half this total.[15] But economic integration with one of the world's largest and most productive economies will require much more than a small nudge to create an acceptable relative equality between North and South in a reasonable number of years.

With the threat of war removed, Korea's international credit rating will likely improve to the highest rating of AA+.[16] And with an expectation of close to 10 percent annual growth, the International Monetary Fund, the Asian Development Bank, Chinese lending institutions and other sources of finance should be willing to provide significant development funding, especially in the energy and transportation sectors, since they will underwrite economic growth in other sectors.

Paved roads and port facilities must be built, vehicles must be imported, and reliable sources of oil and electricity must become available. Some electricity can be transmitted almost immediately across the border from the South, but large investments in energy must be forthcoming. The North has a prodigious supply of bituminous coal in the ground and it is much faster and cheaper to build coal-burning power plants than nuclear installations. Thus, obtaining energy from coal will probably be the most appropriate development strategy in the early stages.

Korea may be reluctant to depend on international banking institutions for capital after what transpired during the Asian Economic Crisis in 1997–1998.[17] However, heavy reliance on these institutions may not be necessary, as injections of money from the Korean Peace Fund and private regional and international investors will boost the overall economy and underwrite conditions for immediate profitability in every sector. Household savings and consumption will be large for at least the first five years; banking institutions may reinvest this huge household savings account directly into their communities. China and Vietnam modernized their economies with low taxes and without excessive foreign debt partly because their bottomless supply of cheap labor invited private foreign investment, while export earnings were reinvested in productive infrastructure.[18]

Employers of unskilled workers in the North will be in a similar attractive bargaining position after reunification. Foreign investment–induced employment opportunities will increase standards of living, while peace fund–underwritten household savings will provide local banks with capital to invest in small- to medium-scale local and regional development projects. Some of the economic activity at this level of entrepreneurship will unite rural and urban areas in economic exchange and create jobs and a healthy flow of goods within the deep structure of the domestic economy.

Private institutional entrepreneurs have already leveraged resources and established extensive internal markets in the North.[19] They can now come out of the shadows, legally purchase ownership, obtain investment, and grow naturally. The development of light industry can be accelerated with relatively small investments. And in rural areas, with quick-payback investments in better seeds, fertilizer, fuel and machinery to replace draft animals, food production will increase dramatically in a few years.

Besides crop loss due to non-hybrid seeds and lack of fertilizer, much of the harvest is lost every year because there is no way to get it to market. It is a sad irony that in an undernourished North Korea, food is sometimes left to rot in the fields. New businesses across the North will soon solve this transportation problem. Japanese rice farming is currently about twice as productive as in North Korea; with this large margin of difference, there is good reason to believe the North can rapidly increase its level of output. Along with temporary relatively inexpensive rice imports and appropriate subsidies, improved agricultural productivity will help keep a lid on subsistence food prices and inflation.[20]

Following China's example, a more productive rural labor force and the growth of household savings may be a crucial first step in economic development. Barry Naughton observes, "As Chinese rural household saving skyrocketed in the 1980s, the supply of funds to the Local Rural Credit Cooperatives expanded drastically."[21] This created a positive feedback relationship whereby savings were invested in profit-making improvements in productivity that in turn produced more savings, which in turn were reinvested, and so forth.

A change in Chinese agricultural policy away from collective farms and toward a system of household responsibility made this outcome possible. Naughton asserts, "Once the household responsibility system was adopted, the output response was phenomenal. The return to household farming was one of the main causes, if not the main cause, of output acceleration."[22] There is every reason to believe this development scenario will also occur in the productive heartland of northern Korea. As in China during the 1980s, the total factor productivity in the North is likely to be astounding.[23] With new personal incentives and moderate inputs, 20–60 percent productivity leaps could be obtained during the initial years of reform and capitalization.

In the long run, however, Haggard and Noland argue that due to the natural limitations of the agricultural sector, the most auspicious path to economic transformation will be to follow the South Korean export-led model of development. This strategy would take advantage of abundant cheap labor and the proximity of the large advanced economies and markets in the region.[24] With Russian sources of energy and South Korean (and Chinese) capital and technology, the comparative advantages in the North will lead to rapid industrial development. However, while combining assets for external trade, rural and urban sectors must also begin employing economies of scale to produce a surplus of something of value to each other.

In order to overcome pre-commercial modes of production, it is essential for the North to become economically integrated through internal trade, only some of which will come from the South (at least initially). Just as South Korea wisely protected its infant domestic industries in the early stages of economic growth, the North will need similar protections in selected growth industries. Development economists and politicians must work together to maximize gains in the shorter-term local economic integration process within the North and also the general longer-term economic reintegration with the South.

Policy and macroeconomic inputs will be especially critical. An upgraded rail system and tarred roads built with the help of military labor will be essential for the movement of goods. With infrastructural improvements, investment and entrepreneurship, it may not be long before the natural division of labor between rural and urban activities is mutually beneficial and the slow process of equalizing prices and salaries between the North and South can begin a new stage.

For an extended period during integration, most pricing should be controlled within moderate boundaries as economic competition takes hold, imports become slowly available, and the oligopoly on production goods is eliminated by competition from new domestic industrial sources of production. Rather than simply abolish and destroy state enterprises (as in Germany), the Chinese model of growing out of the planned economy by allowing dual systems to exist (one public and one private) may create productive competitive synergies during the early stages of economic development.

With capital streaming in, it is not likely to take long for private enterprise to either predominate or motivate efficiencies in state enterprises sufficient to create market competition and, eventually, free-market pricing. If some of what remains of North Korean state enterprise can be reformed or retooled inexpensively and turned profitable, this will eventually bring a higher return when sold to private investors. In some state industries the production technologies may be so ramshackle that their dissolution will be the only reasonable alternative. To compensate for this creative destruction, new employment opportunities will be springing up throughout the economy to provide jobs and incomes for displaced workers.

No matter what condition state production facilities are in, food

Nine. After Reunification

prices must be subsidized until the production capacity of the rural economy improves. Rapid price liberalization in Russia and Germany led to extreme distortions, inflation and hardship. Commodity prices should rise slowly, commensurate with salaries and gradually increasing pay scales throughout the North. Wages should converge gradually over many years. After unification East Germany experienced a rapid rise in wages that led to job loss, high unemployment, and output collapse.[25] Limiting rapid wage increases and managing their relationship to slowly rising commodity prices can prevent this outcome. Intelligent macroeconomic management of this balancing process will be necessary as the North adjusts to South Korean levels of prosperity and the gradual institution of free markets. The disastrous "big bang" or shock therapy strategy of economic transformation experienced in Russia in the 1990s can be avoided by invoking principles of gradualism.

In the early 1980s, just a couple years after China decided to institute capitalist economic reforms, Naughton notes, "Gradual decontrol of consumer goods prices—initially cautious—steadily brought most consumer goods under market price regimes."[26] Since marketization began outside Pyongyang almost 20 years ago, free-market prices for food products and other commodities already exist to some extent in the hinterland. There is evidence that interdependent commodity price fluctuations are already in place between North Korea and China along the border.

There will be distortions and imbalances, and unexpected successes and failures along the way, but a consistent economic philosophy of development will be important. Macroeconomic policies should be flexible and pragmatically adjusted to reflect societal needs and not be promulgated by ideological demagogues from either side of the political-economic spectrum. Phillip Tetlock has shown how more accurate holistic interpretations of empirical data, and solutions to complex problems are more likely to be introduced by pragmatic foxes than ideological hedgehogs. In this context, foxes and hedgehogs refer to two distinctive cognitive styles. Foxes are more open-minded and tend to view a problem from different angles and perspectives and offer various solutions to problems, whereas hedgehogs tend to be intransigent ideologues and offer more simple-minded formulaic solutions.[27]

Indeed, from Chinese economist Barry Naughton's analysis, it appears that foxes (and the unintended consequences of hedgehog miscalculations) were responsible for most of the successes of early Chinese economic transformation. Naughton has argued that after the initial failures of orthodox communist reform strategies, China's economy began to turn around once pragmatic non-ideological macroeconomic policies were instituted after Deng Xiaoping came to power in 1978.[28] The East Asian social-economic hybrid philosophy labeled "Confucian Capitalism" can also serve as a general guide for letting circumstances determine policies, and valuing fairness and social harmony along with making a profit.[29]

Naughton has observed that China's economic reform was "always improvised, never clearly formulated in advance, the program has nevertheless been shaped by a distinctive logic."[30] This was the logic of balanced growth and gradualism. It is better to proceed slowly and with caution and get it right the first time than to alienate the masses by unleashing the shock of free markets all at once and suffer the negative fallout of unintended consequences Germany and Russia experienced by liberalizing too fast.[31]

The effects of a sudden infusion of capital must be carefully gauged so that the new economy does not appropriate this personal account surplus with instantly higher prices. It will be more productive for job creation and the overall economy if this money is saved or invested or spent on durable products and material improvements (building materials, transportation and technology) and improving human capital through education, rather than spent on subsistence or expensive non-essential commodities. Therefore, for some period of time the South Korean government should smooth distortions and enforce reasonable price controls on food and other vital commodities.

After the reunification grace period wears out, gradual economic improvement will co-opt opposition that might otherwise form. Through the Internet and other media channels of free and open communication, everyone will slowly begin to understand what happened during the Kim Jong-il years and to realize the truth about their past. Improvements in standards of living will be the most persuasive argument for northern Koreans that they are heading down the right path.

As noted above, this patient development process will benefit from South Korea's "efficient, market-proven system of regulations and institutions," the skill of experienced administrators, and an economic philosophy

Nine. After Reunification

that has in just two generations managed the rise of a bull-cart rice economy into one of the leading industrial economies in the world today.[32] Their task is to keep a balance so that all aspects of the economy and life in the North evolve gradually and common people are given enough time to adapt to change and entrepreneurs have an opportunity to innovate.

Chinese and South Korean firms should be restrained from flooding northern markets with consumer goods that would instantly devalue North Korean capital stock.[33] Scott Bradford and Kerk Phillips note that "when Germany reunified, as much as two-thirds of the East German capital stock was scrapped as useless. Unfortunately, the situation is likely to be similar in North Korea."[34] Rather than have a free-for-all, it is advisable that economic experts monitor the slow introduction and pricing of new consumer goods.

Although North Korea's marketization from below is a grassroots phenomenon that has been creating profitable informal markets across the North for almost a generation, Mitsuhiro argues that "real marketization" throughout the economy has not yet occurred. He asserts that the "North Korean economy is not a planned or a market economy."[35] Changes need to take place in what remains of the command economy in Pyongyang, where centralized food distribution remains the norm, and in other cities, where marketization has less of a hold.

During this transformation, public controls and incentives must restrain the economic tiger from exaggerations that would alienate people from expanded capitalist market activities, and compensation should be made for market failures. In particular, food must be kept inexpensive and plentiful for years to come in Pyongyang and other urban areas as salaries rise and free-market prices slowly emerge. Rapid increases in agricultural productivity may make subsidies unnecessary. These will be enormously exciting times for northern Koreans as they witness a new abundance and variety of food and other commodities. However, nothing would dampen this enthusiasm more quickly than unreasonably high prices.

Economics and Migration

As economic growth occurs, people will migrate toward money and jobs. Internal migration is a concern among South Korean policymakers, workers' unions, and government officials. The massive migration out of East Germany during its reunification process is often cited and South Koreans fear a similar result. In Eastern Europe the Iron Curtain began to fall after the Hungarian government started to allow East Germans to migrate to the West in May 1989. By August large numbers of East Germans were also crossing through Czechoslovakia and Poland. An estimated five percent of East Germans emigrated in 1989–1990. But this population movement was partly motivated by political fears that will already be resolved by the formation of a greater Korea. And imbalanced migration did not last long; by 1993 the number of emigrants to West Germany and to East Germany reached a balance.[36]

Korea is not likely to experience this level of initial migration pressure because the political status of a unified Korea will be settled and the rewards of reunification will be brought to the North quickly in the form of immediate food aid and other benefits. Before long tablet computers and Internet connections may keep people glued to electronic media and information. And people will know that they must be home when the bank opens and while private property issues are settled. Military personnel will not be disbanded or released from their commitments. New jobs will spring up everywhere that will encourage people to go to work in the North.

Labor migration can be controlled by a recruitment employment policy, media and public opinion, and, if necessary, border restrictions. Most northern Koreans are likely to remain close to home near their families if they see things are getting better. Seoul National University international migration expert Song Young Hoon agrees; he expects North Koreans will follow the established pattern of relying on the security of extended families and household support during periods of change and uncertainty.[37]

Displaced by agricultural technology and wanting a better life, many people will move off the farms and into nearby cities to seek employment in expanding service, light manufacturing, transportation and construction industries. The economic synergy associated with urbanization is a necessary step in the development process. However, migration to Pyongyang will likely be heavy and may need to be managed in order to avoid a serious overburdening of public services and housing.

The rural-urban population distribution is about the same in North

Nine. After Reunification

Korea today as it was in the South 30 years ago. If North Korea follows an urbanization path similar to that of South Korea, 20 percent of its population, or about five million people, will migrate to the cities during the next generation. Urbanization will most likely be faster than this. And with demographically initiated multiplier effects, jobs will spring up everywhere. The housing market will boom as new household savings, combined with greater access to concrete and other building materials, will spur new construction and home improvement.

Some migration may positively impact the overexpanded housing market in the South as some wealthy elites and retired military officers move to the South to live in leisure and anonymity.[38] Others will stay at home and invest in their communities. As large amounts of capital begin flowing into the North and moderate numbers of skilled factory workers and unskilled laborers move to the South, everyone will be better off.[39]

Indeed, with appropriate macroeconomic management, reunification will most likely create a long-term economic boom on the Korean Peninsula similar to the growth South Korea and China have enjoyed over the past three decades. Northern Korea will become a new destination for Chinese and Japanese capital investment as the northeast region is developed. On a small scale this is already happening along the Chinese border.[40] Once fears of expropriation by corrupt officials are eliminated, investment and employment will surge. One projection suggests future pockets of growth like what took place 30 years ago in Shenzhen, China, where a small fishing village was transformed into a manufacturing hub of over four million people.[41] Kaesong, Sinuiju and Rason are likely candidates for rapid growth, along with several small cities along the Pacific coast.

The Pacific coast of northern Korea has similar latitude to the Eastern United States, where cities such as Boston and New York sit in ice-free Atlantic waters. Many northeast Chinese products will find it cheaper to flow through these Korean ports. Zhan and Lee assert, "Considering that China is the largest trading partner of South Korea, and the latter is the third largest trading partner of the former, a prosperous Korea will contribute to the long-time prosperity and stability in the Far East and Northeast Asia."[42]

Since diplomatic relations were formalized twenty years ago, bilateral trade between South Korea and China has increased 35-fold to nearly

$250 billion in 2012; this represents more than the South Korean trade volume with the United States and Japan combined and seventy times that of North Korean trade with China.[43] With double-digit growth rates, South Korea already sends about one-quarter of its annual total exports to China.[44] China is the largest destination for Korean foreign investment and "more than 30,000 South Korean firms have operations in China."[45]

Without the tension of war looming, it seems likely the new Korea may develop stronger, mutually beneficial ties with China, perhaps similar to the relationship between Canada and the United States. Indeed, in May 2012 Korea and China officially launched bilateral free-trade negotiations. Increased trade and commerce will benefit the citizens of both countries.

A unified Korea will also have consequences for the Kaesong Industrial Complex. The 40,000 skilled industrial workers trained there will be free to migrate to higher salaries in the South. But it would be chaotic if all or most workers quit their jobs in Kaesong and milled about southern industrial sites looking for higher paid work. Labor migration could be constricted by an invitation-only (requirement) system, with labor recruiters at the center of this process. Levels of recruitment can be adjusted to meet demand in the South, as northern Koreans gradually replace 600,000 foreign workers.

Even at relatively lower wages, more workers will come to Kaesong to replace those who leave, as an entry into skilled manufacturing. Of course, Kaesong enterprises will have to adapt to growing labor demands over time, but overall business activity will grow enormously as a result of new markets for commodities in the North. The Kaesong industrial region, with its head start, will undoubtedly evolve into a much larger hub of manufacturing and production and will continue to be a place where cheap northern Korean labor meets South Korean capital investment and technology.

There are legitimate fears that wages in the South may decline due to increasingly available cheap labor from the North. Cha notes, "While most Koreans welcome the marriage of northern labor and southern capital as beneficial to the united Korean economy as a whole, South Korean labor groups may be less enthusiastic."[46] Labor pressure on the South will be minimal if labor migration is limited by an invitation-only system to replace foreign workers for the first five years and then con-

Nine. After Reunification

trolled by gradual changes in immigration policy before South Korea completely opens its borders. And the current movement of South Korean capital investment into Vietnam and China may be redirected toward cheap labor in northern Korea, holding workers in place near their families and homes. Indeed, as integration occurs there will be many more benefits to the South Korean worker than costs as the economy grows. A larger, more diversified Korean economy with access to investment capital will produce full employment for at least a generation.

Indeed, there will likely be strong demand for skilled labor from the South, since the extent of underdevelopment in North Korea is so vast.[47] This specialized labor, to teach North Koreans how to use modern machines and new technology, must be paid at levels approaching those in South Korea; these employees should be kept on as managers and people who have the know-how to repair or reprogram equipment. Over time, many South Koreans will undoubtedly establish new homes in the North.

North Korea has about the same per-capita income as Vietnam and India, and about one-third of the Chinese population. As noted, North Korea has a similar rural-urban demographic and industrial structure to that of South Korea in the mid–1980s. And like what happened thirty years ago in the South, investments and new economic opportunities will undoubtedly produce an explosion of innovation and growth in the North. Indeed, as previously noted, the results of an economic study by the investment banking firm Goldman Sachs suggest that a united Korea would create strong synergies between the North and South that might produce enough growth to exceed the GNP of France and Germany in as little as thirty years.[48] A competitive labor force, favorable demographics, and abundant mineral wealth are cited as compelling reasons for this economic synergy.

A majority of the North's export earnings are currently derived from minerals and mining products.[49] Increased investments in extraction industries would produce significantly more earnings, since they are seriously underdeveloped. Edward Yoon observes, "The minerals production sector in North Korea lacks modern equipment and suffers from electricity shortages. Equipment in many mines is decades old and include some materials that date back to the Japanese colonial period."[50]

With capital investment these extraction industries will grow precipitously, as the North has substantial quantities of valuable strategic minerals ($4 trillion known; $10 trillion estimated), including coal, uranium, iron ore, gold, copper, nickel and magnesite, most of which South Korean industries currently must import. Once this mineral industry is developed, the export profits from resource-hungry China will be astronomical.[51]

Without formalizing a separate system in the North, the rapid rise of opportunities and gradual improvements should greatly reduce the demand for immigration to the South. The initial difficulty of finding transportation and the long-term high cost of housing in the South will also play a role. Nevertheless, pragmatic controls of the border will be necessary to contain possible unpleasant developments. Application for permanent residence in the South can be handled on a case-by-case basis for at least the first ten years.

It may be possible to proclaim the border permanently opened within one year and citizens from both sides of the 38th parallel may feel free to come and go as they please with proper identification and approval. A controlled but open border will have enormous symbolic and psychological significance; this freedom will set a new tone for a new nation. Immigration to the South will be naturally regulated by changes occurring in the North. A one-year waiting period will create time for psychological adjustment, food distribution and banking services to become established, and allow employment and other economic opportunities to begin to sprout inside the North.

However much empathy South Koreans may have for the privations incurred by their northern brothers and sisters, it is unlikely they would have much tolerance for large-scale loitering and criminal activities. This can be prevented with permitted travel restrictions for at least the first five years and with penalties for illegal activities and overstaying taken directly out of future peace fund payments.

A RAND study estimated that the economic investment required to limit mass migration to the South would be between $50 and $67 billion (to double the North Korean GDP) within the first four years of reunification.[52] If this estimate is even close to accurate, migration should not be a problem, since vastly more money than this will flow into the North each year for at least the first five years. If after five years immigration pressures on the South become a concern, an open border can be reconsidered; it may be easy to place limitations on migration since everything (including jobs in the South) can be controlled for the first ten years by an invitation-only employment policy and identification cards.

The Demilitarized Zone (DMZ) will be protected (by unarmed guards) as a sanctuary for wildlife and endangered bird species and controlled as a dangerous no-man's-land that contains over a million landmines. The DMZ is approximately 4 kilometers wide and 250 kilometers long and is a valuable natural habitat and wildlife refuge, and an important flyway, wintering and breeding site for three endangered bird species.[53] Portions of the DMZ can be opened to eco-tourism.

Survey data from the former East Germany indicate that home ownership robustly correlates with unwillingness to move.[54] Within one year most northern Koreans may be sitting in a home they personally own, surfing the World Wide Web while looking at a vast array of new jobs in their area. Mass migration into China and then back again over the years suggests this was largely the result of food deficits (hunger) and that Koreans would stay home if they had enough to eat. Once people have adequate diets and new hope, there will be less reason to leave. Local bank accounts, property ownership, and increasing employment opportunities will keep people near their loved ones.

Indeed, after reunification it can be expected that many refugees who have permanently settled in China may return to Korea as private industries develop on the Korean side of the border and the quality of life improves. Many of the Koreans who settled in China were refugees from Japanese colonialism, the Korean War, and the brutalities of the North Korean political regime. If these families wish to return and live in a united Korea, perhaps they should be granted full benefits from the Korean Peace Fund. This would be a messy proposition and invite fraud, but it is the right thing to do and so should be considered. Many of these dislocated families will be coming home anyway. There are over 2 million North Koreans in China; many have found new lives and established deep roots and will remain. Calculating from the lowest payment schedule and assuming one-third are children, if 1.5 million Koreans came home, this would add $12 billion over five years to the total peace fund payout.

Travel tours to the South may be heavy but requests for permanent residence will probably be low to moderate, though perhaps enough to positively impact the labor and housing markets. Labor migration would be good for South Korean industry, as foreign immigration can be phased out for the time being. Businesses have had trouble recruiting people to do 3D (dirty, dangerous and difficult) jobs from the highly educated domestic South Korean labor force and have been compelled to rely on foreign workers. There are almost 600,000 foreigners in South Korea on temporary work visas who currently do the majority of 3D work. North Koreans could be hired to accomplish these tasks at salaries beyond their wildest dreams, and this would be a win-win for Korea. These Korean migrant workers will provide significant remittances to their families in the North. During this era of globalization, such cross-border remittances have come to account for significant income for developing countries around the world. For example, if 400,000 workers sent home $5,000 per year to their families in the North, this would amount to $2 billion annually.

Labor migration will also benefit South Korean small and medium-size companies, which now will be able to hire from a permanent labor force of literate, same-language workers who have a reputation for being hard and dependable workers, and who can be easily trained and retained. Reunification will also resolve for the time being some of the concerns South Koreans have regarding a growing foreign migrant population. The alleged high levels of ethnocentrism and xenophobia among the North Korean population will depress movement toward a multiethnic society for the time being. But this attitude will change over time with education and as Korea continues to open up to the world.

Of course, new problems may arise. Fierce regional rivalries have existed throughout the Korean Peninsula that predate the 1945 partition, but the sense of common ethnic Korean identity may override everything else during this period of unity, opportunity, and economic growth. Prejudice and discrimination will be unavoidable, since northern Koreans speak with a distinct dialect and use traditional words instead of foreign loan words, but funding the efforts and programs of organizations that promote a civil society may ameliorate their effects.

It is reported that the crime rate of North Korean refugees is twice that of the national average. Of course, the reason for this is that with poor education and few marketable skills, North Koreans are having a difficult time fitting into productive employment in the South. These effects have generational remedies, but they can be mitigated in the short term by stronger government retraining and assistance programs, and eliminated in a generation or two through education. However, it is most likely this criminal activity will be eliminated because these migrants will suddenly have job opportunities in the North and will move back to live near their friends and families.

Indeed, perhaps the 24,000 North Korean defectors who live in the South should also be included in the Korean Peace Fund benefits; if they were given $15,000 each over five years, this would cost $360 million. Many of these individuals will return to their families in the North and it would be unfair if they did not, like their friends, have money in their pockets and in private bank accounts. It is even possible to make peace fund benefits available only to those who migrate back to the North.

Labor will migrate in both directions. Many jobs will become available in the North for college graduates and skilled workers in the South, thus relieving current unemployment concerns for at least a generation. Skill and talent will migrate to the North and capture some of the money that will be spent retraining a society that has been taught by an inadequate propaganda-based educational system and worked for decades with low-level technologies in obsolete manufacturing facilities.

These employees from the South will have to be heavily subsidized; this will be a necessary short-term investment because their modern knowledge and technological skills will be critical to the development process. With the amount of money circulating and the growing demand for services and commodity production of all kinds, there will be many more job openings and considerable competition for labor in the North and South. Managed free-passage labor migration will most likely create far more wealth and efficiencies than problems.

A united Korea will have more human and material resources to expand and grow into the 21st century. A non-militaristic and economically unified Korea will advance East Asian regional cooperation and development. At expected levels of growth, in just one generation a unified Korea would become one of the top ten economies in the world. Trade alliances with Japan and China, the world's second and third largest economies, would make Korea the third member of a regional trading bloc of East Asian nations that would account for more than 30 percent of global GDP.

There will be many unforeseen problems to overcome during the long and difficult process of economic integration and development, but it seems clear that unification will result in a much richer Korea. Investment in business enterprises will revitalize economic life and create meaningful and productive jobs in the North. For the first time in twenty years people will have something rewarding to do, as growing economic activity will inspire a plethora of positivity throughout personal and professional life.

Nongovernmental Organizations

A significant portion of the North Korean population will need immediate help and international nongovernmental organizations (NGOs) can be an important conduit to their revitalization and reintegration into Korean society. Many NGOs left North Korea over a decade ago because of restrictions the Kim regime imposed on them.[55] British ambassador John Everard notes that the presence of NGOs reminded the regime of its economic difficulties and therefore they were either treated as a necessary evil or thrown out altogether.[56] After reunification, NGOs should have free access to set up food distribution channels and health care services, empty the prisons and rehabilitate the prisoners, and assess other immediate needs.

We can expect a hundreds of NGOs to flood back into the country. There should be an agency that tracks NGOs and requires reports from them; this would help Korean officials better assess conditions of health and welfare from on-the-ground informants countrywide. These reports may provide valuable empirical data, help inform development needs and assist in the quick response and best use of aid resources. Modern electronic communication devices will make the collection of geographically dispersed ground-level information readily available.

Immediate food distribution will be a top priority. However, it will be important not to disrupt food markets that have already been established and destroy the livelihoods of the very grassroots market entrepreneurs who helped make reunification possible. In the near term, food should be channeled through these people and around them to the most needy. Soon everyone will have access to money to pay for food. Even before roads are tarred, transitional food distribution centers and farmers' markets can be built to keep small-scale food retailers out of the weather. Other private interests may also begin to form a business model for more efficient food distribution and sale. There will be winners and losers, but an overall growing economy will absorb the losers and transform every aspect of society.

Providing an adequate diet is a critical humanitarian public objective. Lacking key proteins, fats, micronutrients and total calories, the World Health Organization estimates 60 percent of children between six months and seven years suffer from moderate to severe malnutrition. The younger generations of North Koreans are 4–8 centimeters (2–3 inches) shorter than their South Korean counterparts; significant stunting is found among the defector population.[57] The provision of adequate diets will bring immediate physical and psychological results. Within the first 5 to 10 years after German reunification, all anthropometric measures of children from East Germany, reflected immediate size increases.[58]

Health care system needs must be assessed. Herbal medicines are widely available but there is a serious shortage of everything else that is standard in modern medical care.[59] Because of inadequate diet and health care, North Koreans, on average, live twelve fewer years than their South Korean counterparts.[60] International humanitarian organizations have vast experience in supplementing health care systems that are severely underfunded and creating workable systems from almost nothing after national disasters. This is the cutting edge of humanitarian work on our planet.

It can be expected that some of the most talented, experienced and compassionate citizens from around the world will converge on North Korea to assist the World Health Organization and North Korean doctors, nurses, and midwives. Hospitals and clinics need to be built and supplied. A temporary, and then a permanent, provisioning system must be set up for the distribution of vaccines, medicines and other attributes of a modern health care system. Over time, the medical proficiency of doctors, nurses and health care professionals must be assessed and a program of modern training established.

North Korea currently holds more people per capita against their will than any other country in the world — six times the world average.[61] Humanitarian NGOs have been trying to get into North Korean prison camps for many years. One of the first challenges following reunification will be to dismantle what has been described as a gulag system of unconscionable abuse and to let an estimated 200,000 prisoners go free. (*Gulag* is a Russian word denoting the savage political prison system in the Soviet Union during the Stalin era.)[62] Cha asserts, "The gulags will be revealed as one of the worst human rights disasters in modern history."[63] Indeed, it is well known that torture and malnutrition have permeated the North Korean prison and detention system.[64] These are damaged people and will need special observation and care by specialists. Buddhist and Christian aid groups, concerned citizens and NGOs can take the lead in this important revitalization and reintegration project.

In December 2010 Victor Cha and David Kang (principal investigators) convened a team of experts to consider the relevance of cross-cultural experiences on the long-term tasks that will be necessary after Korean unification. Among many useful specific recommendations, one of the most important general lessons learned from these sessions was the intrinsic value of listening to and working with the North Koreans themselves rather than imposing preconceived systems and structures on them.[65] This advice applies to Korean government agencies and to NGOs that are mainly operated by people who are foreign to Korean cultural traditions. I have often wondered why architects and planners rarely anticipate walking shortcuts, or at least budget for more sidewalks to be laid after walkers tramp down the grass along more natural routes. This example can be the model for development assistance. Rather than imposing a path, it might be smart to follow a path made by the people. Nobody can understand the needs of northern Koreans better than the people themselves. The success of initial reunification projects will set the tone for appropriate development and bring confidence to the process.

Transportation

One of the first natural expressions of freedom will be a desire to move around and visit distant family members and see places never seen before. As the economy grows, improved transportation will be critical to move people and commodities around the country. South Korea has over 100 times the total length of paved roads; only 3 percent of the roads are paved in the North. Thus, roads will need paving and rail infrastructure must be rehabilitated as quickly as possible, connecting rural to urban areas and linking the major cities.

The North has a more extensive network of rail connections than the South because before the war it was the central industrial region of Korea. Fixing this rail network and paving roads will boost productivity and create a large number of local employment opportunities in the process. A system of public transportation must be implemented that will connect every region with affordable transport. Private entrepreneurs from the South and North will likely meet these demands at a rapid rate.

There will also be immediate demand for new cars among the elite and for less expensive used automobiles. South Korea currently has a shocking 730 times the number of private cars—18,260,000 versus 25,000. As money is withdrawn from bank accounts and provided by overseas families, there will be a surge of demand for automobiles in every price range. Soon gas stations will find new business opportunities, as will repair shops and parts stores. The number of ambulances and trained paramedics should keep pace with automobile imports.

The automobile industry is a foundational synergistic economic pillar in developed societies and will create a significant number of new jobs as it becomes established in the North. Automobile cultures create clusters of companies with complementary interests and a value chain of suppliers, distributors, and support services. And the new freedom to move about the country will create demand for tourist attractions, restaurants and lodging. Improvements in transportation will create new industries across the North that have never existed before and benefit what is sure to become a lucrative tourist industry (see below).

Communication

The introduction of modern digital technology will also make an enormous contribution to cultural and economic reunification. As promised in the Korean Peace Fund model, every North Korean family will receive a tablet computer. Between 6–7 million will be distributed. Competition between Samsung and Apple to stamp their trademark on Korean reunification and world peace on the doorstep of the Chinese market may be fierce, as these are two of the most profitable transnational corporations in the world today. For corporate goodwill both companies may offer these tablet computers at or below their production cost. This would cost the fund around one billion dollars.

The digital communication infrastructure that is now over five years old and has never been turned on must be upgraded and activated, and whatever else needs to be put in place for countrywide and international phone and Internet service must be built or made available.[66] This connection to the outside world will be a vital source of global information and cultural, political, and economic modernization.

Televisions that can access South Korean programming will be in high demand; providing a signal must be a top priority, since TV is not only an important link to the modern world and South Korean news and culture but will also provide important information about social change and development in the North. Television images will provide impressions that will enhance the integration process.

New programming will be developed by and for North Koreans. Grants and the funding of educational institutions in media and communications will produce indigenous uncensored creative efforts and the next generation of reporters and producers in the North. After more than 60 years of isolation, the Hermit Kingdom will suddenly become immersed in world news and modern Korean culture. This will inspire a cultural renaissance and contribute immeasurably to the reunification process.

The Cyber Village initiative and other efforts to bridge the rural-urban technology gap in South Korea suggest new technology can be adopted swiftly and effectively even in remote regions.[67] In one South Korean village where 120 villagers received computers and training from the government, they learned to sell mushrooms directly to urban dwellers and within two years increased their sales volume over sixty-fold from $4,264 to $261,000.[68] Northern Koreans will undoubtedly devise many creative ways to increase efficiency and make money over the Internet. Technology ownership will help alleviate regional disparities, contribute to productivity and ease the culture gap after reunification. The modern digital revolution will make reunification cheaper, quicker, easier and more fun.

Education is a critical development variable. South Korean education experts will be tasked with revamping an antiquated system. Tablet computers will undoubtedly play a central role in educating children from elementary ages onward, as they also soon will in the South. South Korea is experimenting with tablet computers in elementary schools, and according to news reports, will make a serious effort to introduce them countrywide in the next few years. Indeed, experiments in digital learning are ongoing around the world and showing positive results. Tablet computers are just a few years old but it is certain that in time they will contain interactive textbooks and become the digital hub of education at all levels. This will facilitate efforts to equalize the educational systems.

Tourism

Tourism will be a multi-billion-dollar industry that will create jobs and physical improvements in many parts of the North. North Korea has numerous tourist attractions but few tourist amenities. Without first-class tourist services North Korea will likely be a low-cost bargain holiday experience for several years as infrastructure is built. But if the first batches of tourists have a good experience in the early years, word will spread and profits will grow rapidly. Over 10 million tourists visited South Korea in 2012 and spent over $10 billion.

The tourist industry will require large initial investments. But the immediate construction of a supporting infrastructure will likely pay quick dividends, as it can be expected millions of curious people from around the world will want to catch a glimpse of what it was like inside the most closed and isolated society on the planet. Travel agencies and North Korean private businesses will surely be quick to capitalize on this new industry, and Pyongyang will likely become one of the most popular tourist destinations in the world for some time to come as people satisfy their curiosity about the Hermit Kingdom.

Pyongyang contains a host of attractions. Every tourist will want to visit the site of the reunification signing ceremony at Kim Il-sung Square and take a boat ride across the Pothong River to visit the Juche Tower (modeled after the Washington Monument), unless it has been symbolically blown up as suggested in chapter eight. However, a new monument symbolizing unity would attract equal curiosity.

Those with more macabre interests will want to visit the mausoleum in front of Geumsusan Memorial Palace, where the pickled corpses of Kim Il-sung and Kim Jong-il are on display. Pyongyang has many grand monuments and colossal statues, including the Arch of Reunification, Chollima Statue, Triumphal Arch (modeled after the Arc de Triomphe in Paris), the monument of the Korean Workers' Party, and the gargantuan statues of Kim Il-sung and Kim Jong-il. The imposing Tower of Self-Reliance and the sumptuous Mangyongdae Children's Palace will also be of interest.

Communist motifs and grand brutalist monumental architecture in Pyongyang are unique tourist attractions and should be protected from damage. Brutalist architecture grew out of modernist architecture and flourished from the 1950s to the mid–1970s. Examples are typically linear, fortress-like, block concrete constructions.[69] It is important to plan ahead. Beyond their intrinsic historic significance, many unique cultural and material North Korean artifacts and locations should be protected and valued as attractions for future tourist destinations.

The Arirang Mass Games in the Rungrado May Day Stadium is the most incredible performing arts spectacle ever produced, featuring nearly 100,000 children performing gymnastics, acrobatics, and dance and creating gigantic mosaics with individually painted cards.[70] Apart from being a popular North Korean spectacle and appeal to social unity, Heonik Kwon and Byung-Ho Chung argue that the story of Arirang is also a deeply historical piece symbolizing the struggle of Jews, Americans, and everyone trying to remove themselves from oppression, colonial or otherwise.[71] It may be possible to prolong these massive performances for years with modern unification sub-themes.

As children lose interest, over time a scaled-down version of this performance could be continued, perhaps employing technology to flip the cards. A continuing Arirang performance would attract enormous tourist interest. The Revolutionary Opera *Flower Girl* would also be a curious attraction, as would the State Circus featuring daring world-class trapeze acts. A feature film made entirely in North Korea, *Comrade*

Nine. After Reunification

Kim Goes Flying, was recently produced that revolved around circus trapeze acts.[72] There is much in Pyongyang that will be of interest to tourists.

Travel to North Korea may be difficult in the early stages. Pyongyang's Sunan International Airport has only two runways and until 2011 had only four deplaning docks. An international terminal completed in 2011 will need immediate expansion. Upgrades to international standards for passengers and airplane maintenance and storage will be required and new runways built. North Korea currently has only two recently purchased aircraft that are approved for flying over international airspace.

Though tourists can fly into Incheon and take cars or buses north, this is an inconvenience. Short flights from Beijing and other east coast cities in China and from Incheon International Airport to Pyongyang will be in high demand. South Korea's Incheon International Airport is perennially rated one of the best airports in the world and is serviced by a strong fleet of regional airlines. Korean Air, China Southern, Aeroflot, Mandarin and Asiana Airlines, and others will fill the void.

Friendly, welcoming people and monumental attractions will keep tourists coming and North Korea will likely quickly become a popular tourist destination in spite of its initial infrastructural deficiencies. Turning a medieval society into a modern one cannot be accomplished overnight. Or perhaps it can be transformed in some locations, as South Korean and foreign investment will come pouring in after reunification to keep step with tourist demand. With great resolve and cooperation, steady progress can be made and people will begin to see tangible evidence of change in a short time and realize some of the manifold new opportunities awaiting them as members of the global village.

Other Thoughts

An office to coordinate the collection and distribution of in-kind donations should be established months in advance of reunification. Private in-kind donations may be significant and should be welcomed. A major government effort should promote, arrange and monitor goodwill contributions. Last-generation medical technology may come flooding into the country and serve as a bridge to the world-class health care provided in the South.

Corporations will want to brand their products in goodwill and get them in homes and on the shelves. It can be expected an array of companies will seek to enter northern Korean markets and establish a presence; large amounts of less expensive regular-use household commodities will probably be donated and should be wisely distributed.

Pyongyang was once a thriving center of Christianity and Buddhism in East Asia, known as the Jerusalem of Korea. Decades of persecution have not eliminated the desire to worship a higher power. Many underground churches will rise to the surface after reunification to fulfill the human yearning for spiritual awakening.[73] Buddhist and Christian churches from South Korea, the United States and around the world will likely donate hundreds of millions of dollars and church people will expend much effort to help their northern brethren. If it is well publicized in the United States that Korea has the largest Christian denomination (outside China and the Philippines) in Asia, many more tens of millions of dollars may come rolling in from the United States alone, along with a multitude of do-gooder missionaries. Whether one supports or rejects the tenets of Christianity or Buddhism, this charity will be especially beneficial to children and the poor, and should be welcomed.

The process of reunification can also rely on the natural kindness and generosity of individual South Korean people and their abundant national pride. Koreans have demonstrated their ability to organize massive cooperative efforts in the past. The New Village Movement and the Student National Defense Corps were successful mass mobilization movements during the Park era (1961–1979). More recently, over three months during the late 1990s Asian economic crisis 3.5 million Koreans donated 225 tons of gold ($2.17 billion) to help their nation through a difficult period. And in 2008 over a million volunteers from across South Korea cleaned up more than 4,000 tons of oil and tar lumps stretching along 30 beaches from the massive MT *Hebei* oil spill that was estimated at 11,900 tons of oil, about one-third the size of the massive Alaskan *Exxon Valdez* disaster of 1989. The government can rely on this collective devotion and benevolent Korean spirit in times of need. And if reunification occurs, this selfless contribution to their deprived northern brothers and sisters will certainly be needed. Coordinating this goodwill toward beneficial projects will be an important task.

Sudden exposure to South Korean culture will have an enormous influence on North Koreans. Beginning in the 1990s there has been a remarkable cultural renaissance of creativity in South Korea. From Singapore to Vietnam, and from Taiwan to China and Japan, Southeast and East Asians have been tuning in to high-quality Korean cultural contents. This has led to an explosion of goodwill toward South Korea. Culture is like the air we breathe — it is everywhere and all pervasive; it is intangible.

Indeed, the soft power of South Korean culture will be one of the critical change variables responsible for reunification. The rise of popular culture around the world is related to growing economic prosperity and the expansion of a middle class with a household surplus and increased leisure time for recreation and shopping. This describes the South Korean experience over the past two generations of activity, and soon these modernizing influences will captivate a North Korean audience.

From family-oriented historical TV dramas for adults to K-pop for the youth to high-quality cartoon animation for children, there is something for every age group. Besides the powerful impact of *Hallyu* and the surging international interest in K-pop, eye-popping high-quality visual culture is everywhere in South Korea; one sees abundant art and design in architecture, sculptures, and murals, and even concrete walls and temporary ramparts that hide construction projects contain artistic design elements.[74]

Television shows and commercials are of world-class creative and production quality and the indigenous motion picture industry is producing films that rival those of Hollywood, recently outdrawing U.S. films at the box office. These are exciting times. North Korean cultural morbidity will quickly and unalterably be changed by the creative vitality of South Korean culture.

Peace and reunification in Korea under the terms of the Korean Peace Fund will improve the welfare of millions of people and leave the world a safer place. As standards of living rise in the North, Korea will begin to feel whole again — and it will be a much richer whole. In twenty years scholars will look back and see that the Korean Peace Fund was a relatively minor investment compared to the war it may have averted and the great prosperity it unleashed.

Epilogue

"If you want to make peace with your enemy, you have to work with your enemy. Then he becomes your partner."— Nelson Mandela

One of the more important societal roles of the academy is to dispassionately generate possible solutions to complex and contentious problems that are unlikely to percolate out of the normal discussions of politicians and policymakers, who are often immersed in the oppressive daily minutiae of emails, technical details and intermediary disputes, or obliged to follow executive orders. Without these pressures and distractions, I have devised a plan that may have a small chance of diffusing a seemingly intractable international problem.

The original three-page draft of the Korean Peace Fund idea that I shared with a Korean colleague over three years ago was rather primitive. However, the closer I looked into the universal benefits of such an idea, the more it made sense to me. Soon I began to realize a Korean Peace Fund is not only in everyone's best interest but also possible to fund — perhaps not likely, but possible. This book represents an effort to pry open this small window of opportunity.

Material incentive is a powerful motivator in human affairs, and an affordable option in North Korea due to its moderate population size, low per-capita GDP, and relatively small and impoverished elite. The widespread geopolitical benefits of a unified Korea increase the possibility of multilateral cooperation, and the enormous public and private profits from decades of globalization have made these funds available.

Once I realized there is a compelling new political and economic context for peace, I began integrating the supporting social, political, economic and cultural research of other scholars into my incentive fund scheme — a theme that has never been expressed in this detail. However, I do not expect warm applause. Many of the propositions suggested in

Epilogue

this book are controversial, and even compelling new ideas that fall outside the consensus paradigm take time to root.[1] Unfortunately, we may not have much time.

Although it is peaceful in East Asia today, warfare has been an endemic part of the history of civilization and it is important to pause and recount its horrors from time to time in order to recommit ourselves to its prevention. The Korean War (1950–1953) is called "The Forgotten War" in the United States, because it was fought under the banner of the United Nations (although almost 90 percent of allied soldiers were from the United States), and because it is overshadowed by the enormity of World War II and the first televised war in Vietnam. Yet U.S. casualties approached those incurred in Vietnam. And this war may not be forgotten among older generations of Chinese who may remember or have been told about the loss of nearly half a million young men.

Altogether over three million soldiers and civilians perished in Korea during this three-year conflagration. The proportional devastation to the Korean population rivaled that of the wars in Europe. To put the Korean War into relative demographic perspective, the loss of life on the Korean Peninsula is tantamount to a war on U.S. soil that took over 35 million lives, or in China over 150 million. It is estimated up to a quarter of the people living above the 38th parallel were killed, many by the unremitting U.S. carpet-bombing that leveled 22 of 26 North Korean cities; more bombs were dropped than in the entire Pacific theater during World War II. Could something as unimaginable as this happen again? Certainly an unacceptable degree of danger still exists.

War is not inevitable or built into the human genome. Anthropologists have identified numerous human groups that have lived indefinitely without domestic violence and external warfare; without an immediate fear of survival, there is no compelling biological instinct for aggressive behavior. Indeed, natural selection and human evolution have favored those who cooperate with each other at least as much as those who compete. Rather, war is a socially constructed phenomenon in response to existential fear and/or the desire for more money and power. Thus, the Korean Peace Fund model is a modern alternative to war based on a contemporary calculus of materialist incentives, acknowledging personal self-interest and profit, and the particular positive-sum geopolitical, social and economic dynamics of the Korean dilemma. It is a platform for creating peace.

Epilogue

To prevent another war, it is incumbent upon those who influence decisions of this magnitude to consider a full range of peaceful alternatives. Unconstrained by peer pressure or the pedagogical orthodoxies of international relations and political science, I have been free to look for solutions "outside the box" of normal debate. Thus, the Korean Peace Fund model expands the range of available options for creating peace and reunification because it proposes several possibilities that have heretofore been presumed to be exceedingly remote and improbable. Below is a short list of these supposed imponderables:

(1) Global elites will promise billions of dollars to a peace fund.
(2) Governments will then promise billions of dollars to a peace fund.
(3) The Chinese will abandon their support of North Korea.
(4) Kim Jong-un will acquiesce under certain favorable circumstances.
(5) The North Korean military and power elite will also acquiesce.

No matter how persuasive the arguments, this model falls outside the current normal range of discussion in international relations and beyond the polite realm of discourse in the secretive backrooms of public policy. Fortunately, the ultimate success of this pay-for-peace plan does not require an academic or policy consensus. All it would take to test the Korean Peace Fund model is for one outlier billionaire somewhere in the world to provide the necessary initial funding to get the ball rolling.[2] Or, as the late Steve Jobs once proclaimed, someone who has the imagination to "push the human race forward, and while some may see them as the crazy ones, we see genius, because the ones who are crazy enough to think that they can change the world, are the ones who do."[3] After this initial support and publicity, full funding could come much faster than anyone imagines. As we have seen in other realms, ideas that envision the whole oak tree from a small acorn often ignite thresholds that incite a cascading set of events that change everything in their path.

Although this materialist model relies on tangible underlying bedrock incentives to influence human affairs, its greatest weakness is that it also must rely on the intangible reasonableness of political man. For matters of war and peace to be decided by tyrants, the ethnocentric tyranny of misled masses, or intransigent path-dependent institutional prerogatives is equally dangerous. An insightful outlier billionaire may be needed to break this historical-institutional mold of successive wars and instigate a surge of positive impressions and incentives for peace in East Asia.

Money is used to purchase something of value. We have before us an opportunity to transcend gunboat diplomacy with checkbook diplomacy; a fully funded Korean Peace Fund could change the current negative trajectory of world history.

Pulitzer Prize–winning economist Liaquat Ahamed paraphrases the writings of the eminent British journalist Norman Angell who in 1909 wrote, "The commercial and financial linkages between countries are now so extensive that no rational country should contemplate starting a war ... the victor would lose as much as the vanquished."[4] Ahamed later laments, "But trusting too much in the rationality of nations and seduced by the extraordinary economic achievement of the era ... they totally misjudged the likelihood that a war involving all the major European powers would break out."[5]

Despite serious errors of judgment, humankind has done rather well overall. Today we stand atop a new apogee in our long evolutionary climb out of the muck and mud of a difficult past. Indeed, over the past twenty years more people have been able to move out of desperate poverty than at any other time in history. But the political and economic pieces that support this recent climb can come apart again, and very quickly.

The fundamental tool we have repeatedly employed to improve our human condition is an innate ability to confront problems with logic and intuition. Better than all the other animals, we have devised new ways to solve old problems. Through our invention of language and culture, we have displayed a remarkable ability to cooperate with each other, and when challenged by new problems we have exhibited the adaptive flexibility to envision new perspectives and adopt non-programmed behavior to discover their ultimate solutions.

Spanish essayist and philosopher George Santayana once proposed that we must learn from history or else be condemned to repeat it. Let us hope we can learn from the carnage of the world wars of the twentieth century and not let this happen again in East Asia. The Korean Peace Fund model may provide a part of the solution.

In 2012 there were public elections in Russia, the United States, South Korea, and Japan, and an elite transfer of power in North Korea and China. The majority of these heads of state took office in early 2013. Every key political leader who makes important decisions about North Korea is either new or has been given a new vote of confidence. It is possible that if these leaders were to learn about the details of the Korean Peace Fund model, and were to carefully weigh the costs and benefits from their respective national interests, they might each support this fund and create a new era of political and economic cooperation in the region. Not only does the Korean Peace Fund allow everyone to walk away without injury, but it also gives everyone something they want.

Chapter Notes

Preface

1. The United States officially spends over $700 billion on defense per year, more than the total military expenditures of the rest of the world combined.
2. This amounts to about $10 billion per year, or 25 percent of GDP.
3. Without expected reductions, at current rates the United States would spend about $6 trillion during this eight-year period.
4. East Asian educational systems have focused almost exclusively on technical knowledge for a quick two-generation economic catch-up with the West, while ignoring elements of humanistic and liberal arts education that might provide multicultural perspectives, reduce ethnocentrism, and teach tolerance and empathy.
5. See Gi-Wook Shin, *Ethnic Nationalism in Korea: Genealogy, Politics, and Legacy* (Stanford, CA: Stanford University Press, 2006). Of course, this is not a unique propensity and it can be argued that the United States also has a sordid history of race-based nationalism, especially within its ruling class.
6. Research conducted in 1998 by Chinese geneticist Jin Li at the National Human Genome Center at Fudan University in Shanghai has shown that the Chinese did not evolve independently from a unique *Homo erectus* offshoot (Peking Man), but instead are derived, like the rest of humanity, from mitochondrial DNA and Y-chromosome haplotypes contained in the original migrants out of Africa approximately 60,000 years ago. Using genetic markers called microsatellites to compare Chinese populations, and a large sample size including 160 different ethnic groups and over 20,000 individuals, Dr. Jin Li found no evidence for the hypothesis of independent human origin in China. For a brief historical and cultural analysis of Chinese racism, see Martin Jacques, *When China Rules the World: The End of the Western World and the Birth of a New Global Order*, second edition (New York: Penguin, 2012), 294–341; and Frank Dikötter, *The Discourse of Race in Modern China* (London: Hurst, 1992).
7. Suisheng Zhao, *A Nation-State by Construction: Dynamics of Modern Chinese Nationalism* (Stanford, CA: Stanford University Press, 2004).
8. As monstrous as these crimes against humanity are, most of the Japanese military personnel who committed these atrocities died more than a generation ago. Should their grandchildren be held accountable? Should someone born in the 1960s be blamed for something that happened in the 1930s?
9. After the World Bank declined Korean requests for investment capital in the mid-1960s, President Chung-hee Park obtained Japanese reparation money to underwrite the South Korean steel industry, the road connecting Seoul and Busan, and other early development projects. Without original Japanese investment, it is possible that Posco would not be one of the largest and most profitable steel manufacturers in the world today.
10. "Gangnam Style" refers to a song by Psy (a Korean pop star) that in 2012 received more than a billion YouTube hits.
11. See James R. Holmes, "The Sino-Japanese Naval War of 2012," *Foreign Policy*, August 20, 2012, http://www.foreignpolicy.com/articles/2012/08/20/the_sino_japanese_naval_war_of_2012. The Japanese

marine and submarine fleet is newer and tends to have superior capabilities.

12. Eliciting Chinese concern, high-level talks about this issue commenced in Hawaii in March 2013 between U.S. and Japanese military leaders.

13. John J. Mearsheimer, *The Tragedy of Great Power Politics* (New York: W. W. Norton, 2003). Preemptive strikes are one tool of offensive realism.

14. "Sputnik" was the name of the first Soviet satellite launched into orbit in 1957, which ushered in a new era of political and military confrontation between the United States and Russia.

15. It has been estimated that 260,000 to 400,000 U.S. and South Korea troops would be needed to staff missions and stabilize North Korea. See Bruce W. Bennett and Jennifer Lind, "The Collapse of North Korea: Military Missions and Requirements," *International Security* 36, no. 2 (2011): 118.

Introduction

1. Shepherd Iverson, "The Korean Peace Fund," *North Korean Review* 8, no. 2 (2012): 62–75.

2. Marcus Noland, personal communication.

3. South Korean trade volume with China is more than 60 times greater.

4. It is interesting to note that 20 years ago the North Korean government pegged the official exchange rate for the U.S. dollar at 2.16 per North Korean won (based on Kim Jong-il's birthday), where it remains to this day, while the current black market rate is closer to 5,000:1.

5. Beijing has already built a paved road into Rason, giving landlocked Jilin Province better access to the region's northernmost year-round port.

6. If the late Professor Huntington was correct in arguing that without intelligent foresight and proper precautions there may be a military clash between Eastern and Western civilizations (i.e., China and the United States), North Korea is one of the most likely geographical flashpoints for this conflict to begin. See Samuel P. Huntington, *The Clash of Civilizations: And the Remaking of the World Order* (New York: Simon and Schuster, 1996).

7. Victor D. Cha, "China's Rise, the Changing Northeast Asian Security Environment, and U.S.–ROK Strategic Response. An interview" (Washington, DC: Center for Strategic and International Studies, 2010), http://csis.org/files/publication/110114_Chinas_Rise_Changing_NEA_Security.pdf; and Richard Weitz, "Moscow Ponders Korea Unification," *International Journal of Korean Unification Studies* 20, no. 1 (2011): 123–154.

8. Jae Ho Chung, "East Asia Responds to the Rise of China: Patterns and Variations," *Pacific Affairs* 82 (2009): 657–675; David C. Kang, *China Rising: Peace, Power, and Order in East Asia* (New York: Columbia University Press, 2007).

9. Alexander Lukin, "Russia's Korea Policy in the 21st Century," *International Journal of Korean Unification Studies* 18, no. 2 (2009): 30–63.

10. Japan has taken significant military steps to counter North Korea's nuclear and missile threats. See Narushige Michishita, "Japan's Response to Nuclear North Korea," in Gilbert Rozman, ed., *Asia at a Tipping Point: Korea, the Rise of China, and the Impact of Leadership Transitions* (Washington, DC: Korea Economic Institute, 2012): 99–112, http://www.keia.org/sites/default/files/publications/tipping_point_full_book_final_version.pdf.

11. This figure is derived from assuming a price of $75 per barrel of oil. See Index Mundi, http://www.indexmundi.com/g/g.aspx?v=91&c=ja&l=en.

12. United States Naval Institute, "Report: Chinese Develop Special 'Kill Weapon' to Destroy U.S. Aircraft Carriers," March 31, 2009, http://www.usni.org/news-and-features/chinese-kill-weapon.

13. Peter M. Swartz, "Rising Powers and Naval Power," in Philip C. Saunders, Christopher D. Yung, Michael Swaine, and Andrew Nien-Dzu Yang, eds., *The Chinese Navy: Expanding Capabilities, Evolving Roles* (Washington, DC: National Defense University, 2011), 13.

14. The Association of Southeast Asian Nations (ASEAN) is a multilateral institution consisting of twenty-seven countries that meet annually to discuss regional security issues at the foreign-ministry level.

15. In November 2012 China's 18th Communist Party Congress formally elevated Xi Jinping to succeed Hu Jintao as general secretary of the Chinese Communist Party.

16. A change they have not made as of this printing.

17. Displeasure over the April 2012 long-range missile launch by North Korea probably also influenced China's policy reconsideration.

18. Originally pushed out of mainland China by the migration of agriculturalists, the Austronesian Expansion began from the coasts of Taiwan around 3,000 BCE and resulted in populating the islands of the Pacific and all locations where a boat will go, including Madagascar, Hawaii, the Philippines and Jeju Island. The Austronesian language is closely related to the Tai-Kadai language family that is the dominant language group today in Laos, Thailand and the north and east of Burma. Thus, it is possible, if not probable, that Kim Jong-un is a descendent of a relic group of early Southeast Asian coastal settlers.

Chapter One

1. Nicholas Onuf writes, "Standing, security and wealth are the controlling interests of humanity. We recognize them everywhere. They comprehend survival." See *World of Our Making: Rules and Rule in Social Theory and International Relations* (Columbia: University of South Carolina Press, 1989), 278.

2. See Stella Ting-Toomey, "The Matrix of Face: An Updated Face-Negotiation Theory," in William B. Gudykunst, ed., *Theorizing About Intercultural Communication* (Thousand Oaks, CA: Sage, 2005): 71–92.

3. John Stoessinger, *Why Nations Go to War*, tenth edition (Belmont, CA: Thomson Wadsworth, 2008), xiii; Mark Granovetter, "Threshold Models of Collective Behavior," *American Journal of Sociology* 83, no. 6 (1978): 1420–1443.

4. The Black Swan metaphor is used to identify history-changing events that occur predictably. Nassim Nicholas Taleb, *The Black Swan: The Impact of the Highly Improbable* (New York: Penguin, 2008).

5. Alfred L. Kroeber, "Stimulus Diffusion," *American Anthropologist* 42, no. 1 (1940): 1–20. Kroeber introduced the concept of cultural diffusion to the social sciences in 1940. Since then, almost every cultural anthropologist and sociologist in the last three generations has discovered larger, more integrated social networks than they had anticipated before beginning their fieldwork. I suggest we are also underestimating the extent of North Korean social networks, just as the social networking sites Facebook and Twitter were originally underestimated.

6. See KINU (Korea Institute for National Unification), *The White Paper on Human Rights in North Korea, 2011* (Seoul: Korea Institute for National Unification, 2011), http://www.kinu.or.kr/upload/neo board/DATA04/hr20011.pdf.

7. Stephan Haggard and Marcus Noland, *Witness to Transformation: Refugee Insights into North Korea* (Washington, DC: Peterson Institute for International Economics, 2011), 103.

8. Patrick McEachern, *Inside the Red Box* (New York: Columbia University Press, 2010).

9. David M. Kotz and Fred Weir, *Russia's Path from Gorbachev to Putin: The Demise of the Soviet System and the New Russia* (New York: Routledge, 2007).

10. Byung-Yeon Kim, "Markets, Bribery, and Regime Change in North Korea," *EAI Asia Security Initiative Working Paper*, no. 4 (Seoul: East Asia Institute, April 2010).

11. For an account of this quick and efficient system of word-of-mouth (bush telegraph) internal communication, see John Everard, *Only Beautiful Please: A British Diplomat in North Korea* (Stanford, CA: Asia-Pacific Research Center, 2012), 56–58.

Chapter Two

1. Nye defines smart power as a "combination of the hard power of coercion and payment with the soft power of persuasion and attraction." Payment is a gentler form of hard power, and in conjunction with the growing attraction (soft power) of living standards in South Korea and elsewhere, the Korean Peace Fund is a smart-power

Notes—Chapter Two

solution. Joseph S. Nye, *The Future of Power* (New York: Public Affairs, 2011), xiii.

2. Nye's liberal realism is such a synthesis. Also see Giulio M. Gallarotti, *Cosmopolitan Power in International Relations: A Synthesis of Realism, Neoliberalism, and Constructivism* (Cambridge: Cambridge University Press, 2010).

3. New strains of realism have emerged. The "either I kill you or you will kill me" security posture of offensive realism is contrasted with the more cooperative and amicable behavior of defensive realism. For defensive realism, see Stephen Walt, "International Relations: One World, Many Theories," *Foreign Policy*, no. 110 (Spring 1998): 29–45; for offensive realism, see John J. Mearsheimer, *The Tragedy of Great Power Politics*.

It should be noted that Morgenthau and Waltz have often strongly disagreed with the policies derived from their structural and theoretical level of analysis. Hans Morgenthau, *Politics Among Nations: The Struggle for Power and Peace* (New York: Knopf, 1949); *Scientific Man vs. Power Politics* (Chicago: University of Chicago Press, 1967); Kenneth N. Waltz, *Man, the State, and War: A Theoretical Analysis* (New York: Columbia University Press, 2001; orig. 1959); "Realist Thought and Neorealist Theory," in Robert L. Rothstein, ed., *The Evolution of Theory in International Relations* (Columbia: University of South Carolina Press, 1991), 21–38; and Ken Booth, ed., *Realism and World Politics* (New York: Routledge, 2011).

4. Professor Chung-in Moon cites the "positive-sum diplomacy" that resulted in the September 19 Beijing Joint Statement of 2005 as an exception. See Chung-in Moon, *The Sunshine Policy: In Defense of Engagement as a Path to Peace in Korea* (Seoul: Yonsei University Press, 2012), 104–105.

5. For a description of U.S. nuclear policy failures in North Korea, see Gregory J. Moore, "America's Failed North Korea Nuclear Policy: A New Approach," *Asian Perspectives* 32, no. 4 (2008): 9–27; for a perspective on the neoconservative takeover during the Bush administration, and why this ideological anomaly in U.S. foreign policy may be fundamentally disassociated with political realism, see Joshua Muravchik and Stephen M. Walt, "The Neocons vs. the Realists," *National Interest* (September/October 2008): 20–36.

6. Robert O. Keohane, *After Hegemony: Cooperation and Discord in the World Political Economy* (Princeton, NJ: Princeton University Press, 1984); Robert O. Keohane and Joseph Nye, *Power and Interdependence* (New York: HarperCollins, 1977); and David Lake and Robert Powell, *Strategic Choice and International Relations* (Princeton, NJ: Princeton University Press, 1999). For Korea, see Key-young Son, *South Korean Engagement Policies and North Korea: Identities, Norms and the Sunshine Policy* (New York: Routledge, 2006).

7. The statement including North Korea in the "axis of evil" was made by U.S. President Bush on January 29, 2002. Professor Chung-in Moon convincingly argues that the neoconservative foreign policy under the Bush administration was largely responsible for derailing the inter-Korean Sunshine Policy. See Moon, *The Sunshine Policy*, 79–116.

8. For more about Sunshine Policies, see Myounh-Kyu Park and Philo Kim, "Inter-Korean Relations in Nuclear Politics," *Asian Perspective* 34, no. 1 (2010): 111–135; Victor D. Cha and David C. Kang, *Nuclear North Korea: A Debate on Engagement Strategies* (New York: Columbia University Press, 2003); and Terence Roehrig, "Creating the Conditions for Peace in Korea: Promoting Incremental Change in North Korea," *Korea Observer* 40, no. 1 (2009). For an appeal for a reinvigorated engagement policy 2.0, see Moon, *The Sunshine Policy*.

9. The Kaesong Industrial Complex and the Mount Kumgang tourism project (discontinued in 2008 after a South Korean tourist was shot by a North Korean soldier) are the result of this engagement initiative and Sunshine Policy. Professor Chung-in Moon has persuasively argued that the Sunshine Policy might have brought the North and South closer to peace and unification if hardliner political forces had not come to power in the United States (2001) and South Korea (2008).

10. See Alexander Wendt, *Social Theory of International Politics* (Cambridge: Cambridge University Press, 1999).

11. See Onuf, *World of Our Making*; for an erudite philosophical history of constructivism's theoretical roots, see Richard Ned Lebow, *A Cultural Theory of International Relations* (Cambridge: Cambridge University Press, 2008).

12. Kevin Shepard, "Rethinking Engagement on the Korean Peninsula: Confidence to Trust to Peace," *International Journal of Korean Unification Studies* 19, no. 1 (2010): 94–125; and Sangmin Bae and Martyn de Bruyn, "Trust Building through Institutions: European Lessons for Korean Unification," *Academic Papers on Korea* (Washington, DC: Korea Economic Institute, 2010), 149–160.

13. Glenn D. Paige, "Korean Leadership for Nonkilling East Asian Common Security," *Korea Observer*, no. 37 (2006): 547–563; and Glenn D. Paige, "The Nonviolent Approach to Korean Reunification," in Michael Hass, ed., *Korean Reunification: Alternative Pathways* (Los Angeles: Publishinghouse for Scholars, 2012), 71–88.

14. Jae Chang Kim, "A Divided Korea and the Reunification Strategy," *International Journal of Korean Unification Studies* 18, no. 2 (2009): 64–85.

15. Seongji Woo, "North Korea as a Transformer: From a Fortress State to an Amphibious State," *East Asian Institute Working Paper*, no. 8 (2010): 2–22, http://www.eai.or.kr/data/bbs/eng_report/2011041513523127.pdf.

16. Min Cho, "Establishment of a Peace Regime on the Korean Peninsula: A ROK Perspective," *Korea and World Affairs*, no. 31 (2007): 281–300; Tae-Hwan Kwak, "The Korean Peninsula Peace Regime: How to Build It," *Pacific Focus* 24, no. 1 (2009): 43–60; Charles M. Perry and James L. Schoff, "Consensus Building and Peace Regime Building on the Korean Peninsula," *International Journal of Korean Unification Studies* 19, no. 1 (2010): 1–28; and Sanghee Lee, "Toward a Peace Regime on the Korean Peninsula: A Way Forward for the ROK–US Alliance" (Washington, DC: The Brookings Institution, May 2, 2007).

17. Nils P. Gleditsch, "Democracy and Peace," *Journal of Peace Research* 29, no. 4 (1992): 369–376; Young Whan Kihl, *Transforming Korean Politics: Democracy, Reform, and Culture* (Armonk, NY: East Gate Books, 2005); and Scott Turner, "Global Civil Society, Anarchy and Governance: Assessing an Emerging Paradigm," *Journal of Peace Research* 35, no. 1 (1998): 25–42.

18. Charles K. Armstrong, *Korean Society: Civil Society, Democracy and the State*, second edition (New York: Routledge, 2007; orig. 2002), 6.

19. Marcus Noland, "Pyongyang Tipping Point: Currency 'Reform' Sparked an Economic Crisis That the Regime May Not Be Able to Repair," *Wall Street Journal*, April 16, 2010.

20. Amitav Acharya and Barry Buzan, eds., *Non-Western International Relations Theory: Perspectives On and Beyond Asia* (New York: Routledge, 2010), 5.

21. Suk Hi Kim, "Will North Korea Be Able to Overcome the Third Wave of Its Collapse?" in Suk Hi Kim, Terence Roehrig and Bernhard Seliger, eds., *The Survival of North Korea: Essays on Strategy, Economics and International Relations* (Jefferson, NC: McFarland, 2011), 29–32; also see Christopher A. Ford, *The Mind of Empire: China's History and Modern Foreign Relations* (Lexington: University of Kentucky Press, 2010).

22. Russell J. Dalton and Nhu-ngoc T. Ong, "Authority Orientations and Democratic Attitudes: A Test of the 'Asian Values' Hypothesis," *Japanese Journal of Political Science* 6, no. 2 (2005): 1–21. For materialist explanations of culture change, see Marvin Harris, *Cultural Materialism: The Struggle for a Science of Culture* (New York: Random House, 1972); for a concise historical essay on the mutability of culture, see Ha-Joon Chang, *Bad Samaritans: The Myth of Free Trade and the Secret History of Capitalism* (New York: Bloomsbury Press, 2008), 182–202.

23. For an intriguing exposé of inertial political forces, the institutional roots of path dependency, and a critique of conventional wisdom, see Frank Harvey, "President Al Gore and the 2003 Iraq War: A Counterfactual Critique of Conventional 'W'isdom" (Calgary: Canadian Defence and Foreign Affairs Institute, November 2008).

24. For more challenges to conventional wisdom from a career Canadian diplomat, see Daryl Copeland, *Guerrilla Diplomacy:*

Rethinking International Relations (Boulder, CO: Lynne Rienner, 2009).

25. See Paul A. David, "Why Are Institutions the 'Carriers of History'? Path Dependence and the Evolution of Conventions, Organizations and Institutions," *Structural Change and Economic Dynamics* 5, no. 2 (1994): 205–220; and Paul Pierson, "Increasing Returns, Path Dependence, and the Study of Politics," *American Political Science Review* 94, no. 2 (2000): 251–267.

26. Victor Cha, *The Impossible State: North Korea Past and Future* (New York: HarperCollins, 2012), 100.

27. Joshua Cooper Ramo, *The Age of the Unthinkable: Why the New World Disorder Constantly Surprises Us* (New York: Little, Brown, 2009), 9.

28. Waltz, *Man, the State, and War*, 2.

29. South Korea's GDP is almost 35 times larger than North Korea's—$1.12 trillion versus $32.7 billion (2011).

30. Becker extended existing theory to new phenomena; his seminal scholarship in behavioral economics includes *The Economics of Discrimination* (Chicago: University of Chicago Press, 1957); *Human Capital* (New York: Columbia University Press, 1964); *Crime and Punishment* (Chicago: University of Chicago Press, 1968); "A Theory of Social Interactions," *Journal of Political Economy* 82, no. 1 (1974): 1063–1093; and *The Economic Approach to Human Behavior* (Chicago: University of Chicago Press, 1976). Adam Smith, Jeremy Bentham, and others could be cited as early rational choice utilitarian theorists, but it was Becker (and the behaviorist George Homans) who pioneered the use of cost-benefit calculations into social and political realms. Researchers have since refined rational choice theory by introducing subjectivity and including special situations of irrationality and risk. Prospect theory is one example.

31. Steven D. Levitt and Stephen J. Dubner, *Freakonomics: A Rogue Economist Explores the Hidden Side of Everything* (New York: Penguin, 2006), 11.

32. His Nobel Lecture is published in "Nobel Lecture: The Economic Way of Looking at Behavior," *Journal of Political Economy* 101, no. 3 (1993): 402.

33. See Nicolas Guilhot, "The Realist Gambit: Postwar American Political Science and the Birth of IR Theory," *International Political Sociology* 2, no. 4 (2008): 281–304.

34. Morgenthau, *Scientific Man vs. Power Politics*, 134.

35. See Ioannis D. Evrigenis, *Fear of Enemies and Collective Action* (Cambridge: Cambridge University Press, 2008); also see Jan H. Blits, "Hobbesian Fear," *Political Theory* 17, no. 3 (August 1989): 417–431.

36. Brian C. Rathbun, "Uncertain and Uncertainty: Understanding the Multiple Meanings of a Crucial Concept in International Relations Theory," *International Studies Quarterly* 51, no. 3 (2007): 533–557. For a historical and philosophical discussion of realism, see Michael C. Williams, *The Realist Tradition and the Limits of International Relations* (Cambridge: Cambridge University Press, 2005).

37. See Kyo-Duk Lee et al., *Changes in North Korea as Revealed in the Testimonies of Saetomins* (Seoul: Korean Institute of National Unification, 2008). Simply defined, the Juche idea represents the spirit of self-reliance; Suryong is associated with the personality cult and absolute child-like loyalty to the parent-leader; and Songbun is ascribed social status based on family background—the highest family rank is derived from men who fought in the resistance to Japanese occupation or in the Korean War. Although the Songbun system has lost much of its influence among the masses, it remains important among elites. In modern North Korea, family background is irrelevant in marriage selection if someone has access to foreign exchange through their job or connections. It is interesting to note that Kim Jong-un's mother—Mother of Pyongyang—should be ranked as a member of a lower status since her father was a descendent of South Koreans from Jeju Island and she was born in Japan. Of course, this fact is covered up by the propaganda establishment.

38. Nye, *The Future of Power*, xiii.

39. Till Geiger, "The Power Game: Soft Power and the International Historian," in Inderjeet Parmar and Michael Cox, eds., *Soft Power and US Foreign Policy: Theoretical, Historical and Contemporary Perspectives* (New York: Routledge, 2010), 103.

Chapter Three

1. Emma Chanlett-Avery, "North Korea: U.S. Relations, Nuclear Diplomacy, and Internal Situation" (Washington, DC: Congressional Research Service, January 17, 2012), 11.

2. For a partial list of these predictions, see Ralph C. Hassig and Kongdan Oh, *The Hidden People of North Korea: Everyday Life in the Hermit Kingdom* (Lanham, MD: Rowman and Littlefield, 2009), 249–250.

3. Daniel Byman and Jennifer Lind, "Pyongyang's Survival Strategy: Tools of Authoritarian Control," *International Security* 35, no. 1 (2010): 44–74.

4. See Nicholas Eberstadt, *The North Korean Economy: Between Crisis and Catastrophe* (New Brunswick, NJ: Transaction, 2007), 280–312.

5. This is a middle-range guess. Some starvation estimates reach 3 million. Demographers Goodkind and West assert, "The actual demographic toll of the famine remains uncertain owing to the lack of reliable data." Daniel Goodkind and Loraine West, "The North Korean Famine and Its Demographic Impact," *Population and Development Review* 27, issue 2 (2001): 219; also see Stephan Haggard and Marcus Noland, *Famine in North Korea: Markets, Aid, and Reform* (New York: Columbia University Press, 2007). Barbara Demick has written a sensitive ethnographic account of suffering and resolve from six refugee case studies in *Nothing to Envy: Ordinary Lives in North Korea* (New York: Spiegel and Grau, 2009).

6. Mark Manyin and Mary Beth Nikitin, "Foreign Assistance to North Korea" (Washington, DC: Congressional Research Service, March 20, 2012).

7. In September 2002 Kim Jong-il admitted North Korea had abducted 13 Japanese citizens. Further developments and disputes related to these abductions have worsened relations between Pyongyang and Tokyo up to the present.

8. It is estimated China provides 80 percent of North Korean consumer goods, 45 percent of its food and 90 percent of its energy supplies as an indirect subsidy since North Korea cannot finance its $1.25 billion average annual trade deficit. See Jayshree Bajoria, "The China–North Korean Relationship" (New York: Council on Foreign Relations 2012), http://www.cfr.org/china/chinanorthkorearelationship/p11097; also see Julia Joo-A Lee, "To Fuel or Not to Fuel: China's Energy Assistance to North Korea," *Asian Security* 5, no. 1 (2009): 45–72.

9. Andrei Lankov and Seok-hyang Kim, "North Korean Market Vendors: The Rise of Grassroots Capitalists in a Post-Stalinist Society," *Pacific Affairs* 81, no. 1 (2008): 70.

10. See Andrei Lankov and In-ok Kwak, "The Decline of the North Korean Surveillance State," *North Korean Review* 7, no. 2 (2011): 6–21; and Nat Kretchun and Jane Kim, *A Quiet Opening: North Koreans in a Changing Media Environment* (Washington, DC: InterMedia, May 2012), 23, http://audiencescapes.org/sites/default/files/A_Quiet_Opening_FINAL_InterMedia.pdf.

11. Andrei Lankov, *North of the DMZ: Essays on the Daily Life in North Korea* (Jefferson, NC: McFarland, 2007), 139.

12. Haggard and Noland, *Witness to Transformation*, 45–79.

13. Lankov, *North of the DMZ*, 183.

14. The statistics cited in this book are derived from refugee samples of mostly working-class and rural women (75 percent) from two northern provinces who risked their lives crossing the border into China. Drawing inferences from these biased samples about the population still living in North Korea is done with caution.

15. Byung-Yeon Kim and Dongho Song, "The Participation of North Korean Households in the Informal Economy: Size, Determinants, and Effect," *Seoul Journal of Economics* 21, no. 2 (2008): 361–385.

16. Haggard and Noland, *Witness to Transformation*, 50–51.

17. McEachern, *Inside the Red Box*; for speculations about further erosion of totalitarian rule under Kim Jong-un, see Rudiger Frank and Phillip H. Park, "From Monolithic Totalitarian to Collective Authoritarian Leadership? Performance-Based Legitimacy and Power Transfer in North Korea," *North Korean Review* 8, no. 2 (2012): 32–49.

18. Bradley K. Martin, *Under the Loving Care of the Fatherly Leader: North Korea and*

the Kim Dynasty (New York: St. Martin's Press, 2004), 579.

19. Jin-Ha Kim, "On the Threshold of Power, 2012/12: Pyongyang's Politics of Transition," *International Journal of Korean Unification* 20, no. 2 (2011): 22.

20. K.A. Namkung, "US Leadership in the Rebuilding of the North Korean Economy," in Marcus Noland, ed., *Economic Integration of the Korean Peninsula: Special Report* (Washington, DC: Peterson Institute for International Economics, 1998), 233.

21. "VIP" stands for "very important person." See Demick, *Nothing to Envy*, 253.

22. Sunny Lee, "N.Korea in the eyes of Chinese journalist," *Korea Times*, May 8, 2010.

23. Hassig and Oh, *The Hidden People of North Korea*, 5.

24. Kim, "Markets, Bribery, and Regime Change in North Korea," 25.

25. Stephan Haggard, Jennifer Lee, and Marcus Noland, "Integration in the Absence of Institutions: China–North Korea Cross-Border Exchange," *Working Paper* (Washington, DC: Peterson Institute of International Economics, August 2011), http://www.iie.com/publications/wp/wp11-13.pdf.

26. Mimura Mitsuhiro, "Outlook for North Korean Economic Reform and Marketization," *International Journal of Korean Unification Studies* 20, no. 2 (2011): 84–85.

27. Scott Snyder and Kyung-Ae Park, "North Korea in Transition: Evolution or Revolution," in Kyung-Ae Park and Scott Snyder, eds., *North Korea Transition: Politics, Economy, and Society* (Lanham, MD: Rowman and Littlefield, 2013), 284.

28. Kim, "Markets, Bribery, and Regime Change in North Korea," 15.

29. Yoonok Chang, Stephan Haggard and Marcus Noland, "Exit Polls: Refugee Assessments of North Korea's Transition," *Working Paper Series* (Washington, DC: Peterson Institute for International Economics, January 2008), http://www.iie.com/publications/wp/wp08-1.pdf.

30. Haggard and Noland, *Witness to Transformation*, 6–7.

31. Everard, *Only Beautiful Please*, 137; and Stephan Haggard and Marcus Noland, *Hunger and Human Rights: The Politics of Famine in North Korea* (Washington, DC: U.S. Committee for Human Rights in North Korea, 2005).

32. *Chosunilbo*, "N. Korea's Underground Economy Booming," September 21, 2011.

33. Hassig and Oh, *The Hidden People of North Korea*, 201.

34. Jae-Cheon Lim and InJoo Yoon, "Institutional Entrepreneurs in North Korea: Emerging Shadowy Private Enterprises Under Dire Economic Conditions," *North Korean Review* 7, no. 2 (2011): 82–93.

35. Nate Thayer, "North Korea: A Mafia Crime State," unpublished paper, http://natethayer.typepad.com/blog/2011/12/north-korea-a-mafia-crime-state-by-nate-thayer.html.

36. Gary Stradiotto and Sujian Guo, "Market Socialism in North Korea: A Comparative Perspective," *Journal of the Asia Pacific Economy* 12, no. 2 (2007): 188–214. This liberalizing trend may continue if the June 28, 2012, new economic management system policies take effect.

37. Dick K. Nanto and Mark E. Manyin, "China–North Korea Relations" (Washington, DC: Congressional Research Service, December 28, 2010), http://www.fas.org/sgp/crs/row/R41043.pdf.

38. More than 120 small and medium-sized South Korean companies occupy this special economic zone, combining cheap North Korean labor with South Korean capital and technology. North Korean workers' take-home pay is less than $60 per month, with Pyongyang collecting the balance.

39. Semoon Chang and Hwa-Kyung Kim, "Inter-Korean Cooperation," in Suk Hi Kim, Terence Roehrig and Bernhard Seliger, eds., *The Survival of North Korea*, 91–92. The 2006 missile and nuclear tests during the Roh administration also did not elicit a negative economic response in Kaesong.

40. Yonhap News Agency, "Inter-Korean trade surges 36 percent this year," March 16, 2012; and Semoon Chang, "Economic Cooperation between the Two Koreas," *North Korean Review* 8, no. 2 (2012): 6–16.

41. Goohoon Kwon, "A United Korea? Reassessing North Korea Risks," *Goldman Sachs Global Economics Paper 188* (New

Notes — Chapter Three

York: Goldman Sachs, September 21, 2009), 12; also see Scott Snyder, "Changes in Seoul's North Korean Policy and Implications for Pyongyang's Inter-Korean Diplomacy," in Kyung-Ae Park, ed., *New Challenges of North Korean Foreign Policy* (New York: Palgrave Macmillan, 2010), 169–170.

42. Chang and Kim, "Inter-Korean Cooperation," 92.

43. Hyeong Jung Park, "Political Dynamics of Hereditary Succession in North Korea," *International Journal of Korean Unification Studies* 20, no. 1 (2011): 25.

44. Haggard and Noland, *Witness to Transformation*, 115.

45. *Chosunilbo*, "N. Korean Dynasty's Authority Challenged," February 13, 2012.

46. Cha, *The Impossible State*, 445; for a list of internal incidents of dissent, see 452–453.

47. Scott Snyder and See-Won Byun, "China-Korea Relations: China Embraces South and North, but Differently," *Comparative Connections* 11, no. 4 (January 2010): 100.

48. Kim, "On the Threshold of Power, 2012/12," 22.

49. See Andrei Lankov, "Kim Serious About Reforms: Expert," *Starting Points*, September 1, 2012, http://starting-points.blogspot.kr/2012/09/kim-serious-about-reforms-expert.html.

50. Stephan Haggard, "Slave to the Blog: Bad News Edition" (Washington DC: Peterson Institute for International Relations, December 3, 2012).

51. Selig S. Harrison, *Korean Endgame: A Strategy for Reunification and U.S. Disengagement* (Princeton, NJ: Princeton University Press, 2002), 5.

52. Lankov, *North of the DMZ*, 311.

53. Joseph S. Nye, *Soft Power: The Means to Success in World Politics* (New York: Public Affairs, 2004); "Soft Power," *Foreign Policy* 80 (1990): 153–171.

54. Haggard and Noland, *Witness to Transformation*, 103.

55. See Kretchun and Kim, *A Quiet Opening*, 38–43.

56. Ibid., 114.

57. *Titanic*, directed by James Cameron (20th Century–Fox, 1997), and *Gone With the Wind*, directed by Victor Fleming (Warner Brothers, 1940).

58. *Hallyu*, or the Korean wave, refers to the increased popularity of South Korean cultural contents and products. Young Sun Jeon, "Diagnosis and Assessment of North Korea's Sociocultural Sector," *International Journal of Korean Unification Studies* 20, no. 2 (2011): 94.

59. For more on the cultural renaissance in South Korea, see Younghan Cho, "Desperately Seeking East Asia Amidst the Popularity of South Korean Pop Culture in Asia," *Cultural Studies* 25, no. 3 (2011): 383–404; and Chua Beng Huat and Koichi Iwabuchi, eds., *East Asian Pop Culture: Analysis of the Korean Wave* (Hong Kong: Hong Kong University Press, 2008). Motivated by the policy of engagement, in 2003 the K-pop groups Shinwa and Baby VOX performed before an elite Pyongyang audience. A few shots of the controlled stoic response of the audience are illuminating. See http://v.youky.com/v_show/id_XMTA1ODgxODA=.html (on Youku, China's version of YouTube) and, on YouTube, http://www.youtube.com/watch?v=ZH_T4DqdQ3c.

60. DVDs of South Korean movies and TV dramas are purchased inexpensively on the black market. More recently the sale of USB flash drives has replaced the trade in DVDs.

61. Hassig and Oh, *The Hidden People of North Korea*, 5.

62. Lankov, *North of the DMZ*, 117.

63. Kretchun and Kim, *A Quiet Opening*, 52.

64. Marcus Noland, "Telecoms in North Korea: Has Orascom Made the Connection?" *North Korean Review* 5, no. 1 (2009): 62–74; and *Chosunilbo*, "Over 1.5 Million N.Korean Subscribe to Mobile Phones," November 22, 2012.

65. *DailyNK*, "Even i-Pads Are in Pyongyang Now," December 1, 2011, http://www.dailynk.com/english/total_list.php.

66. Stacey Banks, "North Korean Telecommunications: On Hold," *North Korean Review* 1, no. 1 (2005): 88–94; also see Jane Kim, *Selling North Korea in the New Frontiers: Profit and Revolution in Cyberspace*, Emerging Voices, Vol. 22 (Washington, DC: Korea Economic Institute, 2011). Google's CEO Eric Schmidt visited North Korea in January 2013 and commented that

a 3G network exists and it would be "very easy" to make a connection to the Internet. Schmidt was shown Linux-based software and technology that controlled the Internet; only individuals in the government, the military, and universities had access, and then only under direct supervision.

67. Haggard and Noland, *Witness to Transformation*, 32; also see Kretchun and Kim, *A Quiet Opening*, 10–11.

68. Haggard and Noland, *Famine in North Korea*, 173.

69. Cha, *The Impossible State*, 209.

70. Kongdan Oh and Ralph C. Hassig, *North Korea: Through the Looking Glass* (Washington, DC: Brookings Institution Press, 2000).

71. Park and Kim, "Inter-Korean Relations in Nuclear Politics," 127–128; also see Jun Hyeong Park and So Yeol Kim, "NK Public 60%–23% in Favor of Change," *Daily NK*, February 27, 2012, http://www.dailynk.com/english/total_list.php.

72. "Velvet Revolution" refers to the nonviolent political revolution that occurred in Prague, Czechoslovakia, in the winter of 1989.

73. Moon, *The Sunshine Policy*, 141.

74. See Patrick M. Cronin, *Vital Venture: Economic Engagement of North Korea and the Kaesong Industrial Complex* (Washington, DC: Center for a New American Security, February 2012), 18–19, http://www.cnas.org/files/documents/publications/CNAS_VitalVenture_Cronin_0.pdf.

75. Moon, *The Sunshine Policy*, 19.

Chapter Four

1. Kotz and Weir, *Russia's Path from Gorbachev to Putin*, 105–125.

2. According to Kotz and Weir, Gorbachev never gave up on democratic socialism; it was Yeltsin and his capitalist cronies who led to the ultimate demise of the socialist system and the Soviet state.

3. Nancy Ries, *Russian Talk: Culture and Conversation During Perestroika* (Ithaca, NY: Cornell University Press, 1997), 14–15.

4. David E. Hoffman, *The Oligarchs: Wealth and Power in the New Russia* (New York: Public Affairs, 2011), 12.

5. Lankov, *North of the DMZ*, 117.

6. B.R. Myers, *The Cleanest Race: How North Koreans See Themselves and Why It Matters* (New York: Melville House Publishing, 2010), 57.

7. Haggard and Noland, *Witness to Transformation*, 117.

8. Nincic warns that policymakers should be more aware of the counterproductive consequences of coercive measures. He argues that positive inducements are overlooked and under-represented in scholarship on international relations and foreign policy. See Miroslav Nincic, "Getting What You Want: Positive Inducements in International Relations," *International Security* 35, no. 1 (2010): 138–183. A similar unstable equilibrium thesis is made by Byung-Yeon Kim in "Markets, Bribery, and Regime Change in North Korea."

9. Ries, *Russian Talk*, 16.

10. Lankov, *North of the DMZ*, 192.

11. It is estimated that over one billion dollars was spent on the celebrations, including over $800,000 for the construction of skyscrapers for the elite and remodeling projects. *Chosunilbo*, "N. Korea Spends Billions on Lavish Fireworks," April 30, 2012.

12. Alexandre Mansourov, "Part I: A Dynamically Stable Regime," *38 North*, U.S.–Korea Institute, December 17, 2012, http://38north.org/2012/12/amansourov121712/.

13. Haggard and Noland, *Famine in North Korea*, 28. With North Korean structural deficits of more than 25 percent per year, Russia was in effect giving away over $500 million in goods annually before this relationship ended.

14. Even a typhoon struck in August 1997. Estimates of the death toll reach as high as 3 million, but 600,000 to 1,000,000 is a middle-range guess. Goodkind and West, "The North Korean Famine and Its Demographic Impact"; also see Courtland Robinson, Myung Ken Lee, Kenneth Hill and Gilbert M. Burnham, "Mortality in North Korean Migrant Households: A Retrospective Study," *Lancet* 354 (1999): 291–295, and Suk Lee, "The DPRK Famine of 1994–2000: Existence and Impact" (Seoul: Korea Institute for National Reunification, May 2005), http://www.kinu.or.kr/up load/neoboard/DATA05/05–06.pdf.

15. Don Oberdorfer, *The Two Koreas: A*

Contemporary History (New York: Basic Books, 2001), 229.

16. Peter Hayes and David von Hippel, "North Korea's Collapse Pathways and the Role of the Energy Sector," in Suk Hi Kim, Terence Roehrig, and Bernhard Seliger, eds., *The Survival of North Korea* (Jefferson, NC: McFarland, 2011), 150.

17. There were reports of plans for an army coup in 1995 in North Hamgyong province during the height of famine. But it was squelched before any shots were fired and the 6th Army Corps was subsequently disbanded. Ju-whal Choi, "An Insider Perspective: North Korea's Unalterable Stance," *Institute for East Asian Studies* 11, no. 4 (1999). Choi was a North Korean senior colonel who defected to South Korea in 1995.

18. *Chosunilbo*, "Pyongyang Elite Key to Regime's Survival," January 9, 2012.

19. Haggard and Noland, *Witness to Transformation*, 12.

20. Demick, *Nothing to Envy*, 291–292.

21. Lankov, *North of the DMZ*, 93–95.

22. Song Min Choi, "No Electricity, No Water, No Patience," *DailyNK*, January 13, 2012.

23. Relying on Chinese input-output data, Marcus Noland has estimated North Korean inflation exceeding 100 percent after the 2002 economic reforms and in the aftermath of currency reform in 2009. Estimates by the Bank of Korea dispute this, but the data suggest that standards of living have regressed outside the capital city of Pyongyang. Also, a decline in basic commodities signals inflation as more money seeks fewer products. Finally, as North Koreans have become more dependent on markets and money for purchasing food, they become more vulnerable to inflation caused by the vicissitudes of weather-related food production. Marcus Noland, *North Korean Economic Performance in 2011* (Washington, DC: Peterson Institute of International Economics, 2012), http://www.piie.com/blogs/nk/?p=7072.

24. Cha, *The Impossible State*, 161.

25. International Monetary Fund, 2012, http://www.imf.org. North Korea ranks 179th in the world in GDP per capita, just behind Uganda and just ahead of Afghanistan.

26. See Jonathan Watts and Tania Branigan, "North Korea's Leader Will Not Last Long, Says Kim Jong-un's Brother," *The Guardian*, January 17, 2012, http://www.guardian.co.uk/world/2012/jan/17/north-korea-leader-not-long.

27. Seung-Ho Joo, "North Korea under Kim Jong-un: The Beginning of the End of a Peculiar Dynasty," *Pacific Focus* 27, no. 1 (April 2012): 1–9.

28. Cha, *The Impossible State*, 304.

29. David C. Kang, "They Think They're Normal: Enduring Questions and New Research on North Korea — A Review Essay," *International Security* 36, no. 3 (Winter 2011/2012): 162.

30. For a vivid description of North Korean prisons, see Kang Chol-Hwan and Pierre Rigoulot, *The Aquariums of Pyongyang: Ten Years in the North Korean Gulag* (New York: Basic Books, 2001); David Hawk, *Hidden Gulag: Exposing North Korea's Prison Camps* (Washington, DC: U.S. Committee for Human Rights in North Korea, 2003); David Hawk, *Hidden Gulag: The Lives and Voices of "Those Who Are Sent to the Mountains."* 2d ed. (Washington, D.C.: U.S. Committee for Human Rights in North Korea, 2012); and KINU, *The White Paper on Human Rights in North Korea, 2011.*

31. Iverson, "The Korean Peace Fund," 64.

Chapter Five

1. Iverson, "The Korean Peace Fund," 64.

2. Nye, *The Future of Power*, xiii.

3. For an explanation of where hard and soft power merge, see Till Geiger, "The Power Game," 103.

4. Bruce W. Bennett, "A Brief Analysis of the Republic of Korea's Defense Reform Plan," National Defense Research Institute (Santa Monica, CA: RAND Corporation, 2006), http://www.rand.org/pubs/occasional_papers/2006/RAND_OP 165.pdf.

5. Even before this, in the action plan for the 2008 "Mutual Benefits and Common Prosperity" legislation, the Lee administration announced support for a

"Vision 3000" plan for peace with a $40 billion investment over five years.

6. Central Bureau of Statistics, *DPR Korea 2008 Population Census National Report* (Pyongyang: Central Bureau of Statistics, 2009), 14–18.

7. Georgetown North Korean expert and former member of the National Security Council in the Bush administration Victor Cha has noted the elevated importance of the top 200 elites.

8. Lankov and Kwak, "The Decline of the North Korean Surveillance State," 6–21.

9. The percentage is lower because not every important party member lives in Pyongyang.

10. Iverson, "The Korean Peace Fund," 68.

11. Haggard and Noland, *Witness to Transformation*, 45–79.

12. Lim and Yoon, "Institutional Entrepreneurs in North Korea," 82–93; Lawrence E. Grinter, "The Economic Rehabilitation of North Korea: Prospects after Kim Jong-il," *Pacific Focus* 25, issue 3 (2010): 313–330; Un-Chul Yang, "Reform without Transition: The Economic Situation in North Korea since the July 1, 2002, Measures," *North Korean Review* 6, no. 1 (2010): 71–87.

13. Lankov and Kim, "North Korean Market Vendors," 70; also see Stephan Haggard and Marcus Noland, "Reform from Below: Institutional Behavioral Change in North Korea: An Institutional Perspective," *Journal of Economic Behavior and Organization* 73, no. 2 (2010): 133–153.

14. Malcolm Gladwell has elucidated the process by which "innovators," "early adaptors," "connectors," "mavens" and "salesmen" create "word-of-mouth epidemics." Such an epidemic could sweep North Korea into the modern world. Malcolm Gladwell, *The Tipping Point: How Little Things Can Make a Big Difference* (New York: Little, Brown, 2000).

15. Banks, "North Korean Telecommunications," 88–94. For developing news and information on North Korean media and communication technology, see Stanford University professor Martyn Williams' blog at http://www.northkoreatech.org/.

16. Hyung Gu Lynn, *Bipolar Orders: The Two Koreas Since 1989* (London: Zed Books, 2007), 136.

17. See Don Tapscott and Anthony D. Williams, *Macrowikinomics: Rebooting Business and the World* (New York: Portfolio/Penguin, 2010).

18. In fact, it might be preferable if South Korea had no money promised to the fund. This should alleviate any doubt among the North Korean elite that reunification is a global objective.

19. Iverson, "The Korean Peace Fund," 70–71.

Chapter Six

1. Oberdorfer, *The Two Koreas: A Contemporary History*, 305.

2. Richard McGregor describes a pragmatically adaptive top Chinese political authority in *The Party: The Secret World of China's Communist Rulers* (New York: Harper Perennial, 2012); also see Crisis Group Asia Report N°179, *Shades of Red: China's Debate Over North Korea*, November 2, 2009, http://www.crisisgroup.org/~/media/Files/asia/north-east-asia/179_shades_of_red___chinas_debate_over_north_korea.

3. Heungkyu Kim, "From a Buffer Zone to a Strategic Burden: Evolving Sino–North Korea Relations During the Hu Jintao Era," *Korean Journal of Defense Analysis* 22, no. 1 (2010): 55–74.

4. Myeong-hae Choi, "Prospects for China's North Korea Strategy in the Post–Kim Jong-il Era and Implications for South Korea," *International Journal of Korean Unification Studies* 21, no. 1 (2012): 46.

5. Shen Dingli, "Cooperative Denuclearization toward North Korea," *Washington Quarterly* 32, no. 4 (October 2009): 180.

6. Sangit Sarita Dwivedi, "North Korea–China Relations: An Asymmetric Alliance," *North Korean Review* 8, no. 2 (2012): 87.

7. The Philippines have a dispute with the Chinese over the Scarborough Shoal in the South China Sea (now called the West Philippines Sea by the Philippine government). The China-Vietnam dispute is over the Paracel Islands in the South China Sea. It should be noted that China is Vietnam's

Notes — Chapter Six

largest trading partner and that China's aid to the Philippines is four times that of the United States.

8. Since 2008 nongovernmental and semi-governmental exchanges have increased, and more formal negotiations to restore transportation, commerce, and communication activities that have been cut off since 1949 seem to be producing positive results. Taiwan has more in common with China that it does with any other nation and the smooth reunification of Hong Kong may serve as a partial model for the future.

9. Kissinger, now 88 years old, has recently published his own version of China, yesterday and tomorrow. See Henry Kissinger, *On China* (New York: Penguin, 2011).

10. However, even though China succumbed to international pressure, Marcus Noland has noted that UN Security Council sanctions against North Korea were watered down in order to get China's vote, and a subjective "credible information" clause was included that could be invoked to call into question "reasonable grounds" and therefore constrain enforcement.

11. This is not an ordinary school. Students at the heavily guarded Party School of the Central Committee of the Communist Party of China are often senior officials in the Chinese government, 50 years of age or older — the current or future major leaders of the Chinese civilization-state.

12. Shen Dingli, "Lips and Teeth: It's Time for China to Get Tough with North Korea," *Foreign Policy*, February 13, 2013; Deng Yuwen, "Should China Abandon North Korea?" *Financial Times*, February 27, 2013; and Xie Tao, "What's Wrong with China's North Korean Policy," Carnegie Endowment for International Peace, March 26, 2013, http://www.carnegieendowment.org/2013/03/26/what-s-wrong-with-china-s-north-korea-policy/ftjw.

13. See Brookings Institution, "One of China's Top Future Leaders to Watch," http://www.brookings.edu/about/centers/china/top-futureleaders/zhang_dejiang.

14. Sunny Lee, "Chinese Perspectives on North Korea and Korean Unification," *Academic Paper Series* (Washington, DC: Korea Economic Institute, January 24, 2012), 2.

15. Debin Zhan and Hun Kyung Lee, "Chinese People's Understanding of the Korean Unification Issue," *Asian Social Science* 8, no. 3 (2012): 63–74; also see Snyder and Byun, "China–Korea Relations," 99. In a November 2012 meeting of the Korean Global Forum in Seoul, Professor Richard Hu of the University of Hong Kong emphasized that China supports unification via a peaceful "reconciliation and cooperation process" but will not accept a hostile unified nuclear Korea.

16. Stephanie Kleine-Ahlbrandt, "The Diminishing Returns of China's North Korea Policy," *38 North*, U.S.–Korea Institute, November 28, 2012, http://38north.org/2012/08/skahlbrandt081612/.

17. Crisis Group Asia Report N°179, *Shades of Red*, 5–7.

18. Stephan Haggard and Marcus Noland, "Sanctioning North Korea: The Political Economy of Denuclearization and Proliferation," *Working Paper* (Washington, DC: Peterson Institute of International Economics, July 2009), 12; and M. VU Khuong, "Economic Reform and Performance: A Comparative Study of China and Vietnam," *China: An International Journal* 7, no. 2 (2009): 189–226.

19. Mitsuhiro, "Outlook for North Korean Economic Reform and Marketization," 86.

20. *Worldcrunch*, "China Eyes Big Investment Opportunities in North Korea," November 6, 2012, http://worldcrunch.com/business-finance/china-eyes-big-investment-opportunities-in-north-korea/north-korea-jvic-commerce-investing/c2s10050/.

21. South Korean companies have incurred an estimated $1.55 billion in losses. Stephan Haggard, "Chinese Investments in the DPRK: Shanghaied!" (Washington, DC: Peterson Institute for International Economics, August 16, 2012), http://www.piie.com/blogs/nk/?p=7158.

22. The UN Security Council sanctions resolutions 1718 and 1874 were adopted after the 2006 and 2009 nuclear tests respectively. In March 2013 the U.N. approved new sanctions in response to North Korea's February underground nuclear test.

23. Andrei Lankov, "Staying Alive: Why North Korea Will Not Change," *Foreign Affairs* 87, no. 2 (March/April 2008): 9–16.

24. Flora Ji, "Road paved but NKorea economic zone still building power stations, upgrading rail and ports," *Associated Press*, August 22, 2012.

25. It is still uncertain whether these ideas have been implemented. To compare these initial North Korean economic initiatives with those made in China, see Barry Naughton, *Growing Out of the Plan: Chinese Economic Reform, 1978–1993* (Cambridge: Cambridge University Press, 1995).

26. John Delury, "Reform Sprouts in North Korea: Kim Jong Un's timid glasnost may signal shift in emphasis from military to economic development," *YaleGlobal*, July 26, 2012, http://yaleglobal.yale.edu/content/sprouts-reform-north-korea.

27. Stephan Haggard, Marcus Noland, and Jaesung Ryu, "The 'June 28 Directive' and July 26 'Let Us Effect Kim Jong Il's Patriotism...': Not Yet Time to Break Out the Soju," *Working Paper Series* (Washington, DC: Peterson Institute for International Economics, August 6, 2012), http://www.piie.com/blogs/nk/?p=7046.

28. Naughton, *Growing Out of the Plan*, 134.

29. Andrei Lankov notes there has been a Chinese-sponsored improvement in living standards for the Pyongyang elite over the past 5–7 years; the private economy has grown and there are more cars, restaurants and luxury shops. See "North Korea's Pools of Prosperity," *Asia Times*, July 7, 2012. It is uncertain how much of this Chinese money is trickling down to the masses and whether the increasingly more blatant unequal distribution of income has any serious destabilizing effects.

30. See Goohoon Kwon, "A United Korea?" 10, 18; also see Lin Shin, "The Mineral Industry in North Korea," *Minerals Yearbook, 2009* (Reston, VA: U.S. Geological Survey, 2009), http://minerals.usgs.gov/minerals/pubs/country/2009/myb3-2009-kn.pdf. Another mineral valuation by Seoul-based North Korea Resource Institute is close to $10 trillion.

31. For a concise and informative online paper, see Alan Ferrie, "Strategy for the Successful Development of the North Korean Minerals Sector," March 2012, http://sinonk.files.wordpress.com/2012/03/sinonk_alan_ferrie_minerals_sector.pdf.

32. Marcus Noland, "The Economics of Korean Unification," *Working Paper* (Washington, DC: Peterson Institute for International Economics, 2000), http://www.iie.com/publications/wp/wp.cfm?ResearchID=154.

33. For a concise explanation of this international financial competition, see James Rickards, *Currency Wars: The Making of the Next Global Crisis* (New York: Penguin, 2011).

34. Dwivedi, "North Korea–China Relations," 76–93; for his seminal work on alliance formation, see Stephen M. Walt, *The Origins of Alliances* (Ithaca, NY: Cornell University Press, 1987).

35. Also see Jooyoung Song, "Understanding China's Response to North Korea's Provocations: The Duel Threats Model," *Asian Survey* 51, no. 6 (2011): 1134–1155.

36. Bates Gill, "China's North Korean Policy: Assessing Interests and Influences," *Special Report* (Washington, DC: United States Institute of Peace, 2012), 8, http://www.usip.org/files/resources/China%27s_North_Korea_Policy.pdf.

37. Cha, *The Impossible State*, 344.

38. Drew Thompson, *Silent Partners: Chinese Joint Ventures in North Korea* (Washington, DC: U.S.–Korea Institute, February 2011), 7.

39. Cha, *The Impossible State*, 335.

40. Ibid., 338. For more on North Korea's economic dependence on China, see Troy Stangarone and Nicholas Hamisevicz, "The Prospects for Economic Reform in North Korea after Kim Jong-il and the China Factor," *International Journal of Korean Unification Studies* 20, no. 2 (2011): 175–197.

41. It is easy to understand why the two names given to the body of water between Japan and Korea are mutually controversial—they are both ethnocentrically biased. The Sea of Japan is overtly ethnocentric, but the label East Sea is covertly so, as the sea is only east of Korea. My suggestion is to rename this body of water the Sea of Peace.

42. L.C. Russell Hsiao, "Strategic Implications of China's Access to the Rajin Port,"

Notes — Chapter Six

China Brief X, issue 6 (March 18, 2010), http://www.jamestown.org/programs/chinabrief/.

43. This possibility is discussed from a U.S. perspective in Carl E. Haselden Jr., "The Effects of Korean Unification on the US Military Presence in Northeast Asia," *Parameters* (Winter 2002/2003): 120–132.

44. Simon Tisdall, "Wikileaks Cables Reveal China 'Ready to Abandon North Korea,'" *The Guardian*, November 29, 2010, http://www.guardian.co.uk/world/2010/nov/29/wikileaks-cables-china-reunified-korea.

45. Chinese–South Korean trade is now almost one-quarter of a trillion dollars and growing by double digits. For an argument for a neutral Korea after reunification, see Eui-Gak Hwang, *The Search for a Unified Korea: Political and Economic Implications* (New York: Springer, 2010).

46. Georgy Toloraya, "Russian Policy in Korea in a Time of Change," *Korean Journal of Defense Analysis* 21, no. 1 (March 2009): 68.

47. In 2007 I visited my close high school friend in Novosibirsk, who has four Russian American children and had developed a fast-food business that employs over a thousand people. One weekend we drove east for about four hours to visit a Russian oil-drilling platform that sat beside a foreign platform. After several hours of impromptu discussions with various Russians and foreigners, the consensus was that the Russian platform was as much as five times less productive than the foreign platform, mostly due to corruption in buying inferior Russian-manufactured drill bits. Assuming my experience is not uncommon, if President Putin can curtail this corruption and let world-class technology and entrepreneurs develop these Russian oil resources, this would increase investment and production and benefit the entirety of East Asia, as well as the goals of Russia to develop this resource-rich region.

48. Michael Richardson, "Asia's Middle East Oil Dependence: Chokepoints on a Vital Maritime Supply Line," Institute of Southeast Asian Studies, *Trends in Southeast Asia Series*, Vol. 1 (2007), http://www.iseas.edu.sg/tr12007.pdf.

49. Suk Hi Kim, Junhua Jia and Michael Whitty, "The Northeast Asian Energy Situation and the North Korean Factor," *North Korean Review* 7, no. 1 (2011): 78–86.

50. Joshua Pollack, "The Evolution of North Korea's Ballistic Missile Market," *Nonproliferation Review* 18, no. 2 (July 2011): 411–429; and *No Exit: North Korea, Nuclear Weapons, and International Security* (New York: Routledge, 2011).

51. Cha, *The Impossible State*, 228. This four-year projection may be on schedule considering the recent success of its three-stage missile launch in December 2012.

52. Gill, "China's North Korean Policy," 7–8.

53. Even the Chinese government has lost absolute control, since enforcement of export controls has by necessity (due to the gigantic size of exports) been decentralized and there is always the possibility for isolated corruption. In addition, arms traffickers have become more sophisticated and it is sometimes difficult to identify dual-use items and materials. See Evan S. Medeiros, *Chasing the Dragon: Assessing China's System of Export Controls for WMD-Related Goods and Technologies* (Santa Monica, CA: RAND Corporation, 2005), http://www.rand.org/pubs/monographs/2005/RAND_MG353.pdf.

54. Richard A. Bitzinger, "Recent Developments in Naval and Maritime Modernization in the Asia-Pacific: Implications and Regional Security," in Philip C. Saunders, Christopher D. Yung, Michael Swaine, and Andrew Nien-Dzu Yang, eds., *The Chinese Navy: Expanding Capabilities, Evolving Roles* (Washington, DC: National Defense University, 2011), 26, http://www.ndu.edu/press/lib/pdf/books/chinese-navy.pdf.

55. Chi-dong Lee, "U.S. pivots toward Asia due to 'real threats' from Pyongyang: Panetta," *Yonhap News*, September 17, 2012.

56. After an agreement is reached, I propose the construction of an enormous statue on the central island showing three families holding hands — one family each from China, South Korea and Japan (perhaps they could be depicted following Confucius). It can be called the East Asian Family Peace Statue and would attract tourists from around the world. The U.S. Statue of Liberty in New York Harbor stands 93 me-

ters from pedestal to top. I envision a statue of similar size (but with more characters) to symbolize East Asian unity.

57. Jason Lim, "What US doesn't get about Dokdo," *Korea Times*, August 24, 2012.

58. Fareed Zakaria, *The Post-American World* (New York: W. W. Norton, 2008), 125.

59. David Rothkopf, *Superclass: The Global Power Elite and the World They Are Making* (New York: Farrar, Straus, and Giroux, 2008).

60. *Forbes*, "The World's Billionaires," April 2013, http://www.forbes.com/billionaires/.

61. Bloomberg Billionaires Index, http://topics.bloomberg.com/bloomberg-billionaires-index/.

62. For perspective, the global GDP has doubled over the past 20 years and is now more than $70 trillion. Over $300 billion is donated each year by private and public sources to aid developing countries. The €130 billion rescue package, plus €109 billion erasures of Greece's sovereign debt, equals US$315 billion.

63. David Sloan Wilson, *Evolution for Everyone: How Darwin's Theory Can Change the Way We Think About Our Lives* (New York: Random House, 2007); for a social and political science perspective, see Robert Axelrod, *The Evolution of Cooperation* (New York: Basic Books, 1984).

Chapter Seven

1. Haggard and Noland, *Witness to Transformation*, 109–110.
2. Kretchun and Kim, *A Quiet Opening*, 13.
3. Cha, *The Impossible State*, 107.
4. Cheoleon Lee, "Gallup World Poll: Implications of Reunification of Two Koreas," *Gallup Poll Briefing*, October 2006, 46. Among Korean college students I have polled, this percentage is even higher.
5. Max St. Brown, Seung Mo Choi, and Hyung Seok Kim, "Korean Economic Integration: Prospects and Pitfalls," *International Economic Journal* 26, no. 3 (2012): 471–485.
6. Kwon, "A United Korea?" 9.

7. Ibid., 19.
8. This assessment did not include the impact of the Korean Peace Fund; see ibid., 16.
9. Ibid., 13. Kwon conservatively estimates a 7–8 percent growth rate for decades into the future.
10. Yonhap News Agency, "N. Korea threatens nuclear war amid looming regional diplomacy," December 17, 2010.
11. Daniel Kahneman and Amos Tversky, "Prospect Theory: An Analysis of Decision Under Risk," *Econometrica* 47, no. 2 (March 1997): 263–292; and Jack S. Levy, "Prospect Theory, Rational Choice, and International Relations," *International Studies Quarterly* 41, no. 1 (1997): 87–112.
12. For a brief discussion of this dangerous scenario, see Cha, *The Impossible State*, 234–238.
13. Hayes and Bruce, "North Korean Nuclear Nationalism and the Threat of Nuclear War in Korea," 65–89.
14. For an explanation of why North Korea is not likely to start an unprovoked war, see Cha and Kang, *Nuclear North Korea*, 46–54.
15. For details on South Korea's new policy and rules of engagement, see Abraham M. Denmark, "Proactive Deterrence: The Challenge of Escalation Control on the Korean Peninsula," *Academic Paper Series* (Washington, DC: Korea Economic Institute, December 2011), http://www.keia.org.
16. Cha, *The Impossible State*, 243. Cha also envisions how border-area war games could unintentionally escalate into full-scale warfare (243–244).
17. Stewart A. Bremer, "Dangerous Dyads: Conditions Affecting the Likelihood of Interstate War, 1816–1965," *Journal of Conflict Resolution* 36 (1992): 309–341; Jacob Bercovitch and Patrick M. Regan, "The Structure of International Conflict Management: An Analysis of the Effects of Intractability and Mediation," *International Journal of Peace Studies* 4, no. 1 (1999): 1–20; and Gary Goertz and Paul F. Diehl, "The Empirical Importance of Enduring Rivalries," *International Interactions* 18, no. 1 (1992): 151–163.
18. Cha, *The Impossible State*, 455–456. The more than 100,000 documented noncombatant (collateral) civilian deaths in

Iraq did not deter U.S. preemptive policy or mission objectives during the neoconservative foreign policy of the Bush administration. See Iraq Body Count, http://www.iraqbodycount.org/.

19. Nye, *Soft Power: The Means to Success in World Politics*; "Soft Power," 153–171.

20. Martin, *Under the Loving Care of the Fatherly Leader*, 495.

21. Colin Robinson and Stephen H. Baker, "Stand-off with North Korea: War Scenarios and Consequences," unclassified summary of a National Intelligence Estimate (2003), http://www.cdi.org/northkorea/north-korea-crisis.pdf.

22. Huntington, *The Clash of Civilizations*, 28.

23. For a concise argument for re-engagement, see Moon, *The Sunshine Policy*.

24. Ms. Park is the daughter of the assassinated Korean military dictator, Park Chung Hee (1961–1979), who led the economic revolution in South Korea. For an appeal for a more moderate and consistent South Korean political approach, see Jin Ha Kim, "In Search of Balance between Inducements and Sanctions: Evaluating the Lee Myung-bak Administration's North Korean Policy," *International Journal of Korean Unification Studies* 21, no. 1 (2012): 119–161.

25. Richard W. Chadwick, "Tensions on the Korean Peninsula: Cats and Mice or the Mouse that Roars? Four-Power Manipulations on a Fog of Irony and Pathos," paper presented at the International Studies Association Annual Conference, 2011.

26. Korea Economic Institute, *Korea's Economy: 2012* (Washington, DC: Korea Economic Institute, 2012), 26.

27. Cha, *The Impossible State*, 410.

28. Andrei Lankov, "Kim Jong-un's North Korea: What Should We Expect?" *International Journal of Korean Unification Studies* 21, no. 1 (2012): 6.

29. Iverson, "The Korean Peace Fund," 68.

30. Richard W. Chadwick, "Northeast Asian International Politics and Alternative Korean Futures: An Early 21st Century Appraisal," *International Journal of Korean Unification Studies* 11, no. 1 (2002): 1.

Chapter Eight

1. Becker, "Nobel Lecture: The Economic Way of Looking at Behavior," 386.

Chapter Nine

1. Central Bureau of Statistics, *DPR Korea 2008 Population Census National Report*.

2. The first technical business schools could be established by expanding Geoffrey See's (founder of Choson Exchange) entrepreneur program for teaching financial literacy and the role economics, technology and law in a new united Korea.

3. The Korean educational system is ranked second in the world, just behind that of Finland.

4. Hassig and Oh, *The Hidden People of North Korea*, 79.

5. Marcus Noland, Sherman Robinson and Tao Wang, "Modeling Korean Unification," *Journal of Comparative Economics* 28, issue 2 (2000): 401; for work that is more than 15 years old, see Jong-Yun Bae, "The Fiscal Burden of Korean Reunification and its Impact on South Korea's Macroeconomic Stability," *Joint U.S.–Korea Academic Studies*, no. 6 (1996): 185–202; Marc Piazolo, "Could South Korea Afford German-Style Reunification?" *Economics of Korean Reunification* 2, no. 2 (1997): 48–63; and Marcus Noland, ed., *Integration of the Korean Peninsula* (Washington, DC: Institute for International Economics, 1997).

6. Alan J. Auerbach, Young Jun Chun, and Ilho Yoo, "The Fiscal Burden of Korean Reunification: A General Accounting Approach," *Working Paper* (Cambridge, MA: National Bureau of Economic Research, August 2004); Michael Funke and Holger Strulik, "Growth and Convergence in a Two-Region Model: The Hypothetical Case of Korean Unification," *Journal of Asian Economics* 16 (2005): 255–279; and Scott C. Bradford and Kerk L. Phillips, "A Dynamic General Equilibrium Model of Phased Korean Reunification," *Journal of Korean Economy* 6, no. 1 (2005): 27–49.

7. After Noland's challenge, there have been some rather narrow economic analyses that either rely heavily on the Ger-

man model or make simplistic assumptions about migration and foreign investment and neglect to consider practical policy alternatives, even though they may dramatically change outcomes.

8. Holger Wolf, "Korean Unification: Lessons from Germany," in Marcus Noland, ed., *Integration of the Korean Peninsula* (Washington, DC: Institute for International Economics, 1997), 187.

9. Marion P. Spina, "Brushes with the Law: North Korea and the Rule of Law," *Korea Economic Institute* 2, no. 6 (June 2007), http://www.keia.org/publication/brushes-law-north-korea-and-rule-law.

10. Jennifer Hunt, "The Economics of German Reunification," *Dictionary of Economics* (New York: Palgrave Macmillan, 2006).

11. During German reunification 14,000 enterprises were privatized within four years.

12. Colonel David Coghlan, *Prospects From Korean Reunification*, (United States Government: U.S. Army War College, Strategic Studies Institute, 2008), http://www.StrategicStudiesInstitute.army.mil/; Lee, "Gallup World Poll," 46.

13. Noland, "The Economics of Korean Unification."

14. Purchasing power parity (PPP) is a technique used to determine the relative value of currencies and to facilitate international comparisons of income.

15. Ibid.

16. In September 2012 Standard and Poor's cited the smooth transition of power in North Korea as the reason the three major rating companies upgraded South Koreas credit rating from A to A+. For decades the threat of war with North Korea has kept the South Korean rating lower than it otherwise would have been.

17. A majority of Koreans believe this was an IMF-precipitated crisis and the South Korean government is naturally reluctant to become over-leveraged by foreign loans and external capital investments (hot money). Currently about 40 percent of the Korean Exchange (stock market) is capitalized with foreign funds and this would likely increase after reunification.

18. There are no taxes in North Korea and its citizens are unfamiliar with their purpose. It may be expedient to authorize a system of taxation, establish an institutional bureaucratic framework and begin taxing commerce and trade at very low symbolic levels. Perhaps television news reports can explain the social purpose and redistributive function of taxation.

19. See Lim and Yoon, "Institutional Entrepreneurs in North Korea," 82–93.

20. China-imported food staples would relieve domestic pressure.

21. Naughton, *Growing Out of the Plan*, 153.

22. Naughton, *Growing Out of the Plan*, 141; also see Justin Jifu Lin, "Rural Reforms and Agricultural Growth in China," *American Economic Review* 82, no. 1 (1992): 34–51.

23. In economic recognition that total growth is often greater than the sum of the input parts, total factor productivity accounts for the portion of output not explained by the amount of inputs used in production.

24. Haggard and Noland, "Sanctioning North Korea," 12.

25. Gerlinde Sinn and Hans-Werner Sinn, *Jumpstart: The Economic Unification of Germany* (Cambridge, MA: MIT Press, 1992).

26. Naughton, *Growing Out of the Plan*, 10.

27. Phillip E. Tetlock, *Expert Political Judgment: How Good Is It? How Can We Know?* (Princeton, NJ: Princeton University Press, 2005).

28. See Naughton, *Growing Out of the Plan*.

29. See Seok-Choon Lew, "Confucian Capitalism: Possibilities and Limits," *Korea Focus* 5, no. 4 (1997): 80–92; Tae-Yeol Kim and Kwok Leung, "Forming and Reacting to Overall Fairness: A Cross-Cultural Comparison," *Organizational Behavior and Human Decision Processes* 104, no. 1 (2007): 83–95; Chan Sup Chang, "Confucian Capitalism: Impact of Culture and the Management System on Economic Growth in South Korea," *Journal of Third World Studies* (Fall 1998): 53–66; and T.R. Reid, *Confucius Lives Next Door: What Living in the East Teaches Us About Living in the West* (New York: Random House, 1999), 201.

30. Naughton, *Growing Out of the Plan*, 20.

31. For Russia, see Kotz and Weir, *Russia's Path from Gorbachev to Putin*, 155–195; for Germany, see Sinn and Sinn, *Jumpstart*, and I. J. Alexander Dyck, "Privatization in Eastern Germany: Management Selection and Economic Transition," *American Economic Review* 87, no. 4 (1997): 565–597.

32. Wolf, "Korean Unification," 187.

33. Noland, Robinson and Wang, "Modeling Korean Unification." This capital stock may be so miniscule by now that it may not be worth mentioning.

34. Bradford and Phillips, "A Dynamic General Equilibrium Model of Phased Korean Reunification," 41.

35. Mitsuhiro, "Outlook for North Korean Economic Reform and Marketization," 75; also see Stradiotto and Guo, "Market Socialism in North Korea," 188–214.

36. Sodgil Young, Chang-Jae Lee, and Hyoungsoo Zang, "Preparing for the Economic Integration of Two Koreas: Policy Challenges to South Korea," in Marcus Noland, ed., *Integration of the Korean Peninsula* (Washington, DC: Institute for International Economics, 1997), 262. Average incomes in the top ten U.S. states are over 60 percent those of the bottom ten without noticeable internal migration.

37. Gianluca Spezza, "Why North Koreans Won't Be Fleeing South After Unification," interview of Song Young Hoon, *NK News*, February 19, 2013, http://www.nknews.org/2013/02/why-north-koreans-wont-be-fleeing-south-after-unification/.

38. Most economists agree there is a housing bubble in Seoul and surrounding areas. The government has introduced new policies to stimulate the housing market seven times in the past 18 months and introduced stimulus measures for purchasing tens of thousands of unsold homes to slow the bleeding of construction companies. Although it is unlikely that many North Koreans will be able to afford South Korean high-rise homes anytime soon, there will be some who can.

39. Noland, Robinson, and Wang, "Modeling Korean Unification."

40. Haggard, Lee, and Noland, "Integration in the Absence of Institutions."

41. Philip Bowring, "Modeling Korean Unification," *New York Times*, September 27, 2005.

42. Zhan and Lee, "Chinese People's Understanding of the Korean Unification Issue," 70.

43. Jacques, *When China Rules the World*, 366.

44. See Korea Economic Institute, *Korea's Economy: 2012*, 24.

45. Jacques, *When China Rules the World*, 365.

46. Cha, *The Impossible State*, 425.

47. North Korea is so underdeveloped that it can be compared to a post-war zone. As during reconstruction after the Korean War or the war in Europe, there will be jobs for everybody.

48. Kwon, "A United Korea?" 16.

49. Shin, "The Mineral Industry in North Korea."

50. Edward Yoon, "Status and Future of the North Korean Minerals Sector," *Korean Journal of Defense Analysis* 23, no. 2 (June 2011): 191–210.

51. Ferrie, "Strategy for the Successful Development of the North Korean Minerals Sector."

52. Charles Wolf Jr. and Kamil Akramov, *North Korean Paradoxes: Circumstances, Costs, and Consequences of Korean Unification* (Santa Monica, CA: RAND Corporation, 2005).

53. These endangered species included the red-crowned crane, white-naped crane, and the black-faced spoonbill. See Kevin J. Olival and Hiroyoshi Higuchi, "Monitoring the Long-Distance Movement of Wildlife in Asia Using Satellite Telemetry," in Jeffrey A. McNeely, Thomas M. McCarthy, Andrew T. Smith, Linda Olsvig-Whittaker, and Eric D. Wikramanayake, eds., *Conservation Biology in Asia* (Kathmandu, Nepal: Society for Conservation Biology, 2006), 325; also see Joanne Min-Young Park, "Borderwall: Peace and the Future of the Korean Demilitarized Zone," dissertation, Rice University, Houston, Texas, 2008.

54. Rudiger Dornbusch and Holger C. Wolf, "East German Economic Reconstruction," in Olivier Jean Blanchard, Kenneth A. Froot, and Jeffrey D. Sachs, eds., *The Transition in Eastern Europe, Vol. 1* (Chicago: University of Chicago Press, 1994), 155–190.

Notes—Chapter Nine

55. Mi Ae Taylor and Mark E. Manyin, *Non-Governmental Organizations' Activities in North Korea* (Washington, DC: Congressional Research Service, 2011), 5.

56. Everard, *Only Beautiful Please*, 137.

57. Daniel Schwekendiek, *A Socioeconomic History of North Korea* (Jefferson, NC: McFarland, 2011), 108–114; and Sunyoung Pak, "The Growth Status of Refugee Children in China," *Korea Journal* 43, no. 3 (2003): 165–190.

58. Volker Hesse, Manfred Voigt, Anneliese Sälzler, Sylvia Steinberg, Klaus Friese, Eberhard Keller, Ruth Gausche, and Reiner Eisele, "Alterations in Height, Weight, and Body Mass Index of Newborns, Children, and Young Adults in Eastern Germany after German Reunification," *Journal of Pediatrics* 142, issue 3 (2003): 259–262.

59. Schwekendiek, *A Socioeconomic History of North Korea*, 61–67.

60. United Nations, *By Choice, Not By Chance: Family Planning, Human Rights and Development*, State of World Population 2012 (New York: United Nations Populations Fund, 2012).

61. Per 100,000 people, North Korea detains 833 (the second-ranked United States detains 715). International Centre for Prisons, http://prisonstudies.org/.

62. See Aleksandr Solzhenitsyn, *The Gulag Archipelago: 1918–1956* (New York: Harper and Row, 1973).

63. Cha, *The Impossible State*, 170.

64. Hawk, *Hidden Gulag*, 70; KINU, *The White Paper on Human Rights in North Korea*, 2011.

65. See Victor Cha and David Kang, *Approaching Korean Unification: What We Learn from Other Cases* (Washington, DC: Center for Strategic and International Studies, 2011), http://csis.org/files/publication/101217_Cha_ApproachingUnification_WEB.pdf.

66. Banks, "North Korean Telecommunications," 88–94.

67. Sungjae Choo, "Rural Telematics and the Possibilities for Regional Development: The Case of Information Model Village in Weonju, Korea," *Journal of the Korean Geographical Society* 36, no. 5 (2001): 516–526.

68. Choong Soon Kim, *Kimchi and Information Technology: Tradition and Transformation in Korea* (Seoul: Ilchokak, 2007), 175.

69. Over time it is possible many Kim Jong-il monuments may be destroyed. He will be the scapegoat for North Korea's transgressions, and this symbolic destruction may cathartically relieve some of the pent-up anger and hostility throughout Korea and help North Koreans startanew.

70. To view a documentary film that highlights the Mass Games, see *A State of Mind*, directed by Daniel Gordon and distributed by Kino International (2005).

71. In their ideologically provocative Weberian analysis of power and "charismatic authenticity" in North Korea, Heonik Kwon and Byung-Ho Chung provide a perceptive review of the underlying meaning of Arirang: "Arirang depicts the country's revolutionary history as having originated in the communities of displaced Koreans in [Japanese-controlled] colonial Manchuria [1931–1945]: their tragic lives are emblematic of the tragic fate of the whole nation, displaced within and from its homeland by colonial occupation. The communities' sorrows are embraced by a heroic revolutionary leader, through whom the displaced people recover hope and passion for an honorable destiny and national liberation. In striking biblical fashion, the story of Arirang highlights the redemptive aesthetics of exodus and illustrates the prophesy of truth emerging from life in exile. It is by virtue of being a partisan that one is able to glimpse the truth against the misery and despair of colonial displacement." See Heonik Kwon and Byung-Ho Chung, *North Korea: Beyond Charismatic Politics* (Lanham, MD: Rowman and Littlefield, 2012).

72. *Comrade Kim Goes Flying*, produced by Anja Daelemans, Nicholas Bonner, and Ryom Mi Hwa (2012).

73. See Wi Jo Kang, *Christ and Caesar in Modern Korea: A History of Christianity and Politics* (Albany: State University of New York Press, 1997).

74. Korean popular music rose to prominence in East Asia about 15 years ago and is growing in global appeal. Psy's recent international sensation "Gangnam Style" has had over one billion hits on YouTube—this represents almost 15 percent of the world's population!

Epilogue

1. Thomas Kuhn, *The Structure of Scientific Revolutions* (Chicago: University of Chicago Press, 1962).

2. My guess is that $75 million would be sufficient to create an institution and hire the talent that could get the job done within the next few years.

3. The late Steve Jobs, U.S. computer engineer and industrialist, has been quoted as saying, "Here's to the crazy ones, the misfits, the rebels, the troublemakers, the round pegs in square holes ... the ones who see things differently — they're not fond of rules.... You can quote them, disagree with them, glorify or vilify them, but the only thing you can't do is ignore them because they change things ... they push the human race forward, and while some may see them as the crazy ones, we see genius, because the ones who are crazy enough to think that they can change the world, are the ones who do."

4. Liaquat Ahamed, *Lords of Finance: The Bankers Who Broke the World* (New York: Penguin, 2009), 20.

5. Ibid., 22.

Bibliography

Acharya, Amitav, and Barry Buzan, eds. *Non-Western International Relations Theory: Perspectives On and Beyond Asia.* New York: Routledge, 2010.

Ahamed, Liaquat. *Lords of Finance: The Bankers Who Broke the World.* New York: Penguin, 2009.

Armstrong, Charles K. *Korean Society: Civil Society, Democracy and the State.* Second edition. New York: Routledge, 2007; orig. 2002.

A State of Mind. Directed by Daniel Gordon, distributed by Kino International, 2005.

Auerbach, Alan J., Young Jun Chun, and Ilho Yoo. "The Fiscal Burden of Korean Reunification: A General Accounting Approach." *Working Paper.* Cambridge, MA: National Bureau of Economic Research, August 2004.

Axelrod, Robert. *The Evolution of Cooperation.* New York: Basic Books, 1984.

Ayson, Robert, and Brendan Taylor. "Attacking North Korea: Why War Might Be Preferred." *Comparative Strategy* 23, no. 3 (2004): 263–279.

Bae, Jong-Yun. "The Fiscal Burden of Korean Reunification and its Impact on South Korea's Macroeconomic Stability." *Joint U.S.–Korea Academic Studies*, no. 6 (1996): 185–202.

Bae, Sangmin, and Martyn de Bruyn. "Trust Building through Institutions: European Lessons for Korean Unification." *Academic Papers on Korea.* Washington, D.C.: Korea Economic Institute, 2010.

Bajoria, Jayshree. "The China–North Korean Relationship." New York: Council on Foreign Relations, 2012. <http://www.cfr.org/china/china northkorearelationship/p11097>.

Banks, Stacey. "North Korean Telecommunications: On Hold." *North Korean Review* 1, no. 1 (2005): 88–94.

Becker, Gary S. *Crime and Punishment.* Chicago: University of Chicago Press, 1968.

———. *The Economic Approach to Human Behavior.* Chicago: University of Chicago Press, 1976.

———. *The Economics of Discrimination.* Chicago: University of Chicago Press, 1957.

———. *Human Capital.* New York: Columbia University Press, 1964.

———. "Nobel Lecture: The Economic Way of Looking at Behavior." *Journal of Political Economy* 101, no. 3 (1993): 385–409.

———. "A Theory of Social Interactions." *Journal of Political Economy* 82, no. 1 (1974): 1063–1093.

Bennett, Bruce W. "A Brief Analysis of the Republic of Korea's Defense Reform Plan." *National Defense Research Institute.* Santa Monica, CA: RAND Corporation, 2006. <http://www.rand.org/pubs/occasional_papers/2006/RAND_OP165.pdf>.

Bennett, Bruce W., and Jennifer Lind. "The Collapse of North Korea: Military Missions and Requirements." *International Security* 36, no. 2 (2011): 84–119.

Bercovitch, Jacob, and Patrick M. Regan.

"The Structure of International Conflict Management: An Analysis of the Effects of Intractability and Mediation." *International Journal of Peace Studies* 4, no. 1 (1999): 1–20.

Bitzinger, Richard A. "Recent Developments in Naval and Maritime Modernization in the Asia-Pacific: Implications and Regional Security." In Philip C. Saunders, Christopher D. Yung, Michael Swaine, and Andrew Nien-Dzu Yang, eds., *The Chinese Navy: Expanding Capabilities, Evolving Roles*. Washington, D.C.: National Defense University, 2011. <http://www.ndu.edu/press/lib/pdf/books/chinese-navy.pdf>.

Blits, Jan H. "Hobbesian Fear." *Political Theory* 17, no. 3 (August 1989): 417–431.

Bloomberg Billionaires Index. <http://topics.bloomberg.com/bloomberg-billionaires-index/>.

Booth, Ken, ed. *Realism and World Politics*. New York: Routledge, 2011.

Bowring, Philip. "Modeling Korean Unification." *New York Times*, September 27, 2005.

Bradford, Scott C., and Kerk L. Phillips. "A Dynamic General Equilibrium Model of Phased Korean Reunification." *Journal of Korean Economy* 6, no. 1 (2005): 27–49.

Bremer, Stewart A. "Dangerous Dyads: Conditions Affecting the Likelihood of Interstate War, 1816–1965." *Journal of Conflict Resolution* 36 (1992): 309–341.

Brookings Institution. "One of China's Top Future Leaders to Watch." <http://www.brookings.edu/about/centers/china/top-futureleaders/zhang_dejiang>.

Byman, Daniel, and Jennifer Lind. "Pyongyang's Survival Strategy: Tools of Authoritarian Control." *International Security* 35, no. 1 (2010): 44–74.

Carlin, Robert, and John W. Lewis. "North Korea's New Course." *Los Angeles Times*, December 8, 2011. <http://articles.latimes.com/2011/dec/08/opinion/la-oe-carlin-nkorea-20111208>.

Central Bureau of Statistics. *DPR Korea 2008 Population Census National Report*. Pyongyang: Central Bureau of Statistics, 2009.

Cha, Victor. "China's Rise, the Changing Northeast Asian Security Environment, and US–ROK Strategic Response. An interview." Washington, D.C.: Center for Strategic and International Studies, 2010. <http://csis.org/files/publication/110114_Chinas_Rise_Changing_NEA_Security.pdf>.

_____. *The Impossible State: North Korea Past and Future*. New York: HarperCollins, 2012.

Cha, Victor D., and David C. Kang. *Approaching Korean Unification: What We Learn from Other Cases*. Washington, D.C.: Center for Strategic and International Studies, 2011. http://csis.org/files/publication/101217_Cha_ApproachingUnification_WEB.pdf.

_____. *Nuclear North Korea: A Debate on Engagement Strategies*. New York: Columbia University Press, 2003.

Chadwick, Richard W. "Northeast Asian International Politics and Alternative Korean Futures: An Early 21st Century Appraisal." *International Journal of Korean Unification Studies* 11, no. 1 (2002): 17–32.

_____. "Tensions on the Korean Peninsula: Cats and Mice or the Mouse that Roars? Four-Power Manipulations on a Fog of Irony and Pathos." Paper presented at the International Studies Association Annual Conference, 2011.

Chang, Chan Sup. "Confucian Capitalism: Impact of Culture and the Management System on Economic Growth in South Korea." *Journal of Third World Studies* (Fall 1998): 53–66.

Chang, Ha-Joon. *Bad Samaritans: The Myth of Free Trade and the Secret History of Capitalism*. New York: Bloomsbury Press, 2008.

Chang, Semoon. "Economic Cooperation between the Two Koreas." *North Korean Review* 8, no. 2 (2012): 6–16.

Chang, Semoon, and Hwa-Kyung Kim. "Inter-Korean Cooperation." In Suk Hi Kim, Terence Roehrig, and Bernhard Seliger, eds., *The Survival of North Korea: Essays on Strategy, Economics and International Relations*, 86–98. Jefferson, NC: McFarland, 2011.

Chang, Yoonok, Stephan Haggard, and Marcus Noland. "Exit Polls: Refugee Assessments of North Korea's Transition." *Working Paper Series*. Washington, D.C.: Peterson Institute for International Economics, January 2008. <http://www.iie.com/publications/wp/wp08–1.pdf>.

Chanlett-Avery, Emma. "North Korea: U.S. Relations, Nuclear Diplomacy, and Internal Situation." Washington, D.C.: Congressional Research Service, January 17, 2012.

Cho, Min. "Establishment of a Peace Regime on the Korean Peninsula: A ROK Perspective." *Korea and World Affairs*, no. 31 (2007): 281–300.

Cho, Younghan. "Desperately Seeking East Asia Amidst the Popularity of South Korean Pop Culture in Asia." *Cultural Studies* 25, no. 3 (2011): 383–404.

Choi, Ju-whal. "An Insider Perspective: North Korea's Unalterable Stance." *Institute for East Asian Studies* 11, no. 4 (1999). <http://www.ieas.or.kr/vol11_4/choijuwhal.htm>.

Choi, Myeong-hae. "Prospects for China's North Korea Strategy in the Post–Kim Jong-il Era and Implications for South Korea." *International Journal of Korean Unification Studies* 21, no. 1 (2012): 45–73.

Choi, Song Min. "No Electricity, No Water, No Patience." *DailyNK*, January 13, 2012.

Choo, Sungjae. "Rural Telematics and the Possibilities for Regional Development: The Case of Information Model Village in Weonju, Korea." *Journal of the Korean Geographical Society* 36, no. 5 (2001): 516–526.

Chosunilbo. "N. Korean Dynasty's Authority Challenged." February 13, 2012.

_____. "N. Korea Spends Billions on Lavish Fireworks." April 30, 2012.

_____. "N. Korea's Underground Economy Booming." September 21, 2011.

_____. "Over 1.5 Million N.Korean Subscribe to Mobile Phones." November 22, 2012.

_____. "Pyongyang Elite Key to Regime's Survival." January 9, 2012.

Chung, Jae Ho. "East Asia Responds to the Rise of China: Patterns and Variations." *Pacific Affairs* 82 (2009): 657–675.

Coghlan, Colonel David. *Prospects from Korean Reunification*. United States Government: U.S. Army War College, Strategic Studies Institute, 2008. <http://www.StrategicStudiesInstitute.army.mil/>.

Comrade Kim Goes Flying. Produced by Anja Daelemans, Nicholas Bonner, and Ryom Mi Hwa. 2012.

Copeland, Daryl. *Guerrilla Diplomacy Rethinking International Relations*. Boulder, CO: Lynne Rienner, 2009.

Crisis Group Asia Report N°179. *Shades of Red: China's Debate Over North Korea*. November 2, 2009. <http://www.crisisgroup.org/~/media/Files/asia/north-east-asia/179_shades_of_red___chinas_debate_over_north_korea>.

Cronin, Patrick M. *Vital Venture: Economic Engagement of North Korea and the Kaesong Industrial Complex*. Washington, D.C.: Center for a New American Security, February 2012. <http://www.cnas.org/files/documents/publications/CNAS_VitalVenture_Cronin_0.pdf>.

DailyNK. "Even i-Pads Are in Pyongyang Now." December 1, 2011. <http://www.dailynk.com/english/total_list.php>.

Bibliography

Dalton, Russell J., and Nhu-ngoc T. Ong. "Authority Orientations and Democratic Attitudes: A Test of the 'Asian Values' Hypothesis." *Japanese Journal of Political Science* 6, no. 2 (2005): 1–21.

David, Paul A. "Why are Institutions the 'Carriers of History'? Path Dependence and the Evolution of Conventions, Organizations and Institutions." *Structural Change and Economic Dynamics* 5, no. 2 (1994): 205–220.

Delury, John. "Reform Sprouts in North Korea: Kim Jong Un's timid glasnost may signal shift in emphasis from military to economic development." *YaleGlobal*, July 26, 2012. <http://yaleglobal.yale.edu/content/sprouts-reform-north-korea>.

Demick, Barbara. *Nothing to Envy: Ordinary Lives in North Korea*. New York: Spiegel and Grau, 2009.

Denmark, Abraham M. "Proactive Deterrence: The Challenge of Escalation Control on the Korean Peninsula." *Academic Paper Series*. Washington, D.C.: Korea Economic Institute, December 2011. <http://www.keia.org>.

Dikötter, Frank. *The Discourse of Race in Modern China*. London: Hurst, 1992.

Dingli, Shen. "Cooperative Denuclearization toward North Korea." *Washington Quarterly* 32, no. 4 (October 2009): 175–188.

———. "Lips and Teeth: It's Time for China to Get Tough with North Korea." *Foreign Policy*, February 13, 2013.

Dornbusch, Rudiger, and Holger C. Wolf. "East German Economic Reconstruction." In Olivier Jean Blanchard, Kenneth A. Froot, and Jeffrey D. Sachs, eds., *The Transition in Eastern Europe, Vol. 1*, 155–190. Chicago: University of Chicago Press, 1994.

Dwivedi, Sangit Sarita. "North Korea-China Relations: An Asymmetric Alliance." *North Korean Review* 8, no. 2 (2012): 76–93.

Dyck, I. J. Alexander. "Privatization in Eastern Germany: Management Selection and Economic Transition." *American Economic Review* 87, no. 4 (1997): 565–597.

Eberstadt, Nicholas. *The North Korean Economy: Between Crisis and Catastrophe*. New Brunswick, NJ: Transaction, 2007.

Everard, John. *Only Beautiful Please: A British Diplomat in North Korea*. Stanford, CA: Asia-Pacific Research Center, 2012.

Evrigenis, Ioannis D. *Fear of Enemies and Collective Action*. Cambridge: Cambridge University Press, 2008.

Ferrie, Alan. "Strategy for the Successful Development of the North Korean Minerals Sector." March 2012. <http://sinonk.files.wordpress.com/2012/03/sinonk_alan_ferrie_minerals_sector.pdf>.

Forbes. "The World's Billionaires." April 2013. http://www.forbes.com/billionaires/.

Ford, Christopher A. *The Mind of Empire: China's History and Modern Foreign Relations*. Lexington: University of Kentucky Press, 2010.

Frank, Rudiger, and Phillip H. Park. "From Monolithic Totalitarian to Collective Authoritarian Leadership? Performance-Based Legitimacy and Power Transfer in North Korea." *North Korean Review* 8, no. 2 (2012): 32–49.

Funke, Michael, and Holger Strulik. "Growth and Convergence in a Two-Region Model: The Hypothetical Case of Korean Unification." *Journal of Asian Economics* 16 (2005): 255–279.

Gallarotti, Giulio M. *Cosmopolitan Power in International Relations: A Synthesis of Realism, Neoliberalism, and Constructivism*. Cambridge: Cambridge University Press, 2010.

Geiger, Till. "The Power Game: Soft Power and the International Historian." In Inderjeet Parmar and Michael

Cox, eds., *Soft Power and US Foreign Policy: Theoretical, Historical and Contemporary Perspectives*, 83–107. New York: Routledge, 2010.

Gill, Bates. "China's North Korean Policy: Assessing Interests and Influences." *Special Report*. Washington, D.C.: United States Institute of Peace, 2012. <http://www.usip.org/files/resources/China%27s_North_Korea_Policy.pdf>.

Gladwell, Malcolm. *The Tipping Point: How Little Things Can Make a Big Difference*. New York: Little, Brown, 2000.

Gleditsch, Nils P. "Democracy and Peace." *Journal of Peace Research* 29, no. 4 (1992): 369–376.

Goertz, Gary, and Paul F. Diehl. "The Empirical Importance of Enduring Rivalries." *International Interactions* 18, no. 1 (1992): 151–163.

Goodkind, Daniel, and Loraine West. "The North Korean Famine and Its Demographic Impact." *Population and Development Review* 27, issue 2 (2001): 219–238.

Granovetter, Mark. "Threshold Models of Collective Behavior." *American Journal of Sociology* 83, no. 6 (1978): 1420–1443.

Grinter, Lawrence E. "The Economic Rehabilitation of North Korea: Prospects after Kim Jong-il." *Pacific Focus* 25, issue 3 (2010): 313–330.

Guilhot, Nicolas. "The Realist Gambit: Postwar American Political Science and the Birth of IR Theory." *International Political Sociology* 2, no. 4 (2008): 281–304.

Haggard, Stephan. "Chinese Investments in the DPRK: Shanghaied!" Washington, D.C.: Peterson Institute for International Economics, August 16, 2012. <http://www.piie.com/blogs/nk/?p=7158>.

_____. "Slave to the Blog: Bad News Edition." Washington, D.C.: Peterson Institute for International Relations, December 3, 2012.

Haggard, Stephan, Jennifer Lee, and Marcus Noland. "Integration in the Absence of Institutions: China–North Korea Cross-Border Exchange." *Working Paper*. Washington, D.C.: Peterson Institute of International Economics, August 2011. <http://www.iie.com/publications/wp/wp11-13.pdf>.

Haggard, Stephan, and Marcus Noland. *Famine in North Korea: Markets, Aid, and Reform*. New York: Columbia University Press, 2007.

_____. *Hunger and Human Rights: The Politics of Famine in North Korea*. Washington, D.C.: U.S. Committee for Human Rights in North Korea, 2005.

_____. "Reform from Below: Institutional Behavioral Change in North Korea: An Institutional Perspective." *Journal of Economic Behavior and Organization* 73, no. 2 (2010): 133–153.

_____. "Sanctioning North Korea: The Political Economy of Denuclearization and Proliferation." *Working Paper*. Washington, D.C.: Peterson Institute of International Economics, July 2009.

_____. *Witness to Transformation: Refugee Insights into North Korea*. Washington, D.C.: Peterson Institute for International Economics, 2011.

Haggard, Stephan, Marcus Noland, and Jaesung Ryu. "The 'June 28 Directive' and July 26 'Let Us Effect Kim Jong Il's Patriotism...': Not Yet Time to Break Out the Soju." *Working Paper Series*. Washington, D.C.: Peterson Institute for International Economics, August 6, 2012. <http://www.piie.com/blogs/nk/?p=7046>.

Harris, Marvin. *Cultural Materialism: The Struggle for a Science of Culture*. New York: Random House, 1972.

Harrison, Selig S. *Korean Endgame: A Strategy for Reunification and U.S. Disengagement*. Princeton, NJ: Princeton University Press, 2002.

Harvey, Frank. "President Al Gore and the 2003 Iraq War: A Counterfactual Critique of Conventional 'W'isdom."

Calgary: Canadian Defence and Foreign Affairs Institute, November 2008.

Haselden, Carl E., Jr. "The Effects of Korean Unification on the U.S. Military Presence in Northeast Asia." *Parameters* (Winter 2002/2003): 120–132.

Hassig, Ralph, and Kongdan Oh. *The Hidden People of North Korea: Everyday Life in the Hermit Kingdom*. Lanham, MD: Rowman and Littlefield, 2009.

Hawk, David. *Hidden Gulag: Exposing North Korea's Prison Camps*. Washington, D.C.: U.S. Committee for Human Rights in North Korea, 2003.

_____. *Hidden Gulag: The Lives and Voices of "Those Who Are Sent to the Mounatins."* 2d ed. Washington, D.C.: U.S. Committee for Human Rights in North Korea, 2012.

Hayes, Peter, and Scott Bruce. "North Korean Nuclear Nationalism and the Threat of Nuclear War in Korea." *Pacific Focus* 26, issue 1 (2011): 65–89.

Hayes, Peter, and David von Hippel. "North Korea's Collapse Pathways and the Role of the Energy Sector." In Suk Hi Kim, Terence Roehrig, and Bernhard Seliger, eds., *The Survival of North Korea: Essays on Strategy, Economics and International Relations*, 137–159. Jefferson, NC: McFarland, 2011.

Hesse, Volker, Manfred Voigt, Anneliese Sälzler, Sylvia Steinberg, Klaus Friese, Eberhard Keller, Ruth Gausche, and Reiner Eisele. "Alterations in Height, Weight, and Body Mass Index of Newborns, Children, and Young Adults in Eastern Germany after German Reunification." *Journal of Pediatrics* 142, issue 3 (2003): 259–262.

Hoffman, David E. *The Oligarchs: Wealth and Power in the New Russia*. New York: Public Affairs, 2011.

Holmes, James R. "The Sino-Japanese Naval War of 2012." *Foreign Policy*, August 20, 2012. <http://www.foreignpolicy.com/articles/2012/08/20/the_sino_japanese_naval_war_of_2012>.

Hsiao, L.C. Russell. "Strategic Implications of China's Access to the Rajin Port." *China Brief* X, issue 6 (March 18, 2010). <http://www.jamestown.org/programs/chinabrief/>.

Huat, Chua Beng, and Koichi Iwabuchi, eds. *East Asian Pop Culture: Analysis of the Korean Wave*. Hong Kong: Hong Kong University Press, 2008.

Hunt, Jennifer. "The Economics of German Reunification." *Dictionary of Economics*. New York: Palgrave Macmillan, 2006.

Huntington, Samuel P. *The Clash of Civilizations: And the Remaking of the World Order*. New York: Simon and Schuster, 1996.

Hwang, Eui-Gak. *The Search for a Unified Korea: Political and Economic Implications*. New York: Springer, 2010.

Index Mundi. <http://www.indexmundi.com/g/g.aspx?v=91&c=ja&l=en>.

International Centre for Prisons. <http://prisonstudies.org/>.

International Monetary Fund. 2012. <http://www.imf.org>.

Iraq Body Count. <http://www.iraqbodycount.org/>.

Iverson, Shepherd. "The Korean Peace Fund." *North Korean Review* 8, no. 2 (2012): 62–75.

Jacques, Martin. *When China Rules the World: The End of the Western World and the Birth of a New Global Order*. Second edition. New York: Penguin, 2012; orig. 2009).

Jeon, Young Sun. "Diagnosis and Assessment of North Korea's Sociocultural Sector." *International Journal of Korean Unification Studies* 20, no. 2 (2011): 91–120.

Ji, Flora. "Road paved but NKorea economic zone still building power stations, upgrading rail and ports." *Associated Press*, August 22, 2012.

Joo, Seung-Ho. "North Korea under Kim Jong-un: The Beginning of the End of a Peculiar Dynasty." *Pacific Focus* 27, no. 1 (April 2012): 1–9.

Kahneman, Daniel, and Amos Tversky. "Prospect Theory: An Analysis of Decision Under Risk." *Econometrica* 47, no. 2 (March 1997): 263–292.

Kang, Chol-Hwan, and Pierre Rigoulot. *The Aquariums of Pyongyang: Ten Years in the North Korean Gulag*. New York: Basic Books, 2001.

Kang, David C. *China Rising: Peace, Power, and Order in East Asia*. New York: Columbia University Press, 2007.

———. "They Think They're Normal: Enduring Questions and New Research on North Korea — A Review Essay." *International Security* 36, no. 3 (Winter 2011/2012): 142–171.

Kang, Wi Jo. *Christ and Caesar in Modern Korea: A History of Christianity and Politics*. Albany: State University of New York Press, 1997.

Keohane, Robert O. *After Hegemony: Cooperation and Discord in the World Political Economy*. Princeton, NJ: Princeton University Press, 1984.

Keohane, Robert O., and Joseph Nye. *Power and Interdependence*. New York: HarperCollins, 1977.

Khuong, M. VU. "Economic Reform and Performance: A Comparative Study of China and Vietnam." *China: An International Journal* 7, no. 2 (2009): 189–226.

Kihl, Young Whan. *Transforming Korean Politics: Democracy, Reform, and Culture*. Armonk, NY: East Gate Books, 2005.

Kim, Byung-Yeon. "Markets, Bribery, and Regime Change in North Korea." *EAI Asia Security Initiative Working Paper*, no. 4. Seoul: East Asia Institute, April 2010.

Kim, Byung-Yeon, and Dongho Song. "The Participation of North Korean Households in the Informal Economy: Size, Determinants, and Effect." *Seoul Journal of Economics* 21, no. 2 (2008): 361–385.

Kim, Choong Soon. *Kimchi and Information Technology: Tradition and Transformation in Korea*. Seoul: Ilchokak, 2007.

Kim, Heungkyu. "From a Buffer Zone to a Strategic Burden: Evolving Sino–North Korea Relations During the Hu Jintao Era." *Korean Journal of Defense Analysis* 22, no. 1 (2010): 55–74.

Kim, Jae Chang. "A Divided Korea and the Reunification Strategy." *International Journal of Korean Unification Studies* 18, no. 2 (2009): 64–85.

Kim, Jane. *Selling North Korea in the New Frontiers: Profit and Revolution in Cyberspace*. Emerging Voices, Vol. 22. Washington, D.C.: Korea Economic Institute, 2011.

Kim, Jin Ha. "In Search of Balance between Inducements and Sanctions: Evaluating the Lee Myung-bak Administration's North Korean Policy." *International Journal of Korean Unification Studies* 21, no. 1 (2012): 119–161.

———. "On the Threshold of Power, 2012/12: Pyongyang's Politics of Transition." *International Journal of Korean Unification Studies* 20, no. 2 (2011): 1–25.

Kim, Suk Hi. "Will North Korea Be Able to Overcome the Third Wave of Its Collapse?" In Suk Hi Kim, Terence Roehrig, and Bernhard Seliger, eds., *The Survival of North Korea: Essays on Strategy, Economics and International Relations*, 29–32. Jefferson, NC: McFarland, 2011.

Kim, Suk Hi, Junhua Jia, and Michael Whitty. "The Northeast Asian Energy Situation and the North Korean Factor." *North Korean Review* 7, no. 1 (2011): 78–86.

Kim, Suk Hi, Terence Roehrig, and Bernhard Seliger, eds. *The Survival of North Korea: Essays on Strategy, Economics and International Relations*. Jefferson, NC: McFarland, 2011.

Kim, Tae-Yeol, and Kwok Leung. "Forming and Reacting to Overall Fairness: A Cross-Cultural Comparison." *Orga-*

nizational Behavior and Human Decision Processes 104, no. 1 (2007): 83–95.

KINU (Korea Institute for National Unification). *The White Paper on Human Rights in North Korea, 2011.* Seoul: Korea Institute for National Unification, 2011. <http://www.kinu.or.kr/upload/neoboard/DATA04/hr2011.pdf>.

Kissinger, Henry. *On China.* New York: Penguin, 2011.

Kleine-Ahlbrandt, Stephanie. "The Diminishing Returns of China's North Korea Policy." *38 North,* U.S.–Korea Institute, November 28, 2012. <http://38north.org/2012/08/skahlbrandt081612/>.

Korea Economic Institute. *Korea's Economy: 2012.* Washington, D.C.: Korea Economic Institute, 2012.

Kotz, David M., and Fred Weir. *Russia's Path from Gorbachev to Putin: The Demise of the Soviet System and the New Russia.* New York: Routledge, 2007.

Kretchun, Nat, and Jane Kim. *A Quiet Opening: North Koreans in a Changing Media Environment.* Washington, D.C.: InterMedia, May 2012. <http://audiencescapes.org/sites/default/files/A_Quiet_Opening_FINAL_InterMedia.pdf>.

Kroeber, Alfred L. "Stimulus Diffusion." *American Anthropologist* 42, no. 1 (1940): 1–20.

Kuhn, Thomas. *The Structure of Scientific Revolutions.* Chicago: University of Chicago Press, 1962.

Kwak, Tae-Hwan. "The Korean Peninsula Peace Regime: How to Build It." *Pacific Focus* 24, no. 1 (2009): 43–60.

Kwon, Goohoon. "A United Korea? Reassessing North Korea Risks." *Goldman Sachs Global Economics Paper 188.* New York: Goldman Sachs, September 21, 2009.

Kwon, Heonik, and Byung-Ho Chung. *North Korea: Beyond Charismatic Politics.* Lanham, MD: Rowman and Littlefield, 2012.

Lake, David, and Robert Powell. *Strategic Choice and International Relations.* Princeton, NJ: Princeton University Press, 1999.

Lankov, Andrei. "Kim Jong-un's North Korea: What Should We Expect?" *International Journal of Korean Unification Studies* 21, no. 1 (2012): 1–19.

———. "Kim Serious About Reforms: Expert." *Starting Points,* September 1, 2012. http://starting-points.blogspot.kr/2012/09/kim-serious-about-reforms-expert.html.

———. "North Korea's Pools of Prosperity." *Asia Times,* July 7, 2012.

———. *North of the DMZ: Essays on the Daily Life in North Korea.* Jefferson, NC: McFarland, 2007.

———. "Staying Alive: Why North Korea Will Not Change." *Foreign Affairs* 87, no. 2 (March/April 2008): 9–16.

Lankov, Andrei, and Seok-hyang Kim. "North Korean Market Vendors: The Rise of Grassroots Capitalists in a Post-Stalinist Society." *Pacific Affairs* 81, no. 1 (2008): 53–72.

Lankov, Andrei, and In-ok Kwak. "The Decline of the North Korean Surveillance State." *North Korean Review* 7, no. 2 (2011): 6–21.

Lebow, Richard Ned. *A Cultural Theory of International Relations.* Cambridge: Cambridge University Press, 2008.

Lee, Cheoleon. "Gallup World Poll: Implications of Reunification of Two Koreas." *Gallup Poll Briefing,* October 2006.

Lee, Chi-dong. "U.S. pivots toward Asia due to 'real threats' from Pyongyang: Panetta." *Yonhap News,* September 17, 2012.

Lee, Julia Joo-A. "To Fuel or Not to Fuel: China's Energy Assistance to North Korea." *Asian Security* 5, no. 1 (2009): 45–72.

Lee, Kyo-Duk, et al. *Changes in North Korea as Revealed in the Testimonies of Saetomins.* Seoul: Korean Institute of National Unification, 2008.

Lee, Sanghee. "Toward a Peace Regime on the Korean Peninsula: A Way Forward for the ROK-US Alliance." Washington, D.C.: The Brookings Institution, May 2, 2007.

Lee, Sunny. "Chinese Perspectives on North Korea and Korean Unification." *Academic Paper Series*. Washington, D.C.: Korea Economic Institute, January 24, 2012.

———. "N.Korea in the eyes of Chinese journalist." *Korea Times*, May 8, 2010.

Lee, Suk. "The DPRK Famine of 1994–2000: Existence and Impact." Seoul: Korea Institute for National Reunification, May 2005. <http://www.kinu.or.kr/upload/neoboard/DATA05/05-06.pdf>.

Levitt, Steven D., and Stephen J. Dubner. *Freakonomics: A Rogue Economist Explores the Hidden Side of Everything*. New York: Penguin, 2006.

Levy, Jack S. "Prospect Theory, Rational Choice, and International Relations." *International Studies Quarterly* 41, no. 1 (1997): 87–112.

Lew, Seok-Choon. "Confucian Capitalism: Possibilities and Limits." *Korea Focus* 5, no. 4 (1997): 80–92.

Lim, Jae-Cheon, and InJoo Yoon. "Institutional Entrepreneurs in North Korea: Emerging Shadowy Private Enterprises Under Dire Economic Conditions." *North Korean Review* 7, no. 2 (2011): 82–93.

Lim, Jason. "What US doesn't get about Dokdo." *Korea Times*, August 24, 2012.

Lin, Justin Jifu. "Rural Reforms and Agricultural Growth in China." *American Economic Review* 82, no. 1 (1992): 34–51.

Lukin, Alexander. "Russia's Korea Policy in the 21st Century." *International Journal of Korean Unification Studies* 18, no. 2 (2009): 30–63.

Lynn, Hyung Gu. *Bipolar Orders: The Two Koreas Since 1989*. London: Zed Books, 2007.

Mansourov, Alexandre. "Part I: A Dynamically Stable Regime." *38 North*, U.S.–Korea Institute, December 17, 2012. <http://38north.org/2012/12/amansourov121712/>.

Manyin, Mark, and Mary Beth Nikitin. "Foreign Assistance to North Korea." Washington, D.C.: Congressional Research Service, March 20, 2012.

Martin, Bradley K. *Under the Loving Care of the Fatherly Leader: North Korea and the Kim Dynasty*. New York: St. Martin's Press, 2004.

McEachern, Patrick. *Inside the Red Box*. New York: Columbia University Press, 2010.

McGregor, Richard. *The Party: The Secret World of China's Communist Rulers*. New York: Harper Perennial, 2012.

Mearsheimer, John J. *The Tragedy of Great Power Politics*. New York: W. W. Norton, 2003.

Medeiros, Evan S. *Chasing the Dragon: Assessing China's System of Export Controls for WMD-Related Goods and Technologies*. Santa Monica, CA: RAND Corporation, 2005. <http://www.rand.org/pubs/monographs/2005/RAND_MG353.pdf>.

Michishita, Narushige. "Japan's Response to Nuclear North Korea." In Gilbert Rozman, ed., *Asia at a Tipping Point: Korea, the Rise of China, and the Impact of Leadership Transitions*, 99–112. Washington, D.C.: Korea Economic Institute, 2012. <http://www.keia.org/sites/default/files/publications/tipping_point_full_book_final_version.pdf>.

Mitsuhiro, Mimura. "Outlook for North Korean Economic Reform and Marketization." *International Journal of Korean Unification Studies* 20, no. 2 (2011): 69–90.

Moon, Chung-in. *The Sunshine Policy: In Defense of Engagement as a Path to Peace in Korea*. Seoul: Yonsei University Press, 2012.

Moore, Gregory J. "America's Failed North Korea Nuclear Policy: A New

Approach." *Asian Perspectives* 32, no. 4 (2008): 9–27.

Morgenthau, Hans. *Politics Among Nations: The Struggle for Power and Peace.* New York: Knopf, 1949.

———. *Scientific Man vs. Power Politics.* Chicago: University of Chicago Press, 1967.

Muravchik, Joshua, and Stephen M. Walt. "The Neocons vs. the Realists." *National Interest* (September/October 2008): 20–36.

Myers, B.R. *The Cleanest Race: How North Koreans See Themselves and Why It Matters.* New York: Melville House Publishing, 2010.

Namkung, K.A. "US Leadership in the Rebuilding of the North Korean Economy." In Marcus Noland, ed., *Economic Integration of the Korean Peninsula: Special Report.* Washington, D.C.: Peterson Institute for International Economics, 1998.

Nanto, Dick K., and Mark E. Manyin. "China–North Korea Relations." Washington, D.C.: Congressional Research Service, December 28, 2010. <http://www.fas.org/sgp/crs/row/R41043.pdf>.

Naughton, Barry. *Growing Out of the Plan: Chinese Economic Reform, 1978–1993.* Cambridge: Cambridge University Press, 1995.

Nincic, Miroslav. "Getting What You Want: Positive Inducements in International Relations." *International Security* 35, no. 1 (2010): 138–183.

Noland, Marcus, ed. "The Economics of Korean Unification." *Working Paper.* Washington, D.C.: Peterson Institute for International Economics, 2000. <http://www.iie.com/publications/wp/wp.cfm?ResearchID=154>.

———. *Integration of the Korean Peninsula.* Washington, D.C.: Institute for International Economics, 1997.

———. "North Korean Economic Performance in 2011." Washington, D.C.: Peterson Institute of International Economics, 2012. <http://www.piie.com/blogs/nk/?p=7072>.

———. "Pyongyang Tipping Point: Currency 'Reform' Sparked an Economic Crisis That the Regime May Not Be Able to Repair." *Wall Street Journal*, April 16, 2010.

———. "Telecoms in North Korea: Has Orascom Made the Connection?" *North Korean Review* 5, no. 1 (2009): 62–74.

Noland, Marcus, Sherman Robinson, and Tao Wang. "Modeling Korean Unification." *Journal of Comparative Economics* 28, issue 2 (2000): 400–421.

Nye, Joseph S. *The Future of Power.* New York: Public Affairs, 2011.

———. "Soft Power." *Foreign Policy* 80 (1990): 153–171.

———. *Soft Power: The Means to Success in World Politics.* New York: Public Affairs, 2004.

Oberdorfer, Don. *The Two Koreas: A Contemporary History.* New York: Basic Books, 2001.

Oh, Kongdan, and Ralph C. Hassig. *North Korea: Through the Looking Glass.* Washington, D.C.: Brookings Institution Press, 2000.

O'Hanlon, Michael, and Mike M. Mochizuki. *Crisis on the Korean Peninsula: How to Deal with a Nuclear North Korea.* New York: McGraw-Hill, 2003.

Olival, Kevin J., and Hiroyoshi Higuchi. "Monitoring the Long-Distance Movement of Wildlife in Asia Using Satellite Telemetry." In Jeffrey A. McNeely, Thomas M. McCarthy, Andrew T. Smith, Linda Olsvig-Whittaker, and Eric D. Wikramanayake, eds., *Conservation Biology in Asia.* Kathmandu, Nepal: Society for Conservation Biology, 2006.

Onuf, Nicholas. *World of Our Making: Rules and Rule in Social Theory and International Relations.* Columbia: University of South Carolina Press, 1989.

Paige, Glenn D. "Korean Leadership for Nonkilling East Asian Common Security." *Korea Observer*, no. 37 (2006): 547–563.

———. "The Nonviolent Approach to Korean Reunification." In Michael Hass, ed., *Korean Reunification: Alternative Pathways*, 71–88. Los Angeles: Publishinghouse for Scholars, 2012.

Pak, Sunyoung. "The Growth Status of Refugee Children in China." *Korea Journal* 43, no. 3 (2003): 165–190.

Park, Hyeong Jung. "Political Dynamics of Hereditary Succession in North Korea." *International Journal of Korean Unification Studies* 20, no. 1 (2011): 1–30.

Park, Hyeong Jung, and So Yeol Kim. "NK Public 60%–23% in Favor of Change." *DailyNK*, February 27, 2012. <http://www.dailynk.com/english/total_list.php>.

Park, Joanne Min-Young. "Borderwall: Peace and the Future of the Korean Demilitarized Zone." Dissertation, Rice University, Houston, TX, 2008.

Park, Myounh-Kyu, and Philo Kim. "Inter-Korean Relations in Nuclear Politics." *Asian Perspective* 34, no. 1 (2010): 111–135.

Perry, Charles M., and James L. Schoff. "Consensus Building and Peace Regime Building on the Korean Peninsula." *International Journal of Korean Unification Studies* 19, no. 1 (2010): 1–28.

Piazolo, Marc. "Could South Korea Afford German-Style Reunification?" *Economics of Korean Reunification* 2, no. 2 (1997): 48–63.

Pierson, Paul. "Increasing Returns, Path Dependence, and the Study of Politics." *American Political Science Review* 94, no. 2 (2000): 251–267.

Pollack, Joshua. "The Evolution of North Korea's Ballistic Missile Market." *Nonproliferation Review* 18, no. 2 (July 2011): 411–429.

———. *No Exit: North Korea, Nuclear Weapons, and International Security*. New York: Routledge, 2011.

Ramo, Joshua Cooper. *The Age of the Unthinkable: Why the New World Disorder Constantly Surprises Us*. New York: Little, Brown, 2009.

Rathbun, Brian C. "Uncertain and Uncertainty: Understanding the Multiple Meanings of a Crucial Concept in International Relations Theory." *International Studies Quarterly* 51, no. 3 (2007): 533–557.

Reid, T.R. *Confucius Lives Next Door: What Living in the East Teaches Us About Living in the West*. New York: Random House, 1999.

Richardson, Michael. "Asia's Middle East Oil Dependence: Chokepoints on a Vital Maritime Supply Line." Institute of Southeast Asian Studies, *Trends in Southeast Asia Series*, Vol. 1 (2007). <http://www.iseas.edu.sg/tr12007.pdf>.

Rickards, James. *Currency Wars: The Making of the Next Global Crisis*. New York: Penguin, 2011.

Ries, Nancy. *Russian Talk: Culture and Conversation During Perestroika*. Ithaca, NY: Cornell University Press, 1997.

Robinson, Colin, and Stephen H. Baker. "Stand-off with North Korea: War Scenarios and Consequences." Unclassified summary of a National Intelligence Estimate (2003). <http://www.cdi.org/north-korea/north-korea-crisis.pdf>.

Robinson, Cortland, Myung Ken Lee, Kenneth Hill, and Gilbert M. Burnham. "Mortality in North Korean Migrant Households: A Retrospective Study." *Lancet* 354 (1999): 291–295.

Roehrig, Terence. "Creating the Conditions for Peace in Korea: Promoting Incremental Change in North Korea." *Korea Observer* 40, no. 1 (2009).

Rothkopf, David. *Superclass: The Global Power Elite and the World They Are Making*. New York: Farrar, Straus, and Giroux, 2008.

Schwekendiek, Daniel. *A Socioeconomic History of North Korea*. Jefferson, NC: McFarland, 2011.

Shepard, Kevin. "Rethinking Engagement on the Korean Peninsula: Confidence to Trust to Peace." *International Journal of Korean Unification Studies* 19, no. 1 (2010): 94–125.

Shin, Gi-Wook. *Ethnic Nationalism in Korea: Genealogy, Politics, and Legacy.* Stanford, CA: Stanford University Press, 2006.

Shin, Lin. "The Mineral Industry in North Korea." *Minerals Yearbook, 2009.* Reston, VA: U.S. Geological Survey, 2009. <http://minerals.usgs.gov/minerals/pubs/country/2009/myb3-2009-kn.pdf>.

Sinn, Gerlinde, and Hans-Werner Sinn. *Jumpstart: The Economic Unification of Germany.* Cambridge, MA: MIT Press, 1992.

Snyder, Scott. "Changes in Seoul's North Korean Policy and Implications for Pyongyang's Inter-Korean Diplomacy." In Kyung-Ae Park, ed., *New Challenges of North Korean Foreign Policy*, 153–172. New York: Palgrave Macmillan, 2010.

Snyder, Scott, and See-Won Byun. "China-Korea Relations: China Embraces South and North, but Differently." *Comparative Connections* 11, no. 4 (January 2009): 97–106.

Snyder, Scott, and Kyung-Ae Park. "North Korea in Transition: Evolution or Revolution." In Kyung-Ae Park and Scott Snyder, eds., *North Korea Transition: Politics, Economy, and Society*, 275–294. Lanham, MD: Rowman and Littlefield, 2013.

Solzhenitsyn, Aleksandr. *The Gulag Archipelago: 1918–1956.* New York: Harper and Row, 1973.

Son, Key-young. *South Korean Engagement Policies and North Korea: Identities, Norms and the Sunshine Policy.* New York: Routledge, 2006.

Song, Jooyoung. "Understanding China's Response to North Korea's Provocations: The Duel Threats Model." *Asian Survey* 51, no. 6 (2011): 1134–1155.

Spezza, Gianluca. "Why North Koreans Won't Be Fleeing South After Unification." Interview of Song Young Hoon. *NK News*, February 19, 2013. <http://www.nknews.org/2013/02/why-north-koreans-wont-be-fleeing-south-after-unification/>.

Spina, Marion P. "Brushes with the Law: North Korea and the Rule of Law." *Korea Economic Institute* 2, no. 6 (June 2007). <http://www.keia.org/publication/brushes-law-north-korea-and-rule-law>.

St. Brown, Max, Seung Mo Choi, and Hyung Seok Kim. "Korean Economic Integration: Prospects and Pitfalls." *International Economic Journal* 26, no. 3 (2012): 471–485.

Stangarone, Troy, and Nicholas Hamisevicz. "The Prospects for Economic Reform in North Korea after Kim Jong-il and the China Factor." *International Journal of Korean Unification Studies* 20, no. 2 (2011): 175–197.

Stoessinger, John. *Why Nations Go to War.* Tenth edition. Belmont, CA: Thomson Wadsworth, 2008.

Stradiotto, Gary, and Sujian Guo. "Market Socialism in North Korea: A Comparative Perspective." *Journal of the Asia Pacific Economy* 12, no. 2 (2007): 188–214.

Swartz, Peter M. "Rising Powers and Naval Power." In Philip C. Saunders, Christopher D. Yung, Michael Swaine, and Andrew Nien-Dzu Yang, eds., *The Chinese Navy: Expanding Capabilities, Evolving Roles.* Washington, D.C.: National Defense University, 2011.

Taleb, Nassim Nicholas. *The Black Swan: The Impact of the Highly Improbable.* New York: Penguin, 2008.

Tao, Xie. "What's Wrong with China's North Korean Policy." Carnegie Endowment for International Peace, March 26, 2013. <http://www.carnegieendowment.org/2013/03/26/what-swrong-with-china-s-north-korea-policy/ftjw>.

Tapscott, Don, and Anthony D. Williams. *Macrowikinomics: Rebooting Business and the World*. New York: Portfolio/Penguin, 2010.

Taylor, Mi Ae, and Mark E. Manyin. *Non-Governmental Organizations' Activities in North Korea*. Washington, D.C.: Congressional Research Service, 2011.

Tetlock, Phillip E. *Expert Political Judgment: How Good Is It? How Can We Know?* Princeton, NJ: Princeton University Press, 2005.

Thayer, Nate. "North Korea: A Mafia Crime State." Unpublished paper. <http://natethayer.typepad.com/blog/2011/12/north-korea-a-mafia-crime-state-by-nate-thayer.html>.

Thompson, Drew. *Silent Partners: Chinese Joint Ventures in North Korea*. Washington, D.C.: U.S.–Korea Institute, February 2011.

Ting-Toomey, Stella. "The Matrix of Face: An Updated Face-Negotiation Theory." In William B. Gudykunst, ed., *Theorizing About Intercultural Communication*, 71–92. Thousand Oaks, CA: Sage, 2005.

Tisdall, Simon. "Wikileaks Cables Reveal China 'Ready to Abandon North Korea.'" *The Guardian*, November 29, 2010. <http://www.guardian.co.uk/world/2010/nov/29/wikileaks-cables-china-reunified-korea>.

Toloraya, Georgy. "Russian Policy in Korea in a Time of Change." *Korean Journal of Defense Analysis* 21, no. 1 (March 2009): 67–84.

Turner, Scott. "Global Civil Society, Anarchy and Governance: Assessing an Emerging Paradigm." *Journal of Peace Research* 35, no. 1 (1998): 25–42.

United Nations. *By Choice, Not By Chance: Family Planning, Human Rights and Development*. State of World Population 2012. New York: United Nations Populations Fund, 2012.

United States Naval Institute. "Report: Chinese Develop Special 'Kill Weapon' to Destroy U.S. Aircraft Carriers." March 31, 2009. <http://www.usni.org/news-and-features/chinese-kill-weapon>.

Walt, Stephen M. "International Relations: One World, Many Theories." *Foreign Policy*, no. 110 (Spring 1998): 29–45.

———. *The Origins of Alliances*. Ithaca, NY: Cornell University Press, 1987.

Waltz, Kenneth N. *Man, the State, and War: A Theoretical Analysis*. New York: Columbia University Press, 2001; orig. 1959.

———. "Realist Thought and Neorealist Theory." In Robert L. Rothstein, ed., *The Evolution of Theory in International Relations*, 21–38. Columbia: University of South Carolina Press, 1991.

Watts, Jonathan, and Tania Branigan. "North Korea's Leader Will Not Last Long, Says Kim Jong-un's Brother." *The Guardian*, January 17, 2012. <http://www.guardian.co.uk/world/2012/jan/17/north-korea-leader-not-long>.

Weitz, Richard. "Moscow Ponders Korea Unification." *International Journal of Korean Unification Studies* 20, no. 1 (2011): 123–154.

Wendt, Alexander. *Social Theory of International Politics*. Cambridge: Cambridge University Press, 1999.

Williams, Michael C. *The Realist Tradition and the Limits of International Relations*. Cambridge: Cambridge University Press, 2005.

Wilson, David Sloan. *Evolution for Everyone: How Darwin's Theory Can Change the Way We Think About Our Lives*. New York: Random House, 2007.

Wolf, Charles, Jr., and Kamil Akramov. *North Korean Paradoxes: Circumstances, Costs, and Consequences of Korean Unification*. Santa Monica, CA: RAND Corporation, 2005.

Wolf, Holger. "Korean Unification: Lessons from Germany." In Marcus Noland, ed., *Integration of the Korean*

Peninsula, 165–190. Washington, D.C.: Institute for International Economics, 1997.

Woo, Seongji. "North Korea as a Transformer: From a Fortress State to an Amphibious State." *East Asian Institute Working Paper*, no. 8 (2010): 2–22. <http://www.eai.or.kr/data/bbs/eng_report/2011041513523127.pdf>.

Worldcrunch. "China Eyes Big Investment Opportunities in North Korea." November 6, 2012. <http://worldcrunch.com/business-finance/china-eyes-big-investment-opportunities-in-north-korea/north-korea-jvic-commerce-investing/c2s10050/>.

Yang, Un-Chul. "Reform without Transition: The Economic Situation in North Korea since the July 1, 2002, Measures." *North Korean Review* 6, no. 1 (2010): 71–87.

Yonhap News Agency. "Inter-Korean trade surges 36 percent this year." March 16, 2012.

———. "N. Korea threatens nuclear war amid looming regional diplomacy." December 17, 2010.

Yoon, Edward. "Status and Future of the North Korean Minerals Sector." *Korean Journal of Defense Analysis* 23, no. 2 (June 2011): 191–210.

Young, Sodgil, Chang-Jae Lee, and Hyoungsoo Zang. "Preparing for the Economic Integration of Two Koreas: Policy Challenges to South Korea." In Marcus Noland, ed., *Integration of the Korean Peninsula*, 251–272. Washington, D.C.: Institute for International Economics, 1997.

Yuwen, Deng. "Should China Abandon North Korea?" *Financial Times*, February 27, 2013.

Zakaria, Fareed. "North Korea's High-Stakes Bluster." *Washington Post*, March 14, 2013.

———. *The Post-American World*. New York: W. W. Norton, 2008.

Zhan, Debin, and Hun Kyung Lee. "Chinese People's Understanding of the Korean Unification Issue." *Asian Social Science* 8, no. 3 (2012): 63–74.

Zhao, Suisheng. *A Nation-State by Construction: Dynamics of Modern Chinese Nationalism*. Stanford, CA: Stanford University Press, 2004.

Index

Abe, Shinzo 81, 96
accountability of North Korean regime 55–56
Acharya, Amitav 33
agriculture in North Korea 39, 80, 120; *see also* North Korean food supply and distribution; North Korean rural farmers
Ahamed, Liaquat 147
aid to North Korea *see* North Korea, foreign aid to
airline travel to Korea 141
amnesty for human rights abuses 28, 60–61, 95
Arab Spring revolutions 2, 28, 45
Arirang 140, 168n71
Arirang Mass Games 140
Armstrong, Charles 32
Asian Development Bank 119
Asian Economic Crisis (1997–1998) 120, 166n18
"Asian values" hypothesis 33
Association of Southeast Asian Nations (ASEAN) 18, 150(intro.)n14
assumptions in international relations theories 30
Austronesian Expansion 151n18
authoritarian control in North Korea 27–28, 38, 40–41, 50
automobile industry 137
"axis of evil" 31, 152n7

balance-of-threat theory 82
ballistic missiles, Chinese 8, 18; *see also* North Korean nuclear weapons/missile program
banking in North Korea 45–46, 69, 111, 114–116; *see also* North Korean economy
Bates, Gill 82
Becker, Gary 20, 35–36, 105–106
bicycles in North Korea 57
billionaires 11, 19, 22, 87, 146
"black swan" events 53, 94, 151ch1n4
border between North Korea and China 26, 47, 51, 77, 89, 123, 131

bottom-up vs. top-down pressures for reunification 25, 69
Bradford, Scott 125
bribery and corruption in North Korea: among military officers 43, 65; collapse of food delivery system and 39–40; as destabilizing government control 27–28, 42–43; growth of markets and 89–90; illegal foreign cultural content and 49; prevention of, in reunified Korea 118
Buzan, Barry 33
Byman, Daniel 38

cars in North Korea 57, 137, 162n29; *see also* transportation and travel in North Korea
Ceausescu, Nicolae 28, 59
censorship in North Korea 48, 138
Central Committee of the Communist Party of China 27, 72, 74–75, 151n15, 161n11
Cha, Victor 34, 50, 59–60, 83, 85, 93, 99, 128, 136, 164n16
Chadwick, Richard 97, 102
Chang, Yoonok 43
change in North Korea, socioeconomic context for 36–37, 47–52, 51f
Chanlett-Avery, Emma 38
chemical weapons in North Korea 85
Cheonan sinking 44, 93
China: agricultural productivity 121; aid to North Korea 13, 72, 75, 78, 155n8; border with North Korea 26, 47, 51, 77, 89, 123, 131; Central Committee of 27, 72, 74–75, 151n15, 161n11; defense spending 5; foreign policy toward North Korea 72–75, 82–83; free trade with Japan and Korea 99, 128; Hong Kong integration with 92, 116; interests in Korean reunification 15–17, 83–84, 99, 161n15; interests in stability in Northeast Asia 98; investment in North Korea 76, 127–128; Korean Peace Fund contributions 83; market reforms in 77, 121, 122–125; missile program 8, 18; North Korean natural resources and 16, 82–83, 99, 119, 130; North Korean nuclear arms program

185

Index

and 9, 13, 15–16, 85, 163n53; North Korean refugees in 131; relations with Taiwan 73, 161n8; support for North Korean regime 21; territorial disputes 7–8, 75; trade with North Korea 44, 50; trade with South Korea 127–128; trade with United States 86
Choi, Myeong-hae 73
Chongjin port 83
Chung, Byung-Ho 140, 168n71
churches in reunified North Korea 142
civil society in reunified North Korea 32–33, 117–118
coal in North Korea 120; see also North Korean natural/mineral resources
collective political action 32–33, 97
"comfort women" 81
communication in North Korea see North Korea, communication in
Comrade Kim Goes Flying (film) 140–141
"Confucian capitalism" 124
Confucian values 33, 67, 113
constructivist theories 32
consumer goods 13, 39, 43, 55, 123–125, 155n8
cooperation and human nature 87–88
corporations, multinational 18–19, 86–87, 99, 142
corruption in North Korea see bribery and corruption in North Korea
Cosa Nostra (Italy) 44
coup d'état prospects in North Korea 101, 159n17
credit rating 119
Credit Suisse 68
Cronin, Patrick 50
cultural diffusion, generally 151n5
cultural diffusion in North Korea see North Korea, cultural diffusion in
currency of North Korea 13, 55–56, 76–77, 96, 116, 150n4, 159n23; see also foreign currency in North Korea; North Korean economy
Cyber Village initiative 138–139

defection from Soviet Union 54
defector reports on North Korea see North Korean defector reports
defectors and refugees from North Korea see North Korean defectors and refugees
defense spending 5, 16, 63, 98, 149n1, 149n3
Delury, John 77
Demick, Barbara 41
demilitarized zone (DMZ) 131
democratic voting rights in reunified Korea 70
Deng Xiaoping 124
Denmark, Abraham 93
denuclearization of North Korea see North Korean nuclear weapons/missile program
denuclearization of Soviet satellite states 27
deterrence 9, 33, 93, 164n15
digital communication, general effects of 33, 35
digital technology in North Korea see Internet; North Korea, communication in
Dingli, Shen 73
diplomacy to North Korea 31, 33–34, 147
dissent in North Korea 47, 56, 58, 89; see also North Korean defectors and refugees
Dokdo-Takeshima territorial dispute 8, 85–86, 163n56
Dubner, Stephen 35
Dwivedi, Sangit Sarita 73, 82
dynastic transition 9, 96

East Asia see Northeast Asia
East China Sea 7, 81
East Sea/Sea of Japan 83, 162n41
economy, informal see North Korean economy
education in North Korea 69, 112–113, 149n4
electricity supply to North Korea 70, 97, 119–120, 129
elites in North Korea see North Korean party elites
elites in Soviet Union 53–54
empathy for North Korean leadership/elite 25, 37, 51, 95, 103
energy supply in North Korea 39, 57, 70, 84, 119–120, 121, 155n8; see also North Korean natural/mineral resources; nuclear energy in South Korea
engagement between North and South Korea 96, 157n59; see also Sunshine Policy (South Korea)
ethnic/race-based nationalism and prejudice 6–7, 83, 86, 96, 132, 149nn5–6, 162n41
Eurocentrism 33
Everard, John 134
exchange-trust networks in North Korea 43, 51, 89
expropriation of assets 76, 127, 161n21

face-saving solutions to reunification 25, 27, 63–64
family in Korean culture 67, 126, 129
family reunions 136
famine and starvation in North Korea 13, 39–40, 57, 77, 89, 155n5; see also North Korean food supply and distribution
farmers see agriculture in North Korea; North Korean food supply and distribution; North Korean rural farmers
fear as motivator 31–32, 36–37, 82
Ferrie, Alan 80
Flower Girl (North Korean opera) 140

186

Index

food supply and distribution in North Korea *see* North Korean food supply and distribution

foreign aide to North Korea *see* North Korea, foreign aid to

foreign currency in North Korea 41, 44, 46, 57, 83–84, 90; *see also* currency of North Korea; North Korean economy

foreign investment in North Korea 12, 49, 75–76, 120, 141

fragile equilibrium 21, 28, 42

free trade union of China, Japan and Korea 99, 128

G20 19, 70, 87
Gaddafi, Muammar 18, 28, 59
Galbraith, John Kenneth 60
"Gangnam Style" 7, 149n10, 168n74
Geiger, Till 37
geopolitical alliances 81–85
German reunification: costs of 68; migration out of East Germany 126, 131; nutritional improvements 135; privatization of state resources in 118, 122, 125, 166n11; similarities and differences to Korean reunification 91–92, 116, 165–166n7; wage and price increases 123, 124

gift-giving vs. bribery 42–43
glasnost (Soviet Union) 53
global economy: Korean partition as threat to 10, 22, 86–87; multinational corporations' power in 18–19, 34; Northeast Asian conflict and 8

Goldman Sachs study on Korean reunification 91–92, 129; mineral deposits 45

Gorbachev, Mikhail 14, 28, 53–55, 79, 158n2

Guard Command, Korean Peace Fund payments to 65–66

gulag prison system 28, 60–61, 90, 95, 136

Haggard, Stephan 26, 43, 46, 55, 77, 89, 121
hallyu (South Korean popular culture) 48–50, 143, 157n58–59

hard currency, North Korean need for *see* currency of North Korea; foreign currency in North Korea; North Korean economy

hard-power diplomacy 31, 33–35, 37, 51–52, 62, 94, 102

Harrison, Selig 47
Hassig, Ralph 42, 43, 48–49, 50, 114
Havel, Vaclav 50
Hayes, Peter 58
health care in reunified North Korea 98, 134–135, 141

Hebei oil spill 142
Hippel, David von 58
Hoffman, David 55

Hong Kong, reintegration into China 92, 116
human rights abuses in North Korea 28, 60–61, 95, 136

Huntington, Samuel 95, 150n6
Hyundai (corporation) 76, 119

idealism vs. materialism in international relations theories 31–34, 63, 144, 146

identification cards 115
ideology vs. pragmatism in North Korea 36–37, 41, 46, 53–54, 90, 123–124

incentives: in behavioral microeconomic models 35–36; honor and prestige as 14, 27–28, 63–64, 79, 102; individual choice and 78; lack of state-owned resources to act as 59; North Korean natural resources as reunification incentive to South Korea 79–80, 93; overview 20, 25–26; personal security as 28, 37, 59–61, 95, 103; wealth and prosperity as 12, 28, 37, 59; *see also* Korean Peace Fund

individual choice model of social behavior 78

informal economy in North Korea *see* North Korean economy

informal economy in Soviet Union 55
information flows in North Korea *see* North Korea, communication in

infrastructure in North Korea *see under* North Korea

intelligence on North Korea 38
international community: funding for Korean Peace Fund 19, 79, 87, 98, 146, 164n62, 169n2; interests in Korean reunification 15–17, 79, 86–87; role in reunification signing ceremony 106; support for Korean Peace Fund model 70, 75

International Monetary Fund 119, 159n25
international relations theories 20, 30, 158n3
Internet: as educational tool in reunified North Korea 116, 117, 124, 126; effects on Chinese policy toward North Korea 74–75; infrastructure in North Korea 69–70, 138; North Korean access to 97, 138, 157–158n65

Iran 8, 17, 84, 85
Israel 84–85

Japan: citizens abducted by North Korea 155n7; as confounding North/South Korean re-engagement 96; defense spending 5; economy 119; free trade union with China and Korea 99, 128; imperialism and territorial disputes 6–8, 81, 85–86, 162n41; interests for/against Korean reunification 17, 80–82, 99; investment in reunified North Korea 127; reparations to South Korea 80–81, 149nn8–9

187

Index

Jerusalem of Korea 142
Jilin province 16
Jobs, Steve 146, 169n3
Joo, Seung-Ho 59
Juche system 37, 154n37
Juche Tower 107, 140

K-pop (South Korean popular music) 48–49, 108, 143
Kaesong Industrial Project 44, 76, 127, 128, 152n9, 156n38
Kang, David 60, 136
Kim, Byung-Yeon 28, 42
Kim, Jane 49
Kim, Jin-Ha 46
Kim, Seok-hyang 69
Kim Dae-jung 14, 31, 96
Kim family 59–60, 63–64
Kim Il-sung 40, 102
Kim Il-sung Square 107, 140
Kim Jong-il 40–41, 102, 168n69
Kim Jong-nam 59
Kim Jong-un 23, 100, 101; biography 23, 151n18, 154n37; incentives for reunification 14–15, 59–60, 63–64, 102; legitimacy as leader 56; popular support for 50, 77; as potential Nobel Peace Prize winner 10, 14, 60, 102, 107; regency of elder statesmen 99–101; at reunification signing ceremony 107
Kim regime: authoritarian tools used by 38; dynastic transition 96; symbolic destruction of 168n69; vulnerability of 50, 59, 78–79
Kissinger, Henry 73
Kleine-Ahlbrandt, Stephanie 75
Korea see North Korea; reunified Korea; reunified North Korea; South Korea
Korean Peace Fund: administration of 70; as alternative to war 145–146; backfiring possibility 102; empathy in 25, 37, 51, 95, 103; exclusions from payout 21, 78; failure of conventional thinking and 94–95; funding of 16–17, 19, 20, 79, 87, 98, 146, 164n62, 169n2; honor and prestige incentives 14, 25, 27–28, 63–64, 79, 102; inequality in 68; international community support for 70, 75; likelihood of adoption 1, 3; market reforms and reunification 69–71; military receptiveness to 46–47; moral objections to 2, 28, 60–61, 95; as new Sunshine Policy 96; North Korean defectors and 133; overview 62–63; path dependencies and 87; payment allocations 67–68; personal safety incentives 20, 25, 28, 37, 59–61, 95, 103; Price of Peace Equation 63–67; refugees, payments to 131; as a tipping point 97, 104; wealth incentives 12, 28, 37,
59; word-of-mouth campaign 69; see also incentives; reunification of Korea
Korean revolutionary history 168n71
Korean War 11, 145
Kotz, David 53–54
Kretchun, Nat 49
Kroeber, Alfred L. 151n5
Kuril islands territorial dispute 85
Kwon, Goohoon 91–92
Kwon, Heonik 140, 168n71

labor camps 28, 60–61, 90, 95, 136
labor markets in reunified Korea 92, 114, 120–121, 122, 128–129, 167n47
labor migration see reunified Korea, internal migration in
landmines 131
Lankov, Andrei 40, 46, 47, 49, 55, 69, 77, 94, 162n29
lawyers 118
Lee, Hun Kyung 127
Lee, Myung-bak 31, 50, 63, 96, 159–160n5
Lee, Sunny 74
Levitt, Steven 35
liberal realist (smart-power) theory 20, 30–31
Lim, Jae-Cheon 43
Lim, Jason 86
Lind, Jennifer 38
luxury goods 13, 39, 78, 97

malnutrition and stunted growth 135; see also North Korean food supply and distribution
Manju group (descendents of anti-Japanese guerrillas) 45
Mansourov, Alexandre 56
maritime territorial boundary disputes 6, 18, 81, 86
market socialism in North Korea 44, 156n36
marketization of North Korean economy 40–43, 51, 69, 89, 123
Martin, Bradley 94
materialism vs. idealism in international relations theories 31–34, 63, 144, 146
McEachern, Patrick 40
Mearsheimer, John 31
medical care in reunified North Korea 98, 134–135, 141
microeconomic models 35–36
Middle East 84–85
"military first" policies (North Korea) 37, 46, 77
millionaires in South Korea vs. North Korea 64–65
mineral resources in North Korea see North Korean natural/mineral resources

Index

missile program in North Korea *see* North Korean nuclear weapons/missile program
Mitsuhiro, Mimura 42, 76, 125
mobile phones in North Korea 45, 49, 58, 59, 69, 90; *see also* North Korea, communication in
Moon, Chung-in 51
Morgenthau, Hans 20, 31, 36–37, 152n3
Mount Kumgang tourism project 152n9
multinational corporations 18–19, 86–87, 99, 142
"Mutual Benefit and common Prosperity" policy (South Korea) 31

nation-states, power of multinational corporations vs. 18–19, 86–87
nationalism, race-based 6–7, 83, 86, 96, 132, 149n5
natural/mineral resources in North Korea *see* North Korean natural/mineral resources
Naughton, Barry 121, 123–124
neoliberalism 31–32
neorealist policies 31, 34
"new generation" in North Korea 45
New Village Movement 142
Nincic, Miroslav 56
Nobel Peace Prize 10, 14, 60, 101–102, 107
Noland, Marcus 26, 32, 43, 55, 77, 80–81, 89, 116, 121, 165–166n7
nongovernmental organizations (NGOs) in reunified North Korea 114–115, 134–136
non-state actors *see* billionaires; multinational corporations
North Hamgyong revolt (1995) 58
North Korea: agriculture 39, 80, 120; airline travel to 141; alliance with China 82–83; authoritarian control in 27–28, 38, 40–41, 50; as "axis of evil" member 31, 152n7; banking system 45–46, 69, 111, 114–116; border with China 26, 47, 51, 77, 89, 123, 131; as buffer between China and South Korea 72; censorship in 48, 138; centenary celebrations 56, 158n11; chemical weapons 85; children in 64, 65, 103, 109; coup d'état prospects 101, 159n17; culture of 67; dissent in 47, 56, 58, 89; economic disparity with South Korea 34–35, 47–48, 76, 90, 154n29; education in 69, 112–113, 149n4; energy and electricity supply 39, 57, 70, 84, 97, 119–120, 121, 129, 155n8; ethnocentrism of 132; exchange-trust networks in 43, 51, 89; expropriation of South Korean and Chinese assets 76, 127, 161n21; foreign investment in 12, 49, 75–76, 120, 141; human rights abuses 28, 60–61, 95, 136; ideology vs. pragmatism in 36–37, 41, 46, 53–54, 90, 123–124; incentives for making peace 12–14, 25, 28; infrastructure 69–70, 112–114, 122, 137, 138; intelligence on 38; Japanese citizens abducted by 155n7; labor force as asset to South Korea 92, 128, 156n48; literacy levels 69, 132; material benefits of reunification 79–80; outside world awareness 26–27, 47–49, 56–57, 78; path dependencies in 34, 95, 103; as point of conflict between U.S. and China 9, 150n6; political transition and prospects for peace 10, 27; ports 77, 83, 99, 127; prison system 28, 60–61, 90, 95, 136; propaganda 55–56, 90; provinces of 58; public executions 90; radio/television broadcasting in 48–49, 69, 108, 116, 138, 143; re-engagement with South Korea 96; religion in 142; sanctions against 50–51, 74, 76, 161n10, 161n22; shared culture with South Korea 95, 132; smuggling foreign products into 47, 49; socio-economic context for political change 36–37, 47–52, 51f; Songbun social status system 37, 154n37; Soviet material support for 41, 57; stabilizing factors in 57; surveillance in 57, 78; territorial disputes 75, 162n41; as threat to Northeast Asian stability 73–75; transportation and travel in 39, 57, 69; urban residents and Korean Peace Fund 64, 65; *see also* reunified North Korea; *specific headings beginning with* "North Korea" *and* "North Korean"
North Korea, communication in: digital infrastructure and devices 45, 49, 58, 59, 69–70, 90, 126, 138–139; Korean Peace Fund and 69, 97; mobile phone coverage in North Korea 58, 69; prohibition on communicating with outside 49; restrictions on 49–50, 57, 97; smuggling of communication devices 47; word-of-mouth communication 26, 28, 40, 49–51, 69–70, 90; *see also* propaganda in North Korea
North Korea, cultural diffusion in: as accompanying marketized food distribution 40, 90; digital media and 69–70; extent of 26–27; in Korean Peace Fund model 32; South Korean cultural products 47–50, 142–143; *see also* radio/television broadcasting in North Korea; word-of-mouth information dissemination
North Korea, foreign aid to 39; from China 72, 75, 78, 155n8; food aid 39, 43, 126; as Korean Peace Fund component 2; nongovernmental organizations and 134–135; from South Korea 82; withholding of, as hard power strategy 37
North Korea/South Korea border 50, 76, 90, 126, 130–131

189

Index

North Korean bribery and corruption: among military officers 43, 65; collapse of food delivery system and 39–40; as destabilizing government control 27–28, 42–43; growth of markets and 89–90; illegal foreign cultural content and 49; prevention of, in reunified Korea 118

North Korean defector reports: bribery 43, 49; decline of ideology 37; foreign media consumption 48–49; support for Kim regime 50, 56, 58; support for reunification of Korea 89, 95; underground economy/communication networks 69

North Korean defectors and refugees: crime in South Korea and 132–133; Korea Peace Fund payments to 133; market for arranging defections 41; political dissent and 26, 89; repatriation from China 22; return to reunified Korea from China 131; stunted growth of 135

North Korean economy: currency issues 13, 55–56, 76–77, 96, 116, 150n4, 159n23; as lacking resources to distribute among elites 59, 97; marketization of 40–43, 51, 69, 89, 123; private enterprise 40–43, 69; reform initiatives 75–77; state owned enterprises 53–54, 59, 76–77, 97, 118, 122

North Korean elites *see* North Korean party elites

North Korean food supply and distribution: agriculture in North Korea 39, 80, 120–121; corruption and bribery and 42; famine and starvation 13, 39–40, 57, 77, 89, 155n5; as first priority in reunified Korea 70, 114–115, 134–136; food aid to North Korea 39, 43, 114; food distribution in Pyongyang 125; food shortages as potential tipping point 57; government distribution system collapse and marketization of 39–40, 51, 89, 123; malnutrition and stunted growth 135; migration to China and 131; price controls in newly reunified Korea 124

North Korean masses: access to Korean Peace Fund money 114–116; anger over 2009 currency reform 55–56; awareness of economic disparity with elites 57; as labor force in reunified Korea 92, 120–121; literacy and education levels 69; support for reunification 95

North Korean military: ability to devastate Seoul 94; control over banking and natural resources 45–46; coup d'état prospects 101, 159n17; discontent among 56; integration with South Korean military 112–114; Korean Peace Fund allocations to 64–65; Korean Peace Fund distributions 112–113; as labor for infrastructure improvements 114, 122; "military first" policies 37, 46, 77; military spending 5, 149n2; participation in informal economy 43; participation in reunification signing ceremony 107–108; receptiveness to Korean Peace Fund 46–47; retirement of generals after reunification 111; risk-taking behavior toward South Korea/United States 50–51, 93; support of, as necessary to successful revolt 58; *see also* North Korean nuclear weapons/missile program

North Korean natural/mineral resources: China's economic interest in 16, 82–83, 99, 119, 130; coal 120; as incentive to South Korea for reunification 79–80, 93; natural gas and oil 17, 84; post-reunification investments in extractive industries 129–130; uranium 80, 84, 93, 130; value of 45–46, 162n30

North Korean nuclear weapons/missile program: benefits of denuclearization 84–85; as budgetary priority 72; disarmament in reunified Korea 81, 111–112; hard-power diplomacy's failure to deter 33; international opposition to 7–9, 17–18, 73–74, 80–85, 161n15; legitimacy of Korean regime and 56, 59–60; missile and nuclear tests 8, 56, 74, 81, 85, 93, 151n17, 156n39; purchases of components from China 85, 163n53; readiness projections 85, 163n51; sales of nuclear technology and materials 17–18, 84–85; sanctions against 74, 76, 161n10, 161n22; *see also* North Korean military

North Korean party elites: awareness of outside world 26–27, 47–49, 78; Chinese funds for 162n29; discontent among 45, 49–50; empathy for position of 25, 37, 95; fear of regime collapse and reunification 1–2; importance of 160ch5n7; internal vs. external threats to 77; Korean Peace Fund allocations to 64–65; Korean Peace Fund as exit plan for 103; Korean Peace Fund distribution to 107; non-public sources of payouts to 98–99; participation in informal markets 41, 90; personal safety incentives for 60; as political officeholders in reunified Korea 70; as potential economic elites in reunified Korea 54; as regency for Kim Jong-un 100–101

North Korean regime: accountability of 55–56; economic disagreements within 45–46; irrational acts of 93; loss of legitimacy 56; toleration of food marketization 42–43

North Korean rural farmers: agriculture in North Korea 39, 80, 120; Korean Peace

190

Fund and 64, 65; participation in informal markets 13, 35, 40, 77, 135; post-reunification productivity increases 121

North Korean state-owned enterprises: performance of 13, 76–77; privatization of 53–54, 59, 97, 118, 122

North Korean trade: with China 44, 50; with South Korea 12, 31, 44, 80; with Soviet Union 57

North Korean Workers' Party 58, 65–66; *see also* North Korean party elites

North Korean youth and children: children 64, 65, 103, 109; education and military service 112–113; influence of South Korean popular culture upon 48–49; outside world awareness 56

Northeast Asia: cultural legacy and international relations theory 33; economic development and trade 79, 82–83, 86, 98–99, 133–134; North Korea and regional security 5, 73–75, 127; nuclear weapons in 8–9, 17–18, 33, 80

nuclear energy in South Korea 92

nuclear weapons in North Korea *see* North Korean nuclear weapons/missile program

Nye, Joseph 20, 37, 47–48, 62, 151–152n1

Oberdorfer, Don 57, 72
objectivist policies 31
Oh, Kongdan 42, 43, 48–49, 50, 114
oil and natural gas exports 17, 84
Orascom (mobile carrier) 49, 58
outside world awareness in North Korea 26–27, 47–49, 56–57, 78; *see also* North Korea, communication in; North Korea, cultural diffusion in

Panetta, Leon 85
Park, Hyeong Jung 45
Park, Kyung-Ae 42
Park Geun-hye 7, 96, 165n24
path dependence 21, 34, 88, 95, 103, 146
"Peace and Prosperity" policy (South Korea) 31
peace dividends 80
peaceful reunification of Korea *see* Korean Peace Fund; reunification of Korea
people's groups (North Korea) 39–40, 65–66
perestroika (Soviet Union) 53–54, 56
personal responsibility model 121
personal security as incentive 20, 25, 28, 37, 59–61, 95, 103
philanthropy and Korean Peace Fund 19
Philippines 160–161n7
Phillips, Kerk 125
phones 45, 49, 58, 59, 69, 90, 108, 138

Poland 55
political prisoners 28, 60–61, 90, 95, 136
Pollack, Joshua 84
positivitist-rationalist international relations theories 31
pragmatism vs. ideology in North Korea 36–37, 41, 46, 53–54, 90, 123–124
price controls 124
Price of Peace Equation 21, 63–67
prison (gulag) system in North Korea 28, 60–61, 90, 95, 136
prisoner's dilemma 97
private enterprise in North Korea 40–43, 69; *see also* North Korean economy
private property rights in reunified North Korea 69, 97, 117–118, 126
privatization of state resources 53–54, 59, 97, 118, 122
propaganda in North Korea 55–56, 90
prospect theory 93, 154n30
prosperity as incentive 20, 25, 37, 59
provinces of North Korea 58
purchasing power parity 119, 166n14
Putin, Pres. Vladimir 84, 163n47
Pyongyang, North Korea: Chinese support for elites in 162n29; desperation in 58–59; differences from provinces and rural areas 57–58; food distribution in 125; as future tourist destination 139–141; people's groups in 66; post-reunification migration to 126–127

race/ethnic-based nationalism 6–7, 83, 86, 96, 132, 149n5
radio/television broadcasting in North Korea 48–49, 69, 108, 116, 138, 143
railroads in North Korea 16, 77, 79, 122, 137
Ramo, Joshua 34
Rason port/special economic zone 77, 83, 99, 127, 150n5
rational choice theory 154n30
realist political theory 20, 30–31, 34, 36, 152n3
"Reconciliation and Cooperation" policy (South Korea) 31
re-engagement between North and South Korea 96, 157n59
refugees from North Korea *see* North Korean defectors and refugees
remittances 132
reparations from Japan to Korea 80–81, 149nn8–9
repatriation of North Korean defectors 22
retribution for human rights abuses 28, 60–61, 95
reunification of Korea: Chinese attitudes about 74–75; cost of 9, 68; defectors' sup-

Index

port for 89; effects on South Korea economy 118–119; Goldman Sachs study on 91–92, 129; housing market effects 127, 146n38; international interests in 15–17; Kim Jong-un and 14–15; similarities and differences to German reunification 91–92, 116, 165–166n7; similarities and differences to Hong Kong-China reintegration 92; South Korean attitudes about 91; South Korean proposals for 63; synergies for North and South Korea 80, 91–92, 129; top-down and bottom-up pressures for 25, 69; *see also* Korean Peace Fund

reunified Korea: coordination of in-kind donations 141; foreign investment in 75, 119–120; free trade union with China and Japan 99, 128; integration of the military 112–114; internal migration in 126–132; internal upheaval in 71; Korean Peace Fund payouts in 111–112, 115; labor markets in 92, 114, 120–121, 122, 128–129, 167n47; nongovernmental organizations in 134–136; nuclear energy in 93, 120; regional rivalries 132; reunification period overview 110–111; reunification signing ceremony 106–109; transitional laws 117–118

reunified North Korea: churches in 142; civil society in 32–33, 117–118; democratic voting rights 70; education 113, 116, 117, 133, 135, 139, 165nn203; health care 98, 134–135, 141; labor market 92, 114, 120–121, 122, 128–129, 167n47; nongovernmental organizations in 114–115, 134–136; nuclear disarmament 81, 111–112; private property rights in 69, 97, 117–118, 126; role of former party elites in 54, 70; taxation in 166n18; television and radio in 124, 138, 143; tourism 139–141; transportation and travel in 119, 121, 136–137, 139–141; urbanization of 126–127, 129

reunified North Korean economy: automobile industry in 137; international investment in 119–120, 127; precedents for 116–118; privatization of state enterprises 53–54, 59, 97, 118, 122; productivity gains in 121, 166n23; shift to export-led model 121; wage and price increases 122–125

Ri Yong-ho 46
Ries, Nancy 54–55, 56
roads in North Korea 57, 59, 112, 119, 122, 137
Robinson, Sherman 116
Roh Moo-hyun 31, 50
rural population in North Korea *see* North Korean rural farmers
Russia: defense spending 5; energy resources 20, 163n47; interests in Korean reunification 17, 84, 99; interests in stability in Northeast Asia 75, 98; Soviet revolution as model for North Korea 21, 27–28; Soviet Union collapse 21, 27–28, 32, 54–55; wage and price increases 123, 124; withdrawal of aid to North Korea 57, 158n13
Ryu, Jaesung 77

Samsung (corporation) 119
sanctions against North Korea 50–51, 74, 76, 161n10, 161n22
Sawiris, Nuguib 58
Schmidt, Eric 157–158n66
Sea of Japan/East Sea 83, 162n41
self-interest 31–32; *see also* incentives
Senkaku-Diaoyu territorial dispute 7, 85–86
Seoul, South Korea 94, 167n38
Shenzen, China 127
Shim Jae-cheol 9
Sinuiju, North Korea 77, 127
Six-Party Talks 18, 20, 31, 94
smart-power theory 20, 37, 62, 92–94, 102, 151–152n1
smuggling into North Korea 47, 49
Snyder, Scott 42
soft-power cultural change 47–52, 89, 102
Song Young Hoon 126
Songbun social status system 37, 154n37
Songun "military first" policy 41, 46
South Korea: airline travel to 141; attitudes about reunification 91; benefits of Korean reunification 79–80, 91–92, 99; cultural diffusion into North Korea 47–50, 142–143; Cyber Village initiative 138–139; defense spending 5, 16 , 62–63; demographic decline 113; economic disparity with North Korea 34–35, 47, 76, 90, 154n29; education system 113, 165n3; energy dependence 119; failure of economic sanctions against North Korea 50–51; foreign immigration in 128–129, 132; foreign investment 128; generosity of citizens 142; gross domestic product and credit rating 119, 166n16; integration of North Korean military into 112–114; international relations theories held by 31–32; investment in North Korea 44, 76, 128–129, 141, 159–160n5; Korean Peace Fund participation 62–63, 160n18; legal system 117–118; North Korean impressions of prosperity of 50; North Korean labor force as asset to 92, 128, 156n48; North Korean refugees in 132–133; on nuclear arms in North Korea 7–9; nuclear energy industry 92; participation in reunification signing ceremony 108; post-reunification economic effects upon 118–119; post-reunification economic manage-

192

Index

ment by 116–117, 124–125; post-reunification education of North Koreans in 113; re-engagement with North Korea 96, 157n59; reparations from Japan 80–81, 149nn8–9; reunification effects on housing market 127, 146n38; rules of military engagement 9, 93; shared culture with North Korea 95, 132; territorial disputes 8; trade and foreign investment in China 127–128, 150n3, 163n45; trade with North Korea 12, 31, 44, 80; vulnerability to missile attack from North Korea 94; wages and post-reunification labor migration 127–129; *see also* reunification of Korea; reunified Korea

South Korea economy: effects of reunification of Korea 118–119

Soviet Union collapse 21, 27–28, 32, 54–55; *see also* Russia

starvation and famine in North Korea 13, 39–40, 57, 77, 89, 155n5; *see also* North Korean food supply and distribution

state-owned enterprises in North Korea 53–54, 59, 76–77, 97, 118, 122

Stoessinger, John 26

Student National Defense Corps 142

stunted growth and malnutrition 135; *see also* North Korean food supply and distribution

subsidies to North Korea 39

surveillance in North Korea 57, 78

Suryong system 37, 154n37

Swartz, Peter 18

tablet computers 49, 69, 97, 126, 138–139

"tainted blood" punishment system 58

Taiwan 73, 161n8

Tao, Xie 74

Takeshima-Dokdo territorial dispute 8, 85–86

taxation in reunified North Korea 166n18

television in reunified North Korea 138, 143

territorial disputes 6–8, 75, 81, 85

Tetlock, Phillip 123

Thompson, Drew 83

tipping points 10, 26, 53, 57, 69, 95, 104

Toloraya, Georgy 84

top-down vs. bottom-up pressures for reunification 25, 69

tourism in reunified North Korea 139–141

Toyota 86

trade with North Korea *see* North Korean trade

transition economies 92

transportation and travel in North Korea 39, 57, 69

transportation and travel in reunified North Korea 119, 121, 136–137, 139–141

United Nations sanctions against North Korea 74, 161n10, 161n22

United States: alliance with Japan 81; assurances of safety of Kim family 59–60; as confounding North/South Korean re-engagement 96, 152n7, 152n9; interests in Korean reunification 17, 99; military pivot toward the Pacific 18, 73, 83–85; military retreat from Northeast Asia 99; military spending 149n1, 149n3; policies toward North Korea 31; position on North Korean nuclear weapons program 94; preemption model of military intervention 93, 164–165n18; trade with China 86; vulnerability to North Korean nuclear missiles 85

uranium in North Korea 80, 84, 93, 130; *see also* North Korean natural/mineral resources

urbanization of reunified North Korea 126–127, 129

Vietnam: China and 73, 160–161n7; rural reforms and economic transformation 75–76, 116, 120; South Korean investment in 129; territorial disputes 160–161n7; United States and 31; Vietnam War 145

Walesa, Lech 55

Walt, Stephen 82

Waltz, Kenneth 31, 34, 152n3

Wang, Tao 116

war, Korean Peace Fund as alternative to 144–148

"war of terror" 9

wealth *see* prosperity as incentive

Weir, Fred 53–54

word-of-mouth information dissemination: generally 160n14; in North Korea 26, 28, 49–50, 69–70, 90; in Soviet Union 55; *see also* North Korea, communication in; North Korea, cultural diffusion in

World Food Program 43

World Health Organization 135

Yeonpyong shelling 44, 93

Yoon, Edward 129

Yoon, InJoo 43

Yuwen, Deng 74

Zakaria, Fareed 73, 86

Zhan, Debin 127

Zhang Dejiang 74

Zhang Liangui 75

Zhao, Suisheng 6

www.ingramcontent.com/pod-product-compliance
Ingram Content Group UK Ltd.
Pitfield, Milton Keynes, MK11 3LW, UK
UKHW042010140426
5217IPUK00015B/1083